THE
UNOPPOSITE
SEX

THE

UNOPPOSITE

SEX

The End of the Gender Battle

ELISABETH BADINTER

Translated from the French by Barbara Wright

A Cornelia & Michael Bessie Book

Harper & Row, Publishers, New York
Grand Rapids, Philadelphia, St. Louis, San Francisco
London, Singapore, Sydney, Tokyo

Published in France by Editions Odile Jacob under the title *L'un est l'autre*. First published in Great Britain by Collins Harvill 1989 under the title *Man/Woman: The One Is the Other*. It is hereby reprinted by arrangement with Collins Harvill.

FIRST U.S. EDITION

LIBRARY OF CONGRESS CATALOGING-IN-PUBLICATION DATA

Badinter, Elisabeth
  [Un est l'autre. English]
  The unopposite sex: the end of the gender battle / Elisabeth
Badinter; translated from the French by Barbara Wright.—1st U.S.
ed.
    p.   cm.
  Translation of: L'un est l'autre.
  "A Cornelia & Michael Bessie book."
  Bibliography: p.
  Includes index.
  ISBN 0-06-039096-4
  1. Interpersonal relations. 2. Sex role. I. Title.
HM132.B29   1989
305.3—dc20   88-45882

89 90 91 92 93 HC 10 9 8 7 6 5 4 3 2 1

To Michèle, my sister
To Henri, my friend

CONTENTS

PREFACE

For the last fifteen years or so, every specialist in the social sciences has been enthusiastically observing the evolution of the values, desires, and behaviour patterns of men and women in the West. Whereas in other parts of the world one notices a deliberate return to the old values, the industrialized world of the West constitutes a bloc united by similar and accelerated upheavals. These transformations seem so rapid, almost brutal, and so opposed to our recent traditions, that one is tempted to speak of a revolution. A different world order is coming into being, and we are at the same time its interested spectators and its uneasy actors.

Statistics, evidence, and personal experience all demonstrate beyond question that men and women are profoundly modifying the image they have of themselves and of the Other. Their respective attributes – for so long defined by the "nature" of each sex – are becoming more and more difficult to distinguish. Their relations no longer have the same bases, and are following different paths from those laid down by their forefathers. The criteria are disintegrating as they multiply, and we are beginning to lose our bearings – a legitimate cause for perplexity, and even for some anxiety!

Like many others, I have observed these facts, and I thought at first that the change of model that we are experiencing was not fundamentally different from the numerous other changes that have punctuated our history. Even if they formerly took place more slowly and were therefore less perceptible to those who were taking part in them, modifications of habits and representations can never have operated without some feeling of unease, whether explicit or not. But then, with the passing of time, the new order comes to be seen as the self-evident continuation of the old.

This reminder of the past, however, which should be reassuring, is ineffectual here. The upheavals we are experiencing may perhaps be of a nature that is different from a simple evolution – or even revolution – of life style. The change of model does not merely call our behaviours and values into question, it touches on our innermost being: our identity, our nature as a man or as a woman. This is why our anxiety takes the form of a real existential anguish which obliges us to ask once again the great metaphysical question: Who am I? What is my identity, my specific character, as a man or as a woman? How are we to distinguish the One from the Other? How can the One live with the Other?

Descartes was right. The question of Existence makes us dizzy, and as we do not have his genius, we cannot reassure ourselves by a few days of meditation. The answers are in the Good Book, people say, but we can no longer find them, either because we are too much involved in "this great upheaval" to get things in perspective, or because the Good Book, for once, does not contain the answers to the new questions!

How is it, though, that these new questions have arisen?

We have to go back two centuries to discover their remote origin with the birth of the Western democracies. Equality being their principle, they have constantly striven to impose it, and to put an end to power systems founded on the idea of a natural hierarchy among human beings. Even if we recognize that true equality is utopian, it still had sufficient ideological and moral force to enable it to change men's relationships substantially.

All the same, it was not until the twentieth century that equality between the sexes became a real item on the agenda. Two decades have been sufficient to put an end to the system of representations that for several thousand years allowed men to wield power over women: patriarchy. In so doing, we have not only achieved the conditions in which sexual equality has become a possibility, we have also challenged the archaic model of the complementarity of the sexes, and dealt ourselves new cards of identity.

Convinced that the distinction between the sexual roles is the root cause of inequality, we have systematically, meticulously, substituted the principle of sharing for that of the sexual division of labour, so much so that at the same time as the image of a world divided into male and female spheres is disappearing from our environment (the home and the world of work; the nursery and the office . . .), we have the impression that we have lost our most personal frames of reference. Only a short time ago, there were plenty of certainties. *She* gave life; *He* protected it. *She* looked after the children and the home; *He* went off to conquer the world, and made war when necessary. This division of labour had the merit of developing different characteristics in each sex, characteristics which made a powerful contribution to the formation of a sense of identity.

These days, there is only one difference left, but it is an essential difference: it is women who bear children, and never men. But even if we assume that female identity can be limited to the fact that women can bear children,[1] male identity today has become an enigma. What kind of experience, other than sexual, is there that is specific to men and totally unknown to women? Can we be content with a negative definition of the male: the one who doesn't bear children? This type of question, which can only mark our unconscious, raises radically new problems. The challenge to the complementarity of the sexes undoubtedly has consequences that are not merely social or "political". It obliges us to question ourselves about our nature, its malleability, and the ever-increasing part played by culture. In these days of *in vitro* fertilization and possible genetic manipulation, what unalterable factors remain that keep us linked to our most remote ancestors?

If we cannot answer these dizzying questions, we can at least measure the extent of the present phenomenon by examining history and ethnology. No society, we are told, has ever been unaware of the complementarity of the sexes. On the other hand, questions about the nature of these complementary links still remain. Many ethnologists consider that these links have always been asymmetrical, and at the expense of women. Others disagree. It is true that when we look at the strictly historical period of our societies, we find no other traces than those of a patriarchy, which has often taken the form of absolute male power. Since we have put an end to the patriarchal ideology, though, and this kind of power is completely moribund, we have good reason to presume its contingency.

The coincidence between the end of a power system (patriarchy) and a model of relations between the sexes (complementarity), does not mean that they were originally linked. If complementarity seems to be a specific characteristic of humanity, male supremacy, on the other hand, which is in force in the greater part of the world, is only one among other possible ways of practising this complementarity. Even though they are extremely rare, so-called primitive societies still exist which display a balanced complementarity and a "quasi-equality of the two sexes".[2]

Equality within difference, in other words symmetry, is not merely a feminist slogan. It may even be because it despised this symmetry that the fall of patriarchy, in democratic societies, involves the fall of the complementary model. Rightly or wrongly, we consider the distinction of roles to be so closely linked to an unequal relationship between the sexes that, in order to modify the inequality, we will do our utmost to put an end to the distinction, at the risk of altering our "natural" endowments.

The hypothesis that a disjunction can be made between the complementary relationship uniting man and woman and the power system that places the One above the Other, obliges us to question the origin of this power system; to elucidate its underlying logic; and to demonstrate how this logic has proved incompatible with that of those democratic societies currently generating a completely new model: *the resemblance between the sexes.*

This reflection calls for a double, and eminently perilous, approach. In the first place, we must return to the question of origins, which we know to be both a fiction and an almost unknown prehistoric reality. After that, we must venture to describe the evolution of the man/woman relationship in our civilization. Above all, we must try to throw light on the reasons for it. Although this approach is chronological, the important thing is not so much the general view of history as the desire to perceive its driving force.

The question of *power* proves decisive. Indeed, the distribution of *powers* between the sexes does not seem to have been made once and for all by some *Deus ex machina*. It has varied in time and place for reasons which are sometimes still difficult to determine. True, ecological, economic, ideological and scientific revolutions constitute valuable reference points. But they are not enough to make the history of the relationship between the sexes entirely clear. There remain a host of imponderables which escape reason: desires that we can no longer analyse, and things that have never been said and which will always remain unknown.

The risks of our enterprise, therefore, are considerable.

Its sheer scope exposes it to many reproaches: ignorance, superficiality, over-simplification, caricature, etc. To be aware of this risk, however, is not enough to preserve us from it. Moreover, this passionate history carries with it the weight of our own passions. But how are we to free ourselves from those old resentments passed down from generation to generation, or from an unconscious complicity that makes for mutual exclusion?

Last but not least, there is an overtly cultural bias running through this work. The present evolution of the relationship between the sexes seems to us to be so considerable that we are tempted to see it as the beginning of a genuine mutation, a cultural mutation which does not merely upset the power relationships between men and women, but which obliges us to rethink the "nature" of them both. Moreover, now that we are beginning to be faced with so many scientific possibilities, could they not, tomorrow, complete the process of undermining our fragile identities? The prospect of the artificial mother or even of the "pregnant man" raises the spectre of the man-machine and of the denial of nature, which some people quite simply call "the denial of reality".

Still, as opposed to other mutations, this one is less the effect of the pressure of the environment than the result of the confrontation of the desires of man and woman. Women have now stated clearly what it is they no longer want, and this has initiated an unprecedented revolution. Now the ball is in the men's court, and they must agree to think about the "new deal", and state what it is they want, and how they imagine the new sexual contract.

May we hope that a new equilibrium can be established between two equally responsible partners? Or must we fear that once again the wish to dominate will triumph over wisdom?

Only the Utopia of the future can fortify us against the pessimism of History.

PART ONE

The One And the Other

"The man of the future is incomprehensible if we haven't understood the man of the past."

ANDRÉ LEROI-GOURHAN

It is impossible to resist the temptation to return to the earliest societies. This is a dangerous temptation, since even now we know almost nothing of the life style of prehistoric man. Infinite difficulties arise as soon as we try to understand the relationship between the sexes in those times. Of the laws that governed it, of the feelings they experienced, of the conflicts that beset them, we have only flimsy and indirect evidence, which explains the almost total silence of prehistorians on the subject.

Warned by Rousseau[1] against the dangers of ethnocentrism and anachronism, and then by Lévi-Strauss[2] against improper comparisons between archaic cultures and primitive cultures, how should we approach the dark continent of the Palaeolithic Age? How can we understand the relations of man and woman over such a long period, and one which is marked by different civilizations and a diversity of conditions of life and social customs? How can we guess which roles were assigned to the One and which to the Other, the share taken by each in the management of their everyday life and religious or magical practices, in short, the importance of their respective powers?

Prehistoric men have left traces – over more than thirty thousand years – of their material conditions of life and of their spiritual pre-occupations. But the technico-economic vestiges, the tombs or works of art that might serve as guidelines to our history, are only "truncated messages".[3] How can we interpret them, when we are denied any model to compare them with? Imagination is our guide, but it cannot create *ex nihilo*. On the contrary, it is nourished by analogies, and by our inevitable projections.

Speaking of the Magdalenian hunters of Pincevent, André Leroi-

Gourhan readily pointed out their resemblance to groups of Eskimos and Australian or African Bushmen, who until recently lived in the same conditions. To describe the relationships between the men and women of the Palaeolithic Age, we needs must turn for inspiration to the study of certain primitive societies, as well as reflecting on the present evolution of Western society. In other words, we adopt procedures that contemporary anthropology considers dangerous, if not reprehensible.

But how can we do otherwise, so long as we persist in trying to imagine what the sexes were like, and what were the systems of values and of powers of archaic societies that disappeared thousands of years ago? Some degree of fabulation is inevitable, but isn't the essential thing to remain conscious of it?

The closer we get to historic man, the clearer the reference points become. New implements teach us about the economic revolutions and the new relationships that may have become established between the sexes. Paintings and artifacts, sacred or otherwise – whose meaning we perceive more easily – tell still more about the respective place of man and woman. Their evolution indicates changes of perspective and reversals of power relationships. When we look at objects of worship and art, we can guess whether it is the male or the female who is haloed with magical or religious potency, and who possesses the essential procreative power in this prehistoric period. The representation of a new figure is never gratuitous. On the contrary, it indicates a re-evaluation of the powers of the One or of the Other, which modifies the previous power relationship. Such a relationship, then, is never established once and for all, but fluctuates as a function of technical and ideological upheavals.

All the same, when we glimpse this remote period of the history of humanity, we are not merely struck by the evolution of the relationship between the sexes, we are also left with the impression of a relative balance between the powers attributed to each. In contrast to the period that followed, we never feel that one sex was generally oppressed by the other. Although this, perhaps, is where our story begins . . .

I

THE ORIGINAL COMPLEMENTARITY
OF THE SEXES

Everywhere we look, man and woman are not only different, but they complete each other so well that together they are almost all-powerful: the masters of life, the architects of their survival, of their pleasure, and of the necessary emotional warmth without which human beings wither away. Separated One from the Other, they seem both useless and in danger of death, as if all meaning and effectiveness lay in their unity. The One must marry the Other and collaborate with him or her for humanity to be complete, that's to say "accomplished, fulfilled, perfect". Nothing *a priori* indicates the supremacy of the One or the lesser necessity of the Other.

If the complementarity of the sexes is obvious from the point of view of their anatomy, it is less so on the level of their respective functions. But only a minimum of observation is necessary to discover that in every human collectivity there have always been tasks that were reserved to one sex and forbidden to the other.

Even if it varies greatly from one society to another, the sexual division of labour seems to be a constant. Not only does it distinguish human society from the animal world, but we find it operating everywhere in all the multiplicity of societies so far known. This may perhaps constitute an essential rule of human nature. If this were the case, we would be tempted to accord it a status similar to that given by Lévi-Strauss to the prohibition of incest. In showing that this prohibition constitutes the link between the biological and the social, the great anthropologist has shown its universality and necessity. If the same applied to the sexual division of labour, the evolution that we observe in our societies today might well herald a kind of mutation.

Before we decide, though, we must first consider the evidence of anthropologists and primatologists, which seems to tally with what we know about the earliest societies. After that, we shall be able to consider the content and nature of the complementarity of tasks, and ask the important question about the powers of the One and the Other, and the supremacy of the One over the Other.

Man's Specific Characteristics

A Universal Rule of Human Nature?

Ethnologists and anthropologists are the only people who can tell us of the diversity of the cultures they observe directly, and hence of the common points that unite them over and above their many differences. Unanimous in proclaiming the universality of the prohibition of incest, they are no less unanimous in stressing the universality of the sexual division of roles.

Already some thirty years ago, Margaret Mead was writing: "Whether we deal with small matters or with large . . . we find this great variety of ways, often flatly contradictory one to the other, in which the roles of the two sexes have been patterned.

"*But we always find the patterning. We know of no culture that has said, articulately, that there is no difference between men and women except in the way they contribute to the procreation of the next generation*; that otherwise in all respects they are simply human beings with varying gifts, no one of which can be exclusively assigned to either sex . . . However differently the traits have been assigned, some to one sex, some to the other, and some to both, however arbitrary the assignment must be seen to be . . . , although the division has been arbitrary, it has always been there in every society of which we have any knowledge."[4]

Today, Françoise Héritier makes the same observation. The main thing, she says, is to recognize that "in the beginning is binarity", that "everything will be divided into two and attributed to one or the

6

other sex according to two poles which will be organized into opposites".[5] Even more than Margaret Mead, Françoise Héritier stresses the asymmetrical and unequal character of the sexual dichotomy. Men and women, she notes, are always "inverse": woman acts in the opposite way from man, "he is the major sex, she is the minor sex".[6] This, in her eyes, is nothing less than scandalous. Whereas the American anthropologist always questioned the *origin* and *reality* of these differences (are they rooted in nature or in society? "are we dealing with a *must* that we dare not flout because it is rooted so deep in our biological mammalian nature that to flout it means individual and social disease?" or with a *must* that although less deeply rooted is still socially convenient?), Françoise Héritier thinks that the source of the asymmetry of the sexes is to be found in the nature of the One and the Other. "There is little doubt that men's superior physical strength, and especially women's enforced heaviness, immobility and fragility during the greater part of their lives in their role as breeders, were the essential causes at the dawn of humanity."[7] In other words, the dualism of the sexes is rooted in the truth of the body. And then ideology seizes upon this primary dichotomy, which expresses the supremacy of the masculine, and extends it to all levels of life and all aspects of knowledge. Moreover, we find this qualitative binary classification of aptitudes, behaviours and characteristics according to sex *in all societies*.

However, whether or not we assign a positive and negative value to the two sexual poles, we are all agreed in recognizing the universal character of their complementarity, even in those societies that show a marked preference for symmetrical behaviour patterns. Thus in the Manus people of the Admiralty Islands, there is very little differentiation in the roles of men and women; they all participate in the economic and religious life. In this group of puritans, sex and sexual attraction are so devalued[8] that each sex forms a remarkably similar idea of them. And yet, if there is an even-handedness in the economic and religious life of the Manus, everything contributes "to make the woman's lot less attractive than the man's. As the representatives of the disallowed activities of the body, as the sex in fact that does more with its body, women are the more hedged-in . . . Women do not enjoy being women, not because public rewards given men are denied to them – influence, power, wealth are all open to them – but because the sensuous creative significance of the female role of wife and mother is so undervalued."[9]

Here, as everywhere where the feminine is perceived as an evil to be hidden, complementarity reappears strongly, in negative fashion, to the detriment of women and their affective relations with men. The Mundugumor of New Guinea show an aggressivity common to both sexes,[10] with no other complementary character than that of their sexual anatomy; their specifically feminine life seems to us to be loathsome. With the exception of genital sexuality, pregnancy and breast-feeding are abominated, and avoided wherever possible. This makes Margaret Mead say that if the division of a society into two groups (adult men on the one hand, women and children on the other) is almost abolished, it is at an exorbitant price: the survival of the group.

The lesson to be learnt is twofold: the total abandonment of the characteristics specific to either sex is difficult and risky, for in disregarding this truth one risks death. This comment is so obvious that it may seem like a truism to some. And yet, when we observe the behaviour of men and women in our Western society, the obvious facts become blurred, and the comment becomes valid, or even original.

It is true, as Georges Balandier notes, that "the relationships established between the sexes seem to conform to extremely ancient and intangible structures",[11] and that every attempt to "undermine" this system is a far more corrosive revolution than one that merely aims at the elimination of class relationships. Sexual dualism is the paradigm of all dualisms, "the paradigm of the history of the world".

This indicates the degree to which our societies' questioning of sexual dualism touches what is most archaic in us, and threatens to upset the immemorial order of the human world.

The Dividing Line between Primate and Human

In all known human groups, the techno-economic relations between man and woman are strictly complementary. With primitive peoples, these relations are even "strictly specialized".[12] This situation, however, has no parallel in the animal world. Among the carnivores, males and females hunt in the same manner; among the primates, the search for food is individual and shows no trace of sexual specialization.

The anthropologist and primatologist Sarah Hrdy sees this as evidence that animals have more autonomy than human beings. "In many societies, a woman without a man to hunt or earn income, or a man without a wife to do the cooking, is at a considerable disadvantage. By contrast, among all non-human primates each adult is entirely responsible for supplying his or her own food. The only exceptions involve occasional meat sharing among chimpanzees, but even here males tend to monopolize meat from co-operatively hunted prey . . . But in no case does one sex depend on the other for any staple."[13]

But this autonomy of females in regard to their food has great disadvantages when they are mothers. Jane Goodall, who spent years watching the life of the chimpanzee Flo and her children, reports the difficulties she encountered. She had to carry her last-born on her back, look for food while keeping an eye on the baby, spend long hours hunting for termites, teach her older offspring this skill, play with them, groom them, caress them, and protect them from the moods of the males all at the same time.[14]

The human diet implies the sharing of tasks and resources. In all known primitive groups, hunting is normally the men's pursuit, and gathering that of the women.[15] A combination of meat and vegetables is essential to a balanced diet for both sexes. Both, then, exchanged their resources: animal proteins for vegetable proteins. The basic difference between human and primate probably resides in this original exchange, which is both the source of the complementarity of the sexes and of a totally human social phenomenon.

It is generally agreed[16] that this sexual specialization was the "organic solution"[17] to the problem of hominization. To understand the physio-biological origin of complementarity better, we have to go back a very long way, to the time when the female primate was very slowly evolving towards the human model.

Everything begins in Africa, between eight and nine million years ago. Before that, everyone catered for his own needs and moved about alone. According to some, it was when the problem arose of prolonged dry seasons, and hence the emergence of dangerous savannas, that the protohominids had to learn to transport their food to safe places. This, according to many anthropologists, and notably Helen Fisher, was the origin of the bipedalism that gave rise to a triple mutation: physical, sociological . . . and affective.[18] Even though some[19] reject the savanna argument, there is still a relative consensus as to the consequences of bipedalism.

The protohominids' skeleton was gradually modified,[20] walking erect was selecting for changes. Their big toes were rotating and had begun to lie parallel with the other toes. Their ankles had strengthened. Their knees had rotated inward to lie below the midline of their hips. Their pelvises had realigned and strengthened to bear the weight of their upper frames. But the new stance and evolved skeleton created complications for females, complications that were to set them on the road to human life.

The reshaping of their pelvises brought about a reduction in the diameter of their birth canals, which made childbirth difficult for most females and fatal for some. Natural selection stepped in, and new genetic traits appeared. A few females bore their young too soon, and these premature infants had smaller heads that easily navigated the shrinking birth canal. But this did not liberate the females, because premature infants required many extra months or even years of care. Bipedalism obliged them to carry their infants or strap them to their backs. It was harder for them to catch animals and provide food for themselves and for their children. The time had come to make a deal with the males. The sex contract was about to begin.

In the course of the generations, selection operated in favour of the protohominids who copulated during the greater part of their menstrual cycle. Females began to lose their oestrus, and their daily life changed. According to Helen Fisher, the permanent sexual receptivity of the female, and face-to-face copulation, inaugurated one of the most fundamental exchanges of the human race: love. Their sex-appeal enabled the females to survive by forming economic bonds with the males. They learned to share their tasks, to exchange their meat and vegetables. Sexual activity had bonded them, and economic dependence reinforced their bonds.

From then on, a mother could take care of more than one infant at the same time. She moved about less, and spent her life within a limited territory which she knew inside out. While she gathered the vegetables, the men went to find the meat, which they then shared with her and the young, who thus had a better chance of survival.

More than two million years ago, hominids were already clearly differentiated from the anthropoid apes. Owen Lovejoy listed the differences, in the following table:[21]

HOMINIDS	PONGID (APE)
Exclusively ground-dwelling.	Some predominantly in trees – some predominantly on the ground. None exclusively terrestrial.
Bipedal.	Not bipedal.
Pair-bonded, leading to establishment of nuclear families.	Not pair-bonded. No nuclear families except in gibbons.
Increasing immobility of females and young. Possibility of a home base.	Females move to secure food and take infants with them. No home base.
Food sharing.	No food sharing.
Beginnings of tool use and tool making.	Tool use absent or inconsequential.
Brain continues to enlarge,	Brain does not enlarge.
Continuous sexuality.	Sexuality only during oestrus.
Multiple infant care.	Single infant care.

We are, of course, still a long way from *homo sapiens*. But our own characteristics, and in particular the sexual division of labour, are already present, either actually or potentially. It took barely two million years for Australopithecus to give place to Pithecanthropus, and then to Neanderthal and finally Cro-Magnon man, the father of us all, the first representative in Europe of *sapiens sapiens*, more than thirty thousand years ago.

With time, the complementary relationship between the sexes became accentuated and codified, as if it were the hallmark of humanity, the most necessary condition for its survival.

Complementarity at the Time of the Hunter-Gatherers

Prehistorians situate the beginning of the Upper Palaeolithic at around 35,000 BC. It was during this period that *homo sapiens* took possession of the greater part of the world and that prestigious civilizations emerged.[22] At the same time as the cult of the dead established itself,[23] artistic creation[24] developed in prodigious fashion, thus marking the emergence of a spirituality whose complexity we are still only beginning to discover.

During this period, which represents almost ten times the length of our history, climatic changes had repercussions on the conditions of life of our ancestors, and hence very probably on the relations between men and women also. This illustrates just how far everything that may be said about them is conjectural, and no more than approximative.

What nevertheless inclines one to risk an opinion is the certainty that one thing all these civilizations had in common was that they lived from hunting and gathering, a way of life that has still not completely disappeared. Even though we cannot discern a common attitude to the relations between men and women in the thirty or so remaining hunter-gatherer societies, André Leroi-Gourhan observes that the Eskimos, the Australian Aborigines, and the African Bushmen or Pygmies were only recently still living on the same techno-economic bases as the Magdalenian hunters in Pincevent.[25] These conditions of life are favourable both to a certain distance between the sexes and to their complementarity.

Indications of the Separation of the Sexes

There are many African legends that evoke the original separation of the sexes, a radical separation since it is both geographical and economic. Thus in Kenya, the Masai relate that in the beginning, men and women formed two separate tribes who lived apart. The women bred antelopes, the men cattle. Each tribe was independent of the other and they met only fortuitously in the forests for lovemaking. The children born of these unions stayed with their mothers, but when the little males grew up they joined the men's tribe, until the day when, owing to their stupidity and quarrels,[26] the women lost their herds and were obliged to join the men's tribe. At that point they agreed to become the men's wives and to be entirely dependent on them.

In West Africa, the legends sometimes differ as to the cause of the sexes coming together, but there too the myth of the initial separation is frequently found.

While we know that these archaic representations are not too realistic, but speak an ideological language that is sometimes only a simple inversion of reality, it is not unimportant that a great many primitive legends see the keynote of the relationship between the sexes as being their original separation. It is as if these legends had effectively transmitted the distant memory of the time of *homo erectus*.

The hunter-gatherer society of the Upper Palaeolithic was certainly no longer in this stage. But there are certain signs that lead us to think that men and women had two very distinct life styles and that they may have constituted two relatively separate but mutually tolerant societies.

The natural division between hunting and gathering transformed, even though it relied on, the distinction between the sexes. It gave rise to two fields of activity, and perhaps also to two clearly separated types of intelligence. Serge Moscovici reports that among the sub-Arctic Ainu, "male and female activities do not overlap to any significant extent. The women gather and collect in the vicinity of the settlement, while the male hunters range far afield. If the women do occasionally hunt they must be content to catch small animals that can be dispatched with sticks or even with their bare hands, since they are generally forbidden to handle their mates' weapons."[27]

The semi-nomadism of the hunter-gatherers, motivated by the fluctuation of the animal and vegetable resources, had specific effects on the relationship between the sexes. Women and men followed independent paths in their search for food, and shared the territory in such a way that they lived largely separated from each other: the women with their children, and the hunters amongst themselves.

When they were together in their dwelling places, the men and women of the Palaeolithic continued to observe a certain distance. André Leroi-Gourhan speaks of "feminine living space and masculine living space in the prehistoric dwelling".[28]

We may also suppose that men and women did not eat together. Segregation of the sexes at meals is a custom that is still deeply rooted in many primitive populations. In Africa, this prohibition is almost everywhere respected,[29] but it has also existed in cultures as different as those of the Kurds, the Indians in Guiana, Vedic India, Yucatan, etc. Even the distribution of food implied a certain sexual segregation.[30]

In fact, the hunter-gatherers of the Palaeolithic have left us no tangible signs of their life as a "couple". To this day we do not possess the slightest representation of the human couple in parietal and mobiliary art, although it was so rich at that period. André Leroi-Gourhan has constantly expressed his surprise at "the total absence of representations of human or animal couplings, and, furthermore, at the absence of primary sexual characteristics".[31] At the very most, we find indications of the secondary sexual characteristics showing that animals belong to one sex or the other. But there is no known instance of an ithyphallic figure[32] in close proximity to a female figure.[33]

And yet, when we consider the totality of the figurations of the Upper Palaeolithic, there is no lack of feminine and masculine figures. The parietal art of the Magdalenian Age abounds in sexualized representations, realistic or abstract according to the period. But they are arranged in separate groups, as can be seen notably at Lascaux. There, as elsewhere,[34] three decorated zones (the entrance, the central area, the back) constitute quite distinct entities. The male signs are found at the entrance and at the back of the cave. Most of the female signs are at the centre, in or around the principal compositions.[35]

The separation of the sexes in the Palaeolithic Age, then, was apparently operative even in their art. At least, this is the image of themselves our distant ancestors have left us. Women and men seem to have constituted two separate groups, of whose relations and exchanges we know nothing. And yet the essential relationship that ensured the life and survival of the group did exist.

The Signs of Complementarity

The sexual division of labour, however radical it may be, does not exclude the complementarity of the different tasks. On the contrary: the separation of the sexes and of the functions devolving upon each is its most reliable guarantee.

When men and women are working to obtain different resources, they establish their mutual dependence. No section of the collectivity can definitely monopolize its wealth. The regular nourishment of its individuals calls for these resources to be pooled, and for everyone to have access to them once they have been collected. Complementarity is objective, since no section of the group can subsist without the other.

This mutual dependence is a factor in the consideration of the one for the other and, perhaps more than people think, in equality. Among the Masai, a population of hunter-stockbreeders of a semi-patriarchal type, although the meat is the men's property, the women have control over the milk, which is the essential part of their daily nourishment. They can refuse it to anyone who is ill-mannered.

Until 1970–80, most researchers thought of this sexual division of labour in hierarchical terms. Hunting, a collective activity, was supposed to develop men's intelligence more quickly, whereas individual gathering was presumed to have left women in a sort of sub-culture. Edgar Morin and Serge Moscovici in France, and Robin Fox and Lionel Tiger in the United States were, among many others, the eulogists of hunting as a civilizing activity: "A total human phenomenon . . . it was to transform their relation to the environment, the relations between man and man, between man and woman, between adult and young person."[36]

Edgar Morin is right to say that hunting in the savanna developed man's senses and intelligence, by teaching him to interpret sensory stimuli, by confronting him with the most wily animals and by stimulating his strategic aptitudes: vigilance, tenacity, combativity, daring, guile, luring, trapping, stalking.[37] It is indisputable that hunting was a powerful factor in socialization, because through hunting men learnt co-operation, how to make deals, and the rules of distribution. In contrast to the higher apes, whose males are mutually intolerant, hunters had to practise solidarity, friendship, and some measure of equality.

As the women rarely took part in the hunt – having to see to the children and to the individual gathering – it was decreed that they had remained "social and cultural minors". Described as being slower, weaker, less co-ordinated, or subject to moods on account of their menstrual cycle, and as sexual objects that disturbed the group, women, who had not the same motives to band together, were said to have been quite naturally condemned to submit to the men, who were stronger, more intelligent, and more courageous.

A certain number of anthropologists and primatologists – women, for the most part[38] – have called into question the stereotype of the intellectual and social inferiority of women in prehistoric times, and developed a new type of argument.

Adrienne Zilhman[39] describes feminine gathering quite differently. She thinks that it was a dangerous activity, demanding all the more energy and intelligence from women in that they did not possess the physical capacities of their companions. They had to practise the art of the rapid and efficient picking of nourishing plants, learn to use tools, and quicken their perception of danger. Above all, women had to be capable of sustained attention in order to satisfy the needs of their children: to protect them, feed them, amuse them, prepare them for life.[40]

Contrary to what has been said, the feminine sex participated just as much as men in the work of socialization. The women's contribution was different, but essential. Prolonged maternal care is the primary source of human sociability. It is mothers who teach the elementary rules of social life, language and love.

Solidarity and intelligence are not confined to men. Both sexes, each in its own way, have developed these human qualities. Here too, complementarity has played its part to the full, by allowing the needs of the Other to be expressed, and by moderating the effects of inevitable individual inequality.

The invaluable research carried out by Leroi-Gourhan and

Annette Laming-Emperaire on cave art has also contributed to showing that the men of the Palaeolithic were well aware of their complementarity, even if they expressed it in a way that the twentieth-century observer still finds relatively hard to understand. Apart from explicitly human representations, there are abstract or realistic signs symbolizing the two sexes to be found in the cave sanctuaries, and figurations of animals of different species (always the same ones) in pairs.[41] Thus, a whole network of relationships among animals, human figures and signs was discovered, each set divided into two complementary groups. For example, the topographical position of the male figures, which are associated with horses, ibexes and stags, is distinct from the position of the female figures, and of bisons, oxen and mammoths. The division of the figures into a male group and a female group therefore seems highly probable.

Leroi-Gourhan concludes from this that "pairing" was a fundamental principle to which the idea of reproduction is perhaps not foreign. "One has the impression of being faced with a system polished in the course of time – not unlike the older regions of our world, wherein *there are male and female divinities* whose actions do not overtly allude to sexual reproduction, but whose male and female qualities are indispensably complementary."[42]

Finally, despite their apparent distance, masculine and feminine are inseparable. But cave art does not only tell us of their complementarity, it also shows that the One did not have a better place than the Other. So far, no one has been able to detect any kind of hierarchy between the group of the female figures and that of the male figures. At a time when the conditions necessary for survival seem to militate in favour of a certain equilibrium between the sexes, the ideological representation that is art also shows their symmetry, and perhaps even their equality. At all events, there is no reason to think that the men of this era exercised tyrannical power over the women – nor the women over the men.

The Question of Power

Although there is genuine consensus about the necessary sharing of tasks, there is profound, almost violent disagreement as soon as the question arises of the power relationships between men and women in the first societies. As a general rule, complementarity has been thought of more in terms of hierarchy and domination than in terms of equality and symmetry. Moreover, the popular representation of the cave man has more often shown him dragging a woman by the hair, rather than in a situation of equality with her. Even if we forget about caricature and humour, we are still bound to admit that the idea of equality and mutual respect between the sexes is less widespread than that of the supremacy of the One and the oppression of the Other.

In the last few years, certain American anthropologists have put forward a different view of the relation between the sexes in Palaeolithic society. Some[43] insist on the necessity of their co-operation, and think that in the absence of any true system of private property, division of labour could not form the only basis of the exploitation of the One by the Other. Others see the necessity of a balanced diet as the reason for an equal relationship between the sexes. For Adrienne Zilhman, the question of power cannot be dissociated from the problem of resources. Although there has been a great deal of talk about the carnivorous habits of prehistoric man,[44] it is no less certain that vegetables, which it was the women's task to gather, constituted an essential part of his diet, not to say the most important part in some seasons. This weighty argument in favour of the mutual respect of the partners of the two sexes seems not to have registered with the majority of anthropologists. For almost a century, in fact, they have assumed that power descended either in the male or the female line. For some, an obviously matrilineal filiation was the foundation of women's power. For others, it was men's strength and co-operation that led to the exchange of women and to men's power over them and their children.

Whichever hypothesis is adopted, it is not absurd to suppose that the partisans of both have partially projected their own most secret desires on to early societies, or taken their own world as a model. The matriarchal thesis prevailed in the nineteenth century, which extolled the power of the mother, and it has come back into favour among the feminists of our own period. In the same way, the fact that the greater part of the world still lives under a patriarchal system has encouraged anthropologists to see such a system as the original model of power.

The hypothesis we are going to suggest is no doubt in its turn influenced by our observation of the present-day evolution of our societies.

Early Societies neither Matriarchal nor Patriarchal

At the end of the nineteenth century, the evolutionist thesis of an original matriarchy was extraordinarily popular. The German, Bachofen, and the American, Lewis Henry Morgan, postulated that the first families had started as matriarchies, female lines that only recognized the maternal lineage. Shortly afterwards, Friedrich Engels adopted the same thesis.

This theory was founded on the fact that the mother/child filiation is indisputable, whereas paternity can be questioned, or even ignored. It seemed logical, therefore, that lineage should be traced through the woman, and that the man who became a woman's partner should be incorporated into her social group. According to this theory, it was only very much later that primitive peoples began to conceive of the notion of paternity, after which men appropriated the power, property and titles that had belonged to women in their capacity as heads of the family, assigned to themselves the rank of patriarch, and decreed that the patrilineal principle should apply to their children.

This conception, according to Françoise Picq, in a 1979 doctoral thesis, "throws light on the cultural relations of the monogamic patriarchal family and enables us both to imagine its disappearance and to question its legitimacy. Maternal filiation seems natural . . . whereas paternity is only a belief, a presumption, a legal fiction." It was not by chance, then, that the theory of an original matriarchy, which was severely criticized by the anti-evolutionists at the

19

beginning of this century, was taken up again by feminists in the years between 1970 and 1980, sometimes with success.

Most of these feminists rightly stressed the degree to which women played a part in subsistence, tool-making, and traditional cultures. The American anthropologist Evelyn Reed published a book that made quite a stir, *Woman's Evolution*,[45] which repeated almost word for word the arguments put forward by Robert Briffault. In *The Mothers*,[46] Briffault maintained that mothers, in creating affectivity, had made human socialization possible, and that biology, which preceded any kind of economy, was the foundation of their power. But as Briffault had simply produced an enormous ethnological compilation from dubious sources, Reed's work, which merely duplicated it, neither convinced the specialists nor reversed the ideology of an original patriarchy that now prevails.[47]

In actual fact, the first proponents of the matriarchal theory had not defined the powers of the mother clearly enough, nor had they given sufficient indications about which prehistorical period might have been involved in such a power system. The illustrations they casually picked out of the ethnological material often turned out to be either false or unverifiable. Moreover, the place assigned to men by the matriarchal schema was too restricted to be convincing. For several decades now, the work of the prehistorians has clearly demonstrated the importance of the hunters' civilization, from the social and economic as well as the religious and intellectual points of view. We no longer find it credible to envisage the men of the Palaeolithic as brutes subjected to all-powerful mothers. It is true that the matriarchal theories have often been caricatured by their adversaries, notably by making them claim that mothers had political power equivalent to that later enjoyed by fathers. In actual fact, while feminist anthropologists have never said anything of the sort, their adversaries have taken advantage of this caricature to exclude their theories from scientific discussion, even at the expense of obfuscating their most interesting arguments. For the last hundred years, the proponents of an original patriarchy have refused all compromise with the partisans of matriarchy.

When American anthropology at the beginning of this century[48] liquidated evolutionary theories, the theory of maternal rights was rejected with them.[49] Stress was laid on the extreme variety of the phenomena. Others went even further, and contested the original character of motherhood which the champions of maternal rights explained by the ignorance of paternity and the instability of the conjugal bonds. Lowie, and later, Lévi-Straussian anthropology, took the opposite view. For them, it is the family, the universal social unit, that came first, and not the clan.[50] According to them, humanity only really began with the triangular relationship and the power of the father over his wife and child. Recent American socio-biological theories came at the right time to endorse this hypothesis.

In the 1960s, Robin Fox and Lionel Tiger[51] ardently defended the idea that primitive masculine hunting practices were the foundation of human kinship. Co-operation, solidarity, and sharing, they maintained, created an alliance between males from the very beginning, and men learnt to choose a partner from other groups and to assume the role of patriarchal leaders.

In 1973, Edgar Morin developed these themes further. To hunting, exploring, socialized man he opposed tender, routine-minded, less capable woman: "Two silhouettes appear in the hominid landscape: that of the upright man, his weapon held high, confronting an animal, and that of the woman bending over a child or collecting vegetable food . . . the men's group takes upon itself the government and control of society and imposes a *political* domination on the women and young people, which still continues."[52]

Morin, too, thinks that patriarchy was the original family and social structure, because hominization would have strengthened the bonds between man and child. He thinks it unimportant that paternity could be attributed either to the mother's brother[53] or to her companion, for paternity widens the nuclear mother–child relationship by introducing a man into it, and at the same time the principle of the masculine hierarchy. "The great phenomenon which prepared hominization and which, we believe, brought Sapiens into being, is not 'the murder of the father', but the birth of the father."[54]

The family, Morin continues, is linked to a society through the organization of kinship structures and the regulation of sexuality, and both of these provide the society with a new opening on to other societies by means of the law of exogamy.[55]

By determining the distribution of the women, the men put an end to the risk that the women might choose their own partners, that's to say challenge masculine domination on its own ground. By controlling the women's desires, the men's group confirmed its cohesion and domination, Edgar Morin concludes.

Such is the thesis that is most generally accepted today. Everyone agrees with Lévi-Strauss that asymmetry between the sexes characterizes human society. Even Simone de Beauvoir avowed herself convinced by this assumption. In her view, the Golden Age of Woman is only a myth. "Society has always been male; political power has always been in the hands of men . . . The triumph of the patriarchate was neither a matter of chance nor the result of a violent revolution. From humanity's beginnings, their biological advantage has enabled males to affirm their status as sole and sovereign subjects."[56]

For our part, we are convinced neither by the hypothesis of primeval matriarchy nor by that of primeval patriarchy. This is probably because the society we live in suggests another. While there is no question of comparing the incomparable, that's to say the most archaic societies with the most developed ones, we can at least observe that the collapse of patriarchy which we are now witnessing has no counterpart in the emergence of any kind of matriarchy. Our democratic society seems very well able to put up with the absence of an exclusive power residing either in the father or the mother. It would not be absurd, therefore, to imagine that the first societies were also able to do without the one or the other, and to share power in a different way from that observed in the greater part of the present-day world.

However, having confessed one of the reasons for our undertaking, there are arguments that militate in its favour. In the first place, the notions of patriarchy or matriarchy seem too complex and too rigid to be applicable to archaic human societies. That the mother-child bond should be the first and most obvious social relationship does not necessarily imply the existence of matriarchal power,[57] of which, incidentally, we have found no example in the multiplicity of societies so far known.

Those societies that we call "matrilineal"[58] do not seem to be very well adapted to the condition of the reindeer-age hunters, either. While we can still imagine the transmission of the maternal "name", it is more difficult to conceive of the transmission of "land" in a nomadic society, all the more so in that this would presume the notion of individual property, which is far from being established at this period.[59]

As to the mothers' political power, Françoise Héritier thinks that this is nothing but a myth. No known matrilineal society is a matriarchy. Even among the Iroquois,[60] who seem to come closest to it (in this society of hunter-gatherers, the women enjoy rarely-equalled rights and powers), the men consider themselves superior. Françoise Héritier remarks that although "the matrons controlled the life of the large houses and were in charge of the women's work . . . they were *represented* on the Council of Elders *by a man*, who spoke in their name and made their voice heard".[61]

The patriarchal hypothesis, as we understand it today,[62] seems to us to be equally debatable. It presupposes the institution of marriage and the recognition of the biological father, both of which were highly improbable at that time. Without postulating, like Bachofen, a chaotic, lawless state of sexual promiscuity, it is quite likely that women had several partners during their procreative period. We may assume, then, that like certain Melanesian or Australian societies,[63] who considered motherhood to be a social function of the female sex, prehistoric hunters envisaged paternity from the same angle, namely as being collective. All the men would have been either really, or potentially, the "fathers" of the community. It would have been incumbent upon them to protect and feed all the children in the group.

There is nothing in the Upper Palaeolithic societies to prove the existence of one power system rather than another. We do not know whether the men were already exchanging the women to suit their convenience. We can only think that the mothers were responsible for the children, and the men for the adolescent males.

There remains the question of the "political" power over the group, which present-day theoreticians of matriarchy do not claim for the women alone, but which most anthropologists consider the essential criterion, the quintessence of power.

At the moment there is general agreement that this power has always belonged to men, as we know of no society, not even matrilineal ones, in which women clearly dominate men.[64] But this fact gives us no reason to deduce that power was originally paternal.

Masculine power was not necessarily that of the father. And above all, the women of the Palaeolithic Age may well have had other powers of which we know nothing today.

The Multiplicity of Powers

Speaking of non-human primates, Sarah Hrdy uses the term "dominant" to describe the animal that generally wins in a one-to-one relationship. The females, she notes, have far more power than is generally admitted, but it is nevertheless exceptional for them to have any direct control over the behaviour of the males. On the contrary: male primates from generation to generation, or, in the case of humans, from culture to culture, have never stopped dominating the females and transforming their superiority in fighting into political preponderance over the sex that is apparently weaker and less competitive.[65]

The reasons for this domination are of a bio-physiological order. In the majority of primates, the males are bigger than the females and capable of bullying them.

In the same way, sexual dimorphism in the human species has always been observable everywhere. The discovery in 1974[66] of Lucy,[67] who was more than three million years old, and then of her "friends",[68] the following year, in the Afar triangle in Ethiopia, confirmed this fact.

For the first time in history, enough hominid fossils had been discovered in the same place for comparisons between individuals to be made. On examination, half of them were seen to be distinctly bigger and heavier than the others. After some hesitation, Donald Johanson and his colleagues came to the conclusion that the large bones belonged to men, and the small ones to women. The differences were even greater than those between women and men today.[69] This sexual dimorphism in fossils would seem to confirm that the division of labour began more than three million years ago – male dominance also.

But, while granting that physical superiority was from the beginning the cause of men's political power, other types of powers exist in human beings that do not necessarily belong to men. During the prehistoric period we are considering, there are certain signs that give us reason to imagine that women, too, had very great powers. And rather than confine ourselves to the question of the *power* of one sex over the other, it seems preferable to consider the specific *powers* of the One and the Other. It is rather too easy to say that woman was condemned to immanence, whereas transcendence belonged as of right to men.

Prehistoric art demonstrates that this is far from being the case. The evolution of the representation of the sexes proves that there was extreme interest in both moieties of humanity, and even a particular fascination with regard to women.[70] As far back as the Aurignacian Age (30,000 BC), an age that only produced incisions and graffiti, there were already depictions of vulvas, the symbols of fecundity. In the following period, within the limits of the Gravettian and the Solutrean (25,000–15,000 BC), there were increasing numbers of feminine statuettes in bone, ivory and stone; these were found between the Ukraine and central Europe.[71] During this time, the number of masculine statuettes is so small that they hardly rate a mention.

During the Magdalenian period, on the other hand, while human figures become much less common, it is masculine representations that are the more numerous.[72] The increasingly frequent appearance of masked masculine figures who seem to be observing a magic rite marks the importance of hunting. Game was then man's chief source of food, while plants were no more than an interesting adjunct during the summer season. The representation of the sexes is the expression of the new alimentary equilibrium.

Most commentators have emphasized the extraordinary prestige of the hunter, a man capable of facing death, who thereby raised himself above everyday contingencies. That is the foundation of his power over the world and over other human beings. By risking his life in defending the cave against the great carnivores, or in providing its occupants with meat, the male demonstrates his superiority over nature. His physical strength is nothing in comparison with the metaphysical prestige he thus acquires. And when, in the caves, a man is shown as having been conquered by an animal,[73] it is perhaps not so much his weakness that is exhibited as his tragic courage and grandeur.

It seems that still today, wherever societies of hunters still exist, their prestige is infinitely greater than that of the agriculturists, stockbreeders or collectors. Mircea Eliade observes that the Desana of Colombia call themselves hunters, even though seventy-five per cent of their food comes from fishing and horticulture, because in their view, only the hunter's life is worth living.[74] Françoise Héritier explains this as follows: "What men particularly value in men is no doubt the fact that they can shed their blood, risk their lives, take the lives of others, by a decision of their own free will. Women 'see' their own blood flow out of their bodies . . . and they give life (and sometimes die in doing so), without necessarily either wanting to, or being able to, prevent it. This may well be the basis of all symbolic interpretations of the origins of the relations between the sexes."[75]

We would like to suggest another hypothesis about the relation between the sexes in the Palaeolithic. We believe that the physical and metaphysical power of the hunter had its counterpart in the procreative power of the woman. This suggestion is founded on two features characteristic of the art of that period.

In the first place, the large number of feminine statuettes bears witness to an authentic fertility cult which led to the Mother-Goddesses of the Neolithic period. Quite clearly, the artists of the Aurignacian and Gravettian were primarily interested in the maternal aspect of birth and the perpetuation of the species. The Gravettian statuettes, with their enormous stomachs, their hypertrophied breasts descending to the pelvis, represent woman on the point of giving birth. With a few exceptions,[76] those that have incorrectly been called "Venuses" have no faces. Only those parts of the body that participate in fecundity[77] are shown in exaggerated form. "The breasts, the belly, the pelvic region, and the thighs fall within a circle from which extend the tapering torso and legs."[78] This is the magic circle of fecundity. While it is impossible to be sure of the exact function of these "Venuses",[79] we may presume that they represent feminine sacredness, and consequently the magico-religious force of the goddesses.

But if the feminine-maternal exercised such a great fascination over the Palaeolithic artists, it may well also have been for a different reason, specific to that period.

We have seen that Leroi-Gourhan has constantly pointed out the absence of any representation of the sexual act. Not a single procreative couple, no sign of eroticism in the whole of Palaeolithic art. Is this not a sign that procreation was a strictly feminine power? Even if men suspected their part in it, biological paternity at this period could only have been a vague idea[80] that had no common measure with the obviousness of feminine creation. It is not impossible, then, that men imagined the reproduction of the species as a kind of *parthenogenesis*,[81] thus acknowledging that their females possessed the extraordinary power of creating life. Such potency, which they did not possess, could only arouse envy and admiration in the men. It was as good as that of the hunter, and perhaps even better.

It is generally agreed today that prehistoric men had two different kinds of cult: the hunters worshipped an animal divinity, and the women worshipped fertility goddesses. The separation of the sexes gives us reason to assume the existence of secret rites exclusive to the men, which they celebrated before hunting expeditions[82] in the deepest recesses of the sanctuaries. Palaeolithic man probably used animal disguise both for his initiatory dances and for hunting, the better to deceive his prey.[83] This would explain many masculine representations in which the body is bending forward or the profile is extended into a muzzle.

There has been much speculation as to the reasons for the "bestial" stylization of the masculine face. André Leroi-Gourhan[84] does not rule out the notion of a certain striving after assimilation with the animal, in particular with the horse, which was the most frequent male symbol. This hypothesis corresponds perfectly with the fascinating dualistic theory of Henri Delporte: "The representation of the animal would be that of the living world exterior to man. And in contrast and by opposition, man, the human group, *humanity, would be translated by a feminine configuration*, the feminine form being perfectly legitimate since it ensures the renewal and continuance of the species. This opposition between the '*human-woman*' principle and the '*animal-living-world*' principle would explain the fundamental differences that have been observed between the configuration of woman (her features only semi-perceptible, so as to protect her) and that of animals (realism and morphological accuracy), at the same time as the relative lack of masculine representations in Palaeolithic art."[85]

Given that female forms were thought to be more suitable for incarnating the human, it may well follow that there was also the hope that since women had the power of generation, they might also possess that of regenerating the dead. Woman, as the pole of life, dialectically reflects the pole of death.

As far back as the Upper Palaeolithic, shells, emblems *par excellence* of the feminine organs, were placed in tombs. Their arrangement probably corresponded to a magico-religious rite intended to bring the dead back to life.[86] That is why it has often been thought that it may have been the women who were in charge of the funerary rites. Who could be in a better position than they, who gave life, to give it back again?

The recent work by the American anthropologist Annette Weiner[87] on the women of the Trobriand Islands[88] encourages this interpretation. It has thrown light on the importance of the feminine power of regeneration in this matrilineal society.

In the life and death cycle, men and women control the different aspects of the time involved in the continuity of the generations: "Women control the regeneration of matrilineal identity, the essence of person . . . that moves through unmarked cosmic time. Therefore, *the power of women, operating in an ahistorical continuum of time and space*, is particularly meaningful at conception and death. Men control property, a resource contained within sociopolitical fields of action. *The male domain of power and control is situated in historical time and space . . .*"[89]

The Trobriand women, who are responsible for ensuring the continuity of the *dala* (lineage, or sub-clan), therefore have immortality in their power, and this power is theirs alone. Men's aspiration to immortality can only be realized through women's control over the identity of the *dala*. This shows the transcendentalism of the women's role.

True, we cannot legitimately apply the analysis of Trobriand society just as it stands to prehistoric societies. But Annette Weiner's work has the great merit of breaking away from the dominant theories based on the removal of women from positions of power. It puts an end to the idea that they represent no more than the "nature" pole of a universal nature–culture opposition, and are merely one of the numerous objects exchanged at marriage.[90]

In our turn, we would like to suggest the idea that in Palaeolithic societies, control and power may well have been exercised by both men and women. And that where motherhood and death were not purely biological facts but objects of a mystique, the women disposed of very great powers of a cosmic order, quite distinct from the political and social power of the men.

Like Weiner, we may assume that society was divided into two spheres that were separated by sex, but connected; and that in their respective spheres, each controlled different types of resources, and thereby, in various modes and differing degrees, exercised a specific power over the Other.

Honesty requires us to point out that for lack of proof, we can only formulate conjectures. Our own conjecture falls between two contrary propositions. Whereas certain feminists think that in the Palaeolithic all decisions were taken in common, the philosopher Jean Baechler, in an interview published by *Le Monde*, recently stated (1985) that the democratic ideal prevalent among the hunters did not extend to their women, who were "subjected to the domination of their males".

In our hypothesis of the division of powers, in which a kind of equilibrium between the sexes is established, *the One is equal to the Other*. Contrary to what Simone de Beauvoir thought,[91] to call woman the Other is not to abandon the idea of a reciprocal relationship between the sexes, nor is it to consider reciprocity as "inessential". On the contrary: it is because the women probably did constitute a separate group, endowed with specific powers, that they would have been able to have relatively autonomous relations with the men, and not simply a submissive relationship.

Edgar Morin's poetic image of "the upright man, his weapon held high" and "the woman bending over a child",[92] is quite relative. Palaeolithic art did not only show the hunter triumphant. It also showed wounded men on their knees, defeated. On the other hand, there is no trace of a bending woman in a position of humility or submission. The feminine statues emit an impression of strength and serenity quite incompatible with inferior status.

It may be objected that during the Magdalenian period, feminine representations became increasingly rare, until by the end of the Palaeolithic (9000 BC) they were non-existent. This observation may perhaps indicate a loss of feminine prestige and a gain in that of the male hunter. And yet it cannot be a sign of masculine omnipotence because, contrary to the prevailing ideology, the period that followed it actually marked the apogee of feminine prestige.

II

FROM FEMININE ASCENDANCY
TO SHARED POWERS

The period we are now coming to lasted from the tenth millennium until about the end of the second. It started with the climatic revolution marked by the end of the Wurm glaciation, and finished just before the beginning of the historic era. It was divided into three extensive stages, characterized by different cultures and life styles. The oldest, the Mesolithic,[1] covers slightly more than two millennia. The second, the Neolithic,[2] was spread over nearly three millennia, before giving way to the Chalcolithic[3] and the Metal Ages.[4]

During this long period, the relations between man and woman, in so far as we can imagine them with any degree of precision, seem to have evolved first in the direction of the greater prestige of women, and then towards that of men. But what little we do know about the period does not incline us to assume that there was any revolution similar to the one we know occurred later. From the point of view of the sexes, these eight millennia seem to have been a continuation of the ways of the Palaeolithic. The complementary relationship persists in positive fashion, as collaboration, and not yet as the exclusion characteristic of the absolute patriarchy that was more or less generalized by the time the historic period began.

Ascendancy of Women. Power of Mothers

Between the eighth and sixth millennia, there occurred in the Middle East – with a lead of almost two thousand years over the

31

West – a radical transformation in the way of life of the populations, whereby from an economy based on hunting and gathering they moved on to the domestication of plants and animals. The Neolithic period does not merely open a new page in economic history, it also implies "a radical modification of human society, mentalities, and cultural and spiritual life".[5]

This was characterized by a feminine prestige that was probably far greater than that of the preceding period. This feminine and maternal ascendancy is attested by an impressive number of sculptures and representations of imposing feminine figures, whose divine nature becomes more and more clearly apparent. At the same period, masculine representations become less frequent and less interesting, shorn of the hieratic and magical aspect by which we recognize the goddesses.

The cult of the Mother-Goddesses then prevalent all over the Middle East does not imply the rule of an omnipotent matriarchy which reduced men to a position of inferiority. In all probability, men possessed political power and continued to share economic power with the women.

But even if we cannot speak of a matriarchy, we are nevertheless confronted with a system of values in which feminine ascendancy is so well authenticated that it can only embarrass the partisans of an original male power similar to the one we know. The Mother-Goddess is neither a myth nor a legend, nor even a symbol.[6] We only have to observe the numerous stone statuettes in our museums to be convinced of the extreme importance of the feminine values and of their historical reality.

It may perhaps be said that human relationships do not necessarily follow divine representations, and that they are not carbon copies of each other. To this very serious objection, we reply that the Neolithic religions – like other ideologies – were not isolated from the real world. In this period, when men were beginning to "master" nature rather than submit to its effects, women were in the front line. It was they who made the crops grow, as their power of fertility was associated with that of the earth. So it is no wonder that the Divine was represented in feminine form, and it would be surprising if the prestige of divinity had not served the cause of women.

Feminine Agriculture and Masculine Stockbreeding

Today, there is general agreement that agriculture was probably a feminine invention.[7] The men, busy hunting game, and later grazing their herds, were almost always away. But the women, on the other hand, drawing on the knowledge they had gained as collectors, were able to observe the natural phenomena of sowing and germination. It was natural for them to try to reproduce them artificially.

Lewis Mumford has pointed out that there is a marked difference between the earlier and later phases of the Neolithic civilization, which roughly corresponds to the difference between horticulture and agriculture, in other words the difference between the cultivation of flowers, fruit and vegetables and the cultivation of grains.[8] Gardening, being an almost exclusively feminine activity, is the remote origin of agriculture. And this inclines us to think that it was women who took the first steps towards domestication.[9]

And thus, in little patches of garden, long before the systematic cultivation of fields, the first nutritious plants were deliberately planted and harvested, and their surplus seeds replanted. With this work, women did not provide all the necessary food but they did make a continuous, balanced diet possible, because a proportion of the crops could be dried and stored.

Agriculture proper, the cultivation of cereals, that is, began to make a timid appearance in the Fertile Crescent. While seeds of wheat dating from the eighth millennium have been found in Jericho, it is thought that agriculture was not definitely established until about 6500 BC, in Iran, in Turkey and in Palestine. Various kinds of wheat – einkorn and emmer – were grown there, as well as barley, sometimes rye, oats, vetch, chickpeas and vines.[10]

Since there seems to be an organic link between cereals and pottery[11] (as various kinds of receptacles were needed to stock the harvests and food products), most feminist and Marxist authors claim that pottery was invented by women.[12] This is an attractive, but unproven, hypothesis. Nor – whatever Freud may say – is it proven that leather processing, plaiting, or basket making are purely feminine inventions, even though today, in certain tribes, it is still the women who engage in these activities and not the men.

While women were undertaking the first experiments in agriculture, men were beginning to realize that it was a mistake to kill the game systematically, because that led to reproductive difficulties which resulted in the impoverishment of an animal group. In order to protect certain species that were vital for human food, they began to domesticate them.[13]

From then on, man spent far more time building up a herd and guarding it than he did in hunting. While he kept control of most of the meat supply, this was no longer as important as it had been when the climate was cold. Moreover, although stockbreeding took the place of hunting, the prestige of the stockbreeder was nevertheless far less than that of the hunter, who was constantly risking his life.

The complementarity of these tasks was still respected, but the value attached to each was no longer equal. The farther we get from the era of the hunters, the nearer we get to agriculture, and hence to the greater ascendancy of women.

Within a few millennia, the values of life began to take precedence over the fascination with death. The mother became the central figure of the Neolithic societies.

The Reign of the Goddess: Mother and Mistress of Nature

This extends over a long period which runs from the Upper Neolithic[14] until the Bronze Age, and even far beyond in certain regions. Statuettes representing a Mother-Goddess have been found in those countries between the Indus and the Aegean where there was an ancient civilization, and also in eastern Europe. In the southeast of Europe, nearly 30,000 Neolithic figurines in different materials have been discovered, almost all of which represent feminine figures. Everywhere they are women with broad hips and voluminous breasts who could easily be the sisters of the Perigordian "Venuses".

Western Europe is the exception to this rule. There, only two to three hundred crude stone statuettes have been found: it is as if "religiosity had remained archaically linked to the problem of death and of the funerary",[15] instead of being oriented towards life and towards the woman who gives it. This attitude is probably linked to the fact that the peasant economy appeared much later there than in eastern Europe and the Orient.

Everywhere else,[16] comparable beliefs and practices appeared among peoples as diverse as the Asiatic Semites and the Indo-Europeans.

In the Middle East, many feminine statuettes appeared round about 6500 BC.[17] In Çatal Hüyük,[18] the oldest known town (between 6500 and 5600 BC) in the south of Anatolia, houses decorated with feminine reliefs have been found: pregnant women or stylized figures of pairs of breasts.[19] But we only have to contemplate the famous "Potnia" seated on a throne,[20] accompanied by two panthers, her hands on their heads, to understand that this imposing personage is at the same time the mother and the mistress of nature. As Gabriel Camps says, this sixth-millennium Çatal Hüyük Potnia is seen as the genetrix of a thousand other feminine divinities who, from the beginning of the Neolithic Age until the triumph of the male, monotheistic religions, were the focus of the faith of husbandmen and shepherds. (*Illustrated overleaf.*)

In Palestine, certain Potnias dating from 4500 BC had faces deliberately fashioned to produce a terrifying effect.[21] The exaggeration and deformation of their features emphasize their demoniacal character. No doubt this is a way of showing that the omnipotent mother is not necessarily benevolent. Side by side with the generous mother who bestows life and pleasures, there is another who is cruel, and who refuses to satisfy her children, a close association between the symbols of life and death, the goddess and the ogress,[22] the good and the bad breast.

In the fifth millennium, the steatopygic[23] Mother-Goddess, like the "Venuses" that preceded her, is everywhere represented seated hieratically on a throne, sometimes giving birth, sometimes accompanied by a smaller male god, who remains in his humble place. "She is seen by turns as life-giving, food-giving (she holds out her breasts as an offering), erotic, funerary – all of which aspects were later dispersed into multifarious divine figures, which seem only to be the multiple facets of one omnipotent personage."[24]

The goddess was not always represented in the form of an imposing woman with a terrifying gaze. She was also incarnated in plants and animals.[25] In order to engender each *species*, the Great

The Çatal Hüyük goddess, after Mellaart

Mother adopted the forms that corresponded to the animals she coupled with. Her sovereignty extends over all beings, because she has produced them all. It is not surprising, then, that six thousand years ago in Mesopotamia the Goddess Ninhursag was a milch cow, as were the Egyptian goddess Hathor, the mother of Horus, and the Hindu goddess Aditi.[26]

When the goddess has human form, she always has the same three characteristics: nudity, obesity, and accentuated femininity. She is often represented as showing, or pressing, her breasts. Sometimes she is spreading her thighs in a manner that is almost obscene. In every case, the aim of these attitudes is to reinforce the effect produced by the goddess seen as a source of prosperity.

But the goddess did not only pass through various incarnations.

She also evolved as a function of those who accompanied her. Among numerous peoples, she was represented in human form between two animals: quadrupeds or reptiles, birds, etc. These triads may be found from the Mediterranean to India and beyond, and from the Aegean period until Imperial times.[27] Later, the goddess was represented between two human males. She had become the wife of two gods, her consorts. In Minoan Crete, where it was found distasteful to put human and animal forms together, the goddess is sometimes accompanied by male gods, whose powers seem never to surpass or diminish hers. On the contrary, they turn towards her,[28] and contemplate her with respect. However, whether the goddess is surrounded by animals or accompanied by two males, there are two interesting points about this primitive triad. It shows the dominating attitude of the goddess towards her acolytes, and above all it implies that divine polyandry preceded the couple. Mistress of the animals or wife of young gods, she presides over fecundity, and this is what makes her action specifically divine, or at least magico-religious.

Our Mother who is All . . .

In India, in the Vedic era, Aditi was one of the names of the Mother-Goddess. A stanza in the Rig-Veda defines her thus:

> Aditi is the heavens; Aditi is the atmosphere.
> Aditi is the mother; she is the father; she is the son.
> Aditi is all the gods and the five kinds of beings.
> Aditi is what is born; Aditi is what is to be born.

The Great Goddess reigns over the unified cosmos. All past and future beings are dependent on her. This means that her sovereignty extends over the infinity of time and space. While it is too early to speak of monotheism, since Aditi, like the other Mother-Goddesses, is only the first of a numerous pantheon, the fact that she is the mother from whom all the gods issued does nevertheless bring us close to this notion. She alone symbolizes not only the unity of the universe, but also that of life and death.

The ancient religions of India, Persia, and eastern Europe have in common the myth of the Great Mother, the divinity of the waters. Her name is given to the great rivers[29] that irrigate and fecundate the earth. She is also – as in Iran – the goddess of battles, the bellicose divinity who presides over the destruction of human beings. In the very earliest societies, only a limited number of people could find enough to eat. It was the death of some that enabled the others to be born and to grow up. The Mother-Goddess incarnates this cruel necessity and the idea that life and death are linked as the two faces of the same process.

It is also because she incarnates *All* creation that *bisexual* divinities of the earth and of fecundity are to be found in different places. "In such cases the divinity contains all the forces of creation – and this formula of polarity, of the co-existence of opposites, was to be taken up again in the loftiest of later speculation."[30]

The Goddess's bisexuality is the clearest way of saying that she is All, the Whole who does not need to call on any outside contribution in order to procreate. She engenders the universe by parthenogenesis, exactly like God the Father, who succeeded her in the male monotheistic religions.

This apprehension of the Mother-Goddess could not remain without consequences for the relations between man and woman. The mother was the human substitute for the Goddess, and Neolithic man worshipped a god in feminine form. In daily life, beliefs about the origin of children gave credence to the idea that men have little or no part in creation.

Having assembled a great many ethnological and prehistoric stories and legends from all over the world, Mircea Eliade thinks that before the physiological causes of conception were known, men believed that maternity was due to the direct insertion of the child into the mother's womb.[31] It was said that children began their prenatal life in waters, crystals, stones, trees or caves, in the heart of Mother Earth, before being introduced like a "breath" into the womb of their human mothers.[32] From this point of view, the father merely legitimizes these children by a ritual that has all the features of adoption.[33]

Myths and legends may not, of course, say all there is to be said about human knowledge and feelings. For instance, recent studies of

the Trobrianders reveal the fact that their apparent lack of knowledge of biological paternity stemmed more from denial than from
true ignorance. Moreover, one may imagine the father's part in procreation and at the same time be ignorant of the physiological conditions of the process. But this in no way reduces the importance of the
ideological system which holds that women alone - with the aid of
the cosmos or the spirits - have access to creation.

This belief in a kind of parthenogenesis should perhaps be compared, from the psychological and ideological point of view, with the
ritual couvade, still practised in certain primitive societies. When
the mother gives birth, the father takes to his bed. This is a way for
the father to assert his rights over the child. Often he mimes the
birth, cries out in pain, and only resumes his normal life several
weeks after the child is born.[34]

Neolithic civilizations, on the contrary, took only the creative
power of the woman-mother into account. This *parti-pris* - if it
was one - was profoundly rooted in the religious system and the
economic structure of the period. Even if maternal and feminine
sacredness had been known since the Palaeolithic, the discovery of
agriculture must have considerably increased its sway. The fertility
of the earth was then linked to feminine fecundity: women became
responsible for the abundance of the harvests, for they knew the
"mystery" of creation.

The agricultural cultures developed a "cosmic religion",[35] whose
rites were performed by women. Agricultural work itself was a rite,
because it took place on the body of the Earth-Mother and implied
the integration of the worker in certain either favourable or disastrous periods of time.[36]

The mystical solidarity between the fecundity of the earth and
women's creative force is one of the fundamental intuitions of what
Mircea Eliade calls "the agricultural consciousness". Many rites bear
witness to the decisive influence of erotic magic over agriculture:
nakedness, orgies, drops of maternal milk sprinkled over the field
demonstrate this. But given this global conception of life, if the
women's fecundity influences the fertility of the fields, an abundance of crops also helps women to conceive. The dead contribute to
both, and they expect to gain from these two sources of fertility the
energy and substance that will reintegrate them into the vital flux.

The solidarity of the dead (buried, like seeds) with fertility and agriculture,[37] shows once again the omnipotence of the Earth-Mother and, with her, the prestige of women. Their practice of agriculture was the cause of regeneration, for the fertility cults were closely linked with the mortuary cults.

Everything connected with life, and hence with abundance, was then the woman's domain. The source of plant fertility and human fecundity, it was also she who protected humans from death, before protecting the dead. Like the Cretan goddesses who held poppies and other opiates[38] in their hands, the women possessed healing powers, thanks to the plants they had collected.

There is no doubt that women's dominion had never been so great, even though no serious document mentions their political power.[39] We all know some legends about the Amazons[40] or the Lemnian women, the ones warriors and the others mariticides. But these counter-examples are used more as a release of feelings than as historical models of the relation between man and woman.

Despite the hiatus that may exist between representations and daily life, the analysis of religious beliefs that lasted over several millennia is a serious indication of the prestige attached to each sex. And it does seem that the Neolithic period comes under the sign of the reign of the mother, and leaves masculine powers in the relative shade.

To try to understand the relation between the men and women of this era, we have only two certainties at our disposal. The first concerns the men. Between the hunting period of the Palaeolithic and the expansion of wars in the Bronze Age, they were mainly engaged in stockraising, handicrafts, and then agriculture. All these were sedentary activities, important, it is true, but which did not put their lives in jeopardy, as did hunting and war. It is therefore not impossible that during this more peaceful period the masculine sex lost some of its former prestige. It was not a time when virile values were venerated, as the absence of firmly-established masculine gods would seem to show.

The second certainty concerns the obvious religiosity of the Neolithic societies. When the life of human beings is adapted to the rhythm of magico-religious practices and people always pray and sacrifice to a goddess, how could her human incarnation, woman, not have considerable prestige among those who do not incarnate her? How could the ancient habit of invoking "Our Mother which art the Earth" not translate a prestige of the feminine, similar to that of the masculine when people were later to pray "Our Father which art in Heaven . . ."?

It is true that wherever an omnipotent god reigns, man rules the world and the father rules his family.[41] This was not the case with Neolithic woman, of whom it has been said "she reigned, but she did not rule". And yet, considering that economic activity was closely linked to the cult of the Mother-Goddess, it is difficult to see how men could already have exercised any coercive sway over women.

The Couple, or Shared Powers

From the fourth millennium until the end of the second, there seems to have been a period of equilibrium, and even harmony, in the relations between men and women which we do not find again in the subsequent periods. This moment of closeness between the sexes did not begin and end at the same time everywhere.[42] Some suspect that it existed in Jericho from the fifth millennium, and also on the banks of the Danube. Others consider that its effects were still felt well beyond the beginnings of the institution of patriarchy and lasted until the birth of Greek democracy. Some have spoken of a "semi-patriarchal" system in which the father's recognized powers did not exclude those of the mother, or work against the liberty of the feminine sex. But whatever precise name is given to this period of which we still know little, the documents we do possess give the impression of communities in which the sexes held each other in mutual esteem.

Everything leads us to think that men gradually began to demand the right to participate in the various tasks and functions that had previously been the prerogative of women. In one sense, this new collaboration could be seen as the beginning of the dispossession of women, which history was to confirm. But we can also refuse to observe this period merely in terms of the future, and perceive it just as itself, as a pause for breath before the beginning of the long struggle to impose the supremacy of the One over the Other.

This period saw the birth of the new notion of the couple. Gradually, from the west of Europe to the east of Asia, it came to be realized that it takes two to procreate, two to produce. The cult of God-the-Father had not yet been substituted for that of the Mother-Goddess. But it was the couple formed by a god and a goddess that became the object of worship. Men and women shared heaven and earth between them, no longer according to the old schema of the division of specific powers between the One and the Other, but with the view that the One could no longer do without the Other in order to perform the same task.

Production and Reproduction

Some people date the appearance of male agriculture using the ploughshare (as opposed to female agriculture using the hoe) from the sixth millennium, among the Sumerians. They think it spread throughout the Middle East until the sixth millennium, but did not appear in the West until pre-Homeric times, fifteen to twenty centuries BC.

Whatever the chronology, it was probably at a relatively early stage that it became necessary for men to help their women with the heavy work. To clear the ground for planting by making a furrow with a hoe – usually made of wood – demanded considerable effort, if we are to believe the documents from the ancient Egyptian Empire, which show the fellaheen working laboriously with their digging sticks.[43] It was only later that man was able to get animals to help him with agriculture, that he used a swing-plough,[44] and above all that he substituted a metal blade for the wooden ploughshare.[45] But even before the use of the swing-plough became widespread, it is highly possible that men and women were already sharing agricultural tasks. The men took on the exhausting task of clearing the ground, the women the less tiring job of sowing, and at harvest time they worked together. This division of labour was in conformity with the magico-religious rites of the period, and also respected the physical characteristics of each sex.

By the time the technique of the swing-plough was developed in the Bronze Age, enabling the peasant to husband his strength and to sow larger areas,[46] and when the use of the yoke drawn by a pair of oxen was established, agriculture had become the men's domain. The use of the plough with a metal blade made it exclusively theirs. The fields became their property. All that was left to the women was the former garden.

But before this seizure by men of a domain that had originally been feminine, the solidarity between the fecundity of the "glebe" (the soil under cultivation) and that of women was still a salient feature of the agricultural societies. The women therefore still had the prestige of being able to influence and distribute fertility. Their prestige only began to fade with the coming of the plough, which very soon became a male sexual symbol. The fertility of the earth was no longer the result of the action of the feminine principle alone, but of the association of the two principles.

The assimilation of woman to the earth became that of the furrow to the vulva. It was no longer women who possessed a natural affinity with the seed,[47] but man, or more precisely, the virile seed. The plough-phallus gave man an increasingly important role, by making him the one who fertilized the earth. At this period, however, no one was yet thinking of denying the essential part played by women in the process of fertility and fecundation. Sharing was the order of the day, as was the necessity of the couple to carry out the work of creation.

If we are to believe certain ethnologists[48] of the beginning of the century, several Australian populations of the time were still ignorant of the physiological conditions of procreation. Their explanation of conception took no account of the sexual act and they did not grasp – or pretended not to grasp – the role of the father.[49] Paternity was only understood from the social aspect.

Today, there are some who challenge the interpretation of the fathers of ethnology and think that this ignorance of biological paternity was merely feigned. But the problem still remains where prehistoric men are concerned.

Jean Przyluski takes the ignorance of the earliest men for granted because, he says, every pubertal girl had to be deflowered, and no correlation was seen between conception and these male acts. He thinks that it was the practice of stockbreeding that put men on the right track. To get good results from this new activity, they had to observe the behaviour of their domestic animals. They then discovered that they could prevent or promote their multiplication by keeping the sexes apart or together. After which, all men had to do was apply the consequences of this discovery to themselves. They modified their ideas of conception: it was not the fact of having eaten a particular kind of food or of having come into contact with a certain object that made a woman pregnant, but the seed deposited in her, the substance of the male.

"The unisexual fecundity of the earliest times was succeeded by bisexual fecundity; the transmission of life requires the co-operation of both sexes . . . an explanation that was to convulse both law and religion. Until then, a child had been linked to its mother alone; it was a plant or an animal according to the nature of the seed that had engendered it. From then on, the child was linked to its father. It was a little man, and continued the line of its forebears."[50]

Przyluski thinks that this marks the date of the passage from matrilineal filiation to patrilineal filiation, although so radical a transformation must have operated gradually and not without resistance, if the folklore of the populations concerned is anything to go by.[51]

In Greek mythology, there is still the vague memory of a period when children belonged to their mothers. Pierre Vidal-Naquet[52] refers to the myth of Cecrops, the civilizing hero who led the Athenians from barbarity to civilization. Civilized Athens is presented as the reversal of the preceding state. From then on, Athenian women were no longer allowed to vote, children were no longer known by their mothers' names, and women no longer had a name of their own. They were no more than the wives or daughters of Athenian men, whereas "previously, says Clearchus, sexual unions were formed by chance and no one could identify his father, which implies that everyone was known by his mother's name".[53]

While this proposition does not necessarily imply ignorance of the role of the man in procreation, it does indicate that owing to the sexual liberty of the women the biological father was not known, hence the necessary recourse to a matrilineal kinship structure. This would tend to show that the notion of the couple based on marriage, and the patriarchal system that we know, are more recent than people often want to believe. When we remember that Cecrops[54] was credited not only with the establishment of marriage, but at the same time with the discovery of agriculture, writing, and the laws of property, we observe that mythology made the same link between paternity and the development of agricultural practices as do the prehistorians of today.

The Birth of War [55]

During the whole of the Palaeolithic period, prehistoric hunters were always armed, but peace-loving. There is no trace of war to be found in their tombs. In the archaic period of the Neolithic, the population was still sparse, and therefore pacific. Even if traces of aggressivity between men can be found in the Epipalaeolithic, they do not go beyond individual cases, and we cannot yet talk of war.

It is after the beginning of the fully agricultural Middle Neolithic period that warlike manifestations tend to be more common and become collective. The reason for this is simple: the conditions of life and nutrition caused great demographic upsurges. This was the period when villages were built and production increased. Great storage vases for food, unknown in the Early Neolithic, appear, and confirm the existence of large stocks of provisions which would have aroused the envy of those less well provided for.

The overpopulation encouraged by the accumulation of resources, in its turn created the need for more land, and communities fought each other for the possession of territories. Pillage and conquests became widespread.

From the Late Neolithic and the Metal Age on, war left its traces in the collective burial grounds. Their skeletons show clear signs of traumatism and have several deadly arrows deeply implanted in their bones, a sign of desperate fighting.[56]

Indisputably, war was the prerogative and the compulsion of the male sex. The skeletons pierced with arrows are those of men, and there is no mention of similar female skeletons. With the development of agriculture, the warriors took over from the hunters and recovered the prestige and power that men had lost with the decline of hunting. In time, they were to form a prestigious class which specialized in this dangerous and noble activity.

The fact remains that myths are full of stories about warrior women.[57] So are travellers' tales.[58] Unfortunately, most of these examples are still neither verifiable nor convincing. Woman may be members of an army, wear uniform, but never find themselves facing the enemy in the front line. However, in two very different types of civilization there are instances of women's participation in war that are more historical than mythical. The first is the Celtic civilization, which was semi-patriarchal and in which women were given an important role.[59] André Pelletier speaks of the astonishment of the Romans at finding themselves opposed by tribes led by women.[60] He quotes Plutarch, who was surprised at the part they played in the battle between Marius and the Ambrones (a Celtic tribe) in 102 BC near Aix-en-Provence: ". . . where the women meeting them with swords and hatchets, and making a hideous outcry, set upon those that fled as well as those that pursued . . . , and mixing themselves with the combatants, with their bare arms pulling away the Romans' shields, and laying hold on their swords, endured the wounds and slashing of their bodies to the very last with undaunted resolution".[61]

Brazilian culture provides the second example of "Amazonian" practices, or in any case of feminine participation in battles.[62]

But however this may be, the principle of female warriors never excludes the participation of men in war, which, historically, is their specific domain.[63]

> "Mon enfant, ma soeur
> songe à la douceur
> d'aller là-bas vivre ensemble!
> . . . au pays qui te ressemble!"

Religious Dualism

At the end of the fourth millennium and the beginning of the third, the divine dyad began to prevail over the preceding triad. The transition from polyandry to monogamy was gradually being effected.

Among the gods, too, the notion of the heterosexual couple was taking priority in the fertile areas, while the divine triad persisted as a relic of the past among less favoured peoples.

In Egypt, the divine couple made its appearance during the third millennium. Osiris became at the same time the spirit of grain and the spirit of water.[64] His marriage to Isis, the great goddess of universal fertility, symbolizes the union of the water (the Nile) and the earth. By their lovemaking, Isis and Osiris fertilized all nature. But we will notice, in the legend as recorded by Alexandre Moret, an early appropriation of feminine powers. It was Osiris, not Isis, who was supposed to have revealed to mankind all the nutrient and textile plants, as well as the arts of agriculture and irrigation.

In Babylon,[65] at the same time, the agrarian gods took on a male aspect. From Mesopotamia to Anatolia and Syria, a beardless young god appeared, dressed in a short robe, who was associated with the sacred couple in order to play his own specific role of agrarian god. Soon afterwards, the young, specialized god was "absorbed" by the Great God. He was the lover of the Great Goddess and presided over universal fertility.

In all the Indo-European mythologies, we observe an early tendency towards the formation of couples[66] of the Jupiter-Juno type, namely matrimonial unions resembling monogamy.[67] After having been the mistress of the animals, the goddess became the wife of two male consorts, and then formed a couple with only one husband. The coupled goddesses Demeter and Kore, a unisexual dyad formed of an old and a young goddess,[68] gave way to a heterosexual couple, Astarte and Adonis.

The divine bisexual couple is proof of the transformation of ideas about generation. It no longer belongs exclusively to the feminine sex, which was how the unisexual dyad still interpreted it. The mother could no longer give birth to a child without the intervention of a male.[69]

But the balance of powers within the divine couple seems precarious. Whereas in the ancient triads the goddess took precedence over her masculine acolytes, the opposite was the case with the dyads, in which the importance of the masculine god gradually increased until he often became more influential than his partner. This evolution of the way in which the gods were depicted says a great deal about the power relationship within the human couple. Even though feminine representations persist throughout the Metal Ages and the historical period, we are obliged to recognize that the notion of the couple, which is indissociable from love, is also at the origin of the diminution of the powers of women.

Before feminine prestige declined, it is possible to imagine that the relations between men and women were relatively well balanced. This exceptional period in the history of their relations is characterized by the sharing of heaven and earth. A divine couple, both procreator and producer, man and woman, seemed to be joined together by a complicity and symmetry that was not to be found again for a long time in the Western world, in particular, because people soon forgot that the feminine also may incarnate the Divine, and that transcendence is not simply a masculine prerogative.

Interaction, Equivalence and Equality of the Sexes

Recent studies of archaic Greece[70] all insist on the ambivalence and interaction of the sexes that we can still see at the turn of the fourth century BC in certain religious and social practices.

Jean-Pierre Vernant was one of the first to point out the ambivalence of the sexes as seen in the mythical story of the relations between a complementary god and goddess: Hermes and Hestia.[71] Hermes, as we know, is the god of travel, and Hestia the goddess of the hearth, the centre of the domestic space around which human space is oriented and organized. She is the "inside". He is the "outside", elusive and ubiquitous. Her domain is the house. He travels all over the world to work, make war, engage in commerce and participate in public life. They would seem to be opposed in every respect, but Jean-Pierre Vernant suggests that the opposition is more apparent than real, since characteristics of each god can be found in the other. Hermes may also express permanence, and Hestia mobility.

This ambiguity is also found in the main social institutions, in marriage,[72] for instance, as in meals.[73] Vernant concludes that the polarity of the fixed and the mobile, of the inside and the outside, etc., is not only shown in the interplay of domestic institutions, but is also part of the nature of man and woman: "Neither Hestia nor Hermes can be taken in isolation. They fulfil their functions as a couple, the existence of the one implies that of the other, for each is seen as the necessary counterpart of the other. *Moreover, this very complementarity of the two deities assumes an opposition or an inner tension in them both*, which confers a fundamentally ambiguous character on the nature of their godhood."[74]

To fulfil her function of permanence in time, Hestia, the virgin goddess, must also appear as the Mother, the source of life and creation. Hermes, the god of space and movement, must have a home to settle in. The One is not only the complement of the Other. Part of the One is also necessarily to be found in the Other. In this sense, if man and woman are opposed, the better to complete each other, they must also be resemblant, in order to understand each other and to become allies.

The interaction of the sexes or cases of inversion are not only to be found in myths; they can also be observed in the Greek drama (notably in Aristophanes), and in certain educational traditions. Vidal-Naquet[75] points out that during the rites of passage Athenian ephebes had to wear a female garment, the "black chlamys", until they had taken the oath and become entitled to the uniform of the hoplite. The opposite held good for the passage from the condition of a girl to that of woman, which was effected through the intermediary of a male disguise. In both cases, the boy and the girl had for a moment to incarnate "the Other", as if to mark the bisexual duality of human nature, before they were received and incorporated into their own group.

Sparta too was familiar with the rites of inversion. Vidal-Naquet quotes Plutarch: "The girl was put into the hands of a woman ... who close-cropped her hair, dressed her in a man's garment and shoes and made her lie down on a straw mattress, alone and with no light."[76] In Sparta, the logic of the interaction of the sexes was linked to their equivalence. Nicole Loraux, in a very fine article,[77] has shown the association between the bed and war, the equal value of the hoplite and the mother of a newborn baby. Both had undergone athletic training in order to give the best of themselves when the time was ripe. While this may have gone without saying for the future warrior, the depiction of girls or pregnant women in training in the *Parthenos* constitutes an exception that is characteristic of Sparta.

But Nicole Loraux also finds this same equivalence between war and childbirth on private Athenian tombs. "On the funerary reliefs in Athenian cemeteries, the dead person is represented as he was in life; no allusion is made to his actual death – although there are two exceptions to this rule. One is the death of a soldier, the other the death of a woman in childbirth."[78] She also points out that "in the Greek cities, the conjugal bed was nothing to joke about." All the more so in that the place of reproduction, *lokhos*, was also the word for an ambush, and later for a small unit of the army.[79]

How could equivalence and symmetry be better expressed?

Euripides too recognized the equivalence of childbirth and combat. Nicole Loraux quotes his Medea, speaking of the pain of being a woman, and exclaiming: "They tell us that we lead a safe life at home, while they are at war, fighting. Rather than give birth one single time, I would prefer to be three times in the front line."[80]

Further evidence can be seen in the use of words in the classical period. For example, the word *ponos*, which means "pain borne", is applied both to the young man who is learning to harden himself and to labour pains. In this combat, the woman reverses certain signs of virility. "In order to face war, and also to accede to the status of a citizen, the Greek man girds himself; the woman in labour, on the contrary, has ungirded her waistband . . . The fact remains that even if it is reversed, the sign that links maternity to combat is there."[81]

In both cases, man and woman suffer, and risk death. This is enough to raise them to the same level of transcendence. It is also enough to allow the resemblances to triumph over the differences. By means of two apparently opposed activities, man and woman live through a common experience which unites them in the same concept of Humanity, instead of isolating them in their sexual specificity.

Although the Greeks officially confined women to their reproductive role and separated them from men, "no people foresaw better than the Greeks that the distribution of the masculine and the feminine was rarely established once and for all: from Hesiod to Hippocrates ... did they not choose to divide humanity into female-women, virile-men, men-women, women who act like men?"[82]

Whether we speak of the interaction or the equivalence of the sexes, we are talking about their equality. In the archaic period we are now concerned with, we may assume a state of institutional equilibrium between man and woman which resembles neither the anarchy of a society without laws nor the oppression that was to be found later. Patriarchy – if it already existed – had still not entered its oppressive stage. Matrimonial exchanges took place according to very free rules. In the world of Homer and of heroic legend, the contrast between legitimate spouse and concubine seems far less marked than in the classical age.[83] The norms and the rules of conduct allowed such latitude of choice that we cannot speak of a single model of marriage at that time, although this had become the case by the end of the sixth century in the democratic city of Athens.[84] The many different levels in the status of women formed a sufficiently flexible hierarchy for women not to be confined within one narrow model formulated by men.

All this was favourable for the mutual respect between the sexes that we observe at the same period in other types of societies. In Vedic literature, the balance between the Mother-Goddess Aditi and the great masculine gods was almost equal.[85] Written documents dating from 2000–400 BC (notably the Rig-Veda) show that the Aryan settlers in India seem to have had a high regard for their women. Even though they imposed patriarchy when they invaded the country, their wives were not servile, and their condition was far better than it became later. The birth of daughters was welcomed with joy, they were given as good an education as boys, and scholarly women were encouraged and venerated.[86] At the time of the Rig-Veda they were taught the martial arts. Some distinguished themselves on the field of battle,[87] others were remembered as great queens. Above all, girls were never segregated, either within the family or within the group. They had the same sexual liberty as boys, and illegitimate children were accepted without shame by both family and society. Although based on the patriarchal system, the status of Vedic women was infinitely more enviable than that of Frenchwomen in the seventeenth century.

51

We can say the same of the condition of Celtic women in the Iron Age until the Roman invasion of Gaul in the first century AD. We learn from Celtic law that while this society was already patriarchal, "its women enjoyed prerogatives that would have made Roman women of the same period die of envy: there was an equilibrium between the roles of the sexes that in no way depended upon the superiority of one sex to the other but was based on an equality within which each felt at ease."[88]

Thus ends – on an egalitarian note – the first phase of the history of man and woman. Although it is made up of several stages, this long period of nearly 30,000 years has one constant. While the sexual division of labour and of functions was always present, there is no moment in which we see the One being crushed because the Other has monopolized all the powers. Even though individual tyrannies most certainly have existed, we have not been able to discover a single unmistakably oppressive ideological system. From the Palaeolithic to the Iron Age, men and women shared the tasks with varying degrees of equity, but without ever giving the impression that the One was no more than the pale reflection of the Other, or, worse still, the evil to guard against. Even during the period of great feminine prestige, men, with their superior physical strength, still had their part to play in the body politic, in contrast to the historic period when women were excluded from it.

From the initial separation of powers, which characterizes the Palaeolithic, to the power-sharing of its last period, we find no trace of the sex war that was soon to begin. Separation did not mean exclusion, but the reciprocal need of the other. And as for the sharing of responsibilities, that may well be one of the signs of solidarity and mutual consideration.

Nevertheless, it does seem that this state is not "natural" to the relations between the sexes. The balance between the protagonists is always precarious, at the mercy of a technical or scientific discovery, or even of an ideological cataclysm. The period that follows is full of these changes, but from then on, the history of man and woman is inscribed in terms of conflicts, indeed of the elimination of the One by the Other, to the point of dangerously compromising their complementary relationship.

PART TWO

The One Without the Other

"The world of men and the world of women are like the sun and the moon: they may perhaps see each other every day, but they never meet."

M. MAMMERI

The story that follows covers – depending on the regions – no more than three or four millennia, which was time enough for patriarchy to achieve absolute supremacy, before disappearing in one part of the world. It starts in the East, the cradle of our civilization, and ends in the West. If it is objected that patriarchy is still very much alive in the greater part of the universe, and more so than ever in the Islamic countries of the Middle East where it all began, we would answer that the Neolithic revolution took two thousand years to reach the West. And above all, that even if it is only in one region of the globe that a power system is killed, this suffices to show its relativity and fragility. To be able to establish itself and to endure, "absolute" patriarchy[1] presupposes the combination of a certain number of ideological conditions. The only purpose of these is to establish men's power. It would be better to say men's omnipotence, since in certain societies the notion of power is so intimately linked with men. Maurice Godelier has even used the term "patriarchal despotism" to describe the region stretching from Gibraltar to Japan.[2] But as we shall see, traces of it are also to be found in many other parts of the world.

In these patriarchal systems, men are not satisfied with possessing the most important powers, with reigning over the family as well as over the body politic, in other words like God Almighty over the universe. They also have to impose a system of representations and values to justify such an imbalance. This is the beginning of a conception of the sexes that is hierarchized in the extreme. If man rules the world as well as ruling his wife, it is because he is the best representative of creation and of the creator. If he exercises his power harshly, it is because the woman who used to be his helpmeet has become the embodiment of a permanent danger against which he must be on his guard.

The moment one is convinced that one embodies Good, against the Other who embodies Evil, any excessive power becomes blameless, because it is justified in advance by either theology or morality. It becomes a sacred duty to reduce an evil otherness to its simplest expression, to render it innocuous in order to prevent it from doing harm.

Even when reduced to nearly nothing, though, woman still constituted a danger in man's imagination. Even though she no longer incarnated the Divine, even though her part in procreation was minimized to the extreme and she no longer had any right to determination either over her own life or over the direction of the world, she was still seen as a threatening source of disorder and anarchy. In extreme cases, she was assimilated to Satan.

It seems that the harsher the attitude of a patriarchal society towards the female sex, the more this is an expression of its fear. Fear of castration, but fear too of a women's revolt that would shatter the beautiful edifice ordained by men – for their own benefit. The logic of exclusion protects them from the competition of women. It reassures them about their own specificity and forbids comparison with the opposite sex. Indeed, there can be no comparison of what is naturally dissimilar, not to say radically different, heterogeneous.

But men had no need to be afraid, it would seem. True, there was the odd individual rebellion here or there, always quelled in time, but History has no record of any collective revolt by the female sex. For 2,500 years, women adopted as their own the ideological system of their masters, probably because there were many who were quite satisfied with passivity, irresponsibility and security, even if this was often at the cost of tears, guile, and hatred. Contrary to the men's fears, they did not escape from oppression by means of violence or disorder. They took advantage of the evolution of the men's system of values, and then turned it to their own account. If we somewhat oversimplify, we may say that while the patriarchal logic of the exclusion of the female sex begins in the West with Athenian democracy in the fifth century BC, the end of this logic is rooted in the French Revolution, when democracy was intended to apply to everyone.

Nevertheless, the funeral did not take place so soon. Patriarchy's death agony lasted for two centuries, during which the female sex's timid advances were followed by periods of considerable regression. But the violent spasms of this moribund system did not prevent its end. This took place yesterday . . . but no one has yet gone out into the streets to celebrate the event, perhaps because people were afraid that if they made too much noise they would bring the dead back to life; perhaps too because men's disarray touches women to the heart.

I

ABSOLUTE PATRIARCHY OR
THE CONFISCATION OF ALL POWERS

Patriarchy does not only designate a type of family based on male kinship and paternal power. The term also designates every social structure that has its source in the power of the father. In such an organization, the Prince of the City or the chief of the tribe has the same power over the members of the community as the father over the members of his family. The analogy is so close that rulers are wont to call themselves "the fathers of the people".

The powers of the father and, with him, the chief, vary from one society to another. They seem to be more moderate among the Masai in Africa than they were in the France of Louis XIV. Whether tyrannical or liberal, however, the father decides, controls, and sees that his law is enforced. The minimal patriarchal system can be recognized when fathers exchange their daughters for daughters-in-law (or brothers exchange their sisters for wives), with or without the consent of the parties concerned. Gradually, women became commodities. They were bought and sold, and were the property of their husbands. The main characteristic of the patriarchal society in its most absolute form is the strict control of female sexuality. Female adultery is an obsession with the men. The idea of bequeathing their name and property to a child of alien blood so appals them that they will commit the worst extremities on the person of their wives to avoid such an outrage.

Historically, patriarchy can be discerned everywhere in the Middle East in the Bronze Age. But this does not exclude the possibility that the exchange of women began much earlier, in both East and West.[3] But the power system did not appear in all its rigour and plenitude – as an absolute power[4] – until a little later, when a veritable religious revolution began to operate: the substitution of an

Almighty God for the former goddesses. In less than a thousand years, Brahma, Jehovah, Zeus and Jupiter imposed themselves on believers as the fathers of humanity, and reduced mothers to the status of minors. It was as if men had invented God, to make it easier to impose paternal power.

Divine Power: God the Father

God Drives out the Goddess

The equilibrium of the couple formed by a god and a goddess was precarious. Quarrels began to replace their former harmonious understanding and put an end to the equality of divine powers.

One of the best illustrations of this growing imbalance is the mythical conflict that opposes Demeter, the Earth-Mother, to her husband Hades, the god of Hell, with regard to the custody of their daughter Persephone.[5]

According to Phyllis Chesler, Demeter is the mother who tries to keep her female child under her own roof, and who considers all marriage a misfortune that puts an end to the free, happy life of the little girl and subjects her to the yoke of the male. One version of the legend has it that on the day when Persephone was gathering poppies to celebrate her first menstrual period, Hades, her father, came to rape her and carry her off underground, to the great wrath of her mother. A Homeric hymn relates that Demeter wept for her abducted daughter, refused to be comforted, and abstained from food and drink. This was the first revolt of the Great Goddess against the god who was to supplant her.

Françoise d'Eaubonne thinks that this myth also symbolizes the rejection by a preponderantly female community of the burgeoning male power. She sees proof of this in Demeter's threats to the patriarchal Sun God, who justifies the abduction of the girl. "Yes, if that be the natural fate of girls, let all mankind perish. Let there be no crops, no grain, no corn, if this maiden is not restored to me."[6]

Françoise d'Eaubonne rightly points out that this is the sort of protest that women who cultivated the land might have made against the androcentrist claims of the shepherds, and that its source dates from before the appearance of the first plough, as it assumes that agriculture is entirely feminine.

In any case, the power of the Great Goddess must still have been considerable, because "owing to this agrarian blackmail," she obtained the return of her daughter for six months of the year. It was Zeus who sorted things out by persuading Hades that this division was fair. This compromise between the god and the goddess may also symbolize the "contract" drawn up between man and woman for the management of the nourishing soil. This, according to Françoise d'Eaubonne, is the beginning of "semi-patriarchy".

Demeter's victory did not last long. The transformations taking place in human societies turned the wind into the men's direction. The Bronze Age added other religious concepts to the cult of fecundity and of the nourishing earth, which were so dear to the first neolithic civilizations.

The new importance of wars made the warrior chief pre-eminent.[7] The dagger or the sword had replaced the hunter's bow. It is these "ceremonial" objects that are found in the tombs of high-ranking personages. In this Bronze Age, "the cult of the hero appears in several parts of Europe, and also throughout the Orient. Physical force is extolled. Quite often the societies are dominated by a warrior aristocracy."

The warrior chief was not the only hero. The Bronze Age also celebrated the artisan "who could handle fire as he pleased, who made rocks liquid, and then turned them into swords, or axes . . . The sun, the creative force *par excellence*, also became the object of particular veneration."

At all events, the cult of the hero, the master of the world and of the elements, was substituted for the worship of the Earth-Mother, who had to be content with receiving the seed passively. Everywhere that the Bronze Age established itself, we see the goddess first becoming a subordinate wife, and then disappearing from the divine scene altogether. In some cultures she was gradually eliminated from the Pantheon, in others, either masculinized or driven out by the male god.

Thus in Egypt, the goddess Isis merged into the person of the god Osiris, who then reigned alone. Among the Celts, the new mythological legends corresponded to the development of new mental structures. When a former feminine myth became embarrassing it was ridiculed, or else reversed and the role given to a male character. Jean Markale points out that to begin with, the sun, if it was not a goddess, was for the Celts at least a feminine power.[8] The solar hero became the Sun-God in the place of the original goddess, who was relegated to the rank of a cold, sterile star, the moon. The roles were reversed. The same was to happen to the Sow-Goddess and the Boar-Goddess of the Celtic legends. In the beginning, they symbolized prosperity and love. Later, men suppressed the image of the good goddess and kept "only the image of the lowest kind of sexuality, attached to the idea of blood and putrescence". Also among the Celts, the Doe-Goddess, symbol of fertility, was replaced by the Stag-God, and in general, most of the great goddesses were turned into gods. Thus the unfortunate Ishtar, the principal goddess of the Babylonians and Assyrians, became a male deity under the name of Ashtar. Similar downfalls occurred in other civilizations: in India, the male god Agni was promoted to became the origin of the Aryan race, and was said to have been the discoverer of fire, whereas the Rig-Veda still attributed these privileges to the gentle Agira.

The tragic Greeks have left us their brilliant testimony to the combat of the gods in which the older ones were overthrown and the Olympian religion triumphed at the expense of the maternal cult.

A Homeric hymn celebrates the glory of the Earth-Mother thus:

> Mother of all things, the well-founded Earth,
> My Muse shall memorize; who all the birth
> Gives food that all her upper regions breed,
> All that in her divine diffusions feed . . .
> Fair children, and fair fruits, thy labour's sweat,
> O great in reverence; and referr'd to thee,
> For life and death is all the pedigree
> Of mortal humans . . .[9]

But already for Sophocles, man, the male, had become the first wonder of the world.

Yesterday's Great Goddess had been vanquished, as Aeschylus's tragedies show. In *The Eumenides*, Clytemnestra has been assassinated by her son Orestes to avenge her murder of his father, Agamemnon. At Orestes' trial, which takes place in the court of Athena, two worlds confront each other: is it more serious to kill one's mother than to murder one's husband?

Apollo, the new sun god, is Orestes' advocate. He pleads the pre-eminence of the father over the mother and the legitimacy of the act of vengeance. In his eyes, the killing of a woman, the murderess of her lord and master, is excusable, if not legitimate.

On the other side of the court, the Eumenides bring the accusation. They want to avenge Clytemnestra's death in the name of the old maternal values. For them, Orestes is guilty of the worst crime that exists. According to the law of blood (which they embody), the murder Orestes committed is more serious than that committed by Clytemnestra, who was only the murderess of her husband, whose blood was alien to hers. A mother is worth more than a father.

Athena refuses to judge, and votes in favour of Orestes. In fact, she allows the law of the father to triumph, thus showing that the maternal reign has come to an end. Unlike other religions, however, the new truth does not abolish respect for the old. Athena calms the Eumenides, and offers them a home in her town, Athens, where they will be honoured ever after.

Such was not the fate of the Arabic goddesses.[10] When the prophet Mohammed, Allah's messenger, began his mission, the Arab pantheon was occupied by several gods, but goddesses still played a very important part in it. In *The Book of Idols*, by Ibn al-Kalbi, a key document on pre-Islamic religions, three goddesses, Al-Lat, Al-Uzza and Al-Manat, are described as having great power in the seventh-century Arab pantheon. Al-Uzza, the most important one, was respected from Arabia to Mesopotamia. She was the Earth-Mother, analogous to Demeter, who controlled fertility. The two other goddesses were also influential throughout Arabia.

The cult of these goddesses represented a thorny problem for Mohammed. If Allah and Islam were to triumph, they had to be liquidated both ideologically and concretely. The names of the three goddesses became words that were devoid of power. To Arab minds, they first became "the daughters of Allah". But Allah's protests:

"Would God have daughters, and you sons?" reduced these god-desses to nothingness.

At the same time as the verbal elimination of the goddesses, the destruction of their sanctuaries was being undertaken. That of Al-Manat was destroyed in the year 8 of the Hegira. "Ali destroyed her and expropriated her of all she possessed." The other two goddesses received much the same treatment, and only then did the God Allah fully establish his power.

Occulted in classical Greece, expropriated by Islam, among the Jews the goddess's downfall was total. Between the omnipotent Lilith, condemned to hell for having refused to obey Adam, and Eve, the dispossessed women who would become "only the image of Adam's castrated form, and not the image of the feminine part of god,"[11] there was no longer any place for the worship of a goddess. On the contrary: every form of feminine power had become a syno-nym of maleficence.

The Religion of the Father

Genesis opens with the celebrated words: "In the beginning God [Elohim] created the heaven and the earth. And the earth was with-out form, and void; and darkness *was* upon the face of the deep. And the Spirit of God moved upon the face of the waters." Not only is there no longer any trace of a goddess, but the God of the Jews cre-ates the earth "without form, and void", deprived of its fecundating characteristics. What comes first is the "spirit", which creates by the power of the word. It said "Let there be light," and there was light.

The Earth-Mother's sensuality was made superfluous by this new process of creation. At the very most it could be used as "clay" in the hands of the divine Artisan, to model Adam.

The twelfth chapter of *Genesis* introduces us into a new religious world. The history of the religion of Israel begins with Abraham, who is chosen by God to be the father of the people of Israel and to take possession of the land of Canaan. The first words the Eternal addresses to him are an invitation to substitute the divine Father for the flesh and blood human father: "Get thee out of thy country, and from thy kindred, and from thy father's house . . ." This shows that paternal filiation had already ousted that of the mother (which is not even mentioned) in the Chaldean civilization in which Abraham lived.[12] It is also probable that the ancestors of the Hebrews observed the customs of the patriarchs.

But the Jewish religion is, *par excellence*, that of the patriarchs. It is characterized by the cult of the "god of the father", constantly invoked in *Genesis*. "The 'god of the father' is primitively the god of the immediate ancestor, whom his sons recognize. By revealing himself to the ancestor, he certified a sort of kinship."[13]

In the beginning, he was a god of the nomads who was linked neither to a sanctuary nor to a territory, but to a group of men whom he accompanied and protected. The men of the Bible moved from water hole to water hole, slept in tents, and lived from the produce of their herds.

It has been observed that the history of the Hebrew people attaches great prestige to pastoral techniques and considers the earth accursed. The Eternal accepts Abel's offering but not that of Cain: the keeper of sheep is superior to the tiller of the ground.

The pastoral life, though, unlike the settled life of agriculture, is not conducive to any high regard for the feminine sex. The biblical woman has been called "mistress of her home and of her children",[14] and the four "Matriarchs" of Israel (Sarah, Rebecca, Rachel and Leah) have been tenderly described. But when God orders the sacrifice of Isaac, he speaks to the father. The *Genesis* text (chapter 22) does not once mention Sarah.

André Chouraqui calls the biblical family "endogamous, patrilineal, patriarchal, patrilocal, extended and polygamous . . . The father, like the God he worshipped, had all rights over the men and women in his house. In some circumstances he could sell his children or offer them up as a sacrifice."

Even if Mosaic law tends to restrain paternal absolutism, and the fifth commandment ("Honour thy father and thy mother") does something to re-establish equality between the two parents, it was not until the coming of Christianity that the mother once again became the object of a cult.

Jean Markale was right to stress the fact that strictly speaking the cult of the Virgin Mary is revolutionary: "Patriarchal society suppressed the Mother-Goddess, replacing her sometimes by force, with a warlike father god; he was jealous of her superiority, and popular thought re-created her in the role of Mother of God and men; she was constantly invoked, ever-present and ever-triumphant."[15]

The cult of Mary does not only constitute homage paid to the mother, it also indicates that if a woman had been responsible for the fall of humanity (Eve), another had contributed to its salvation (Mary). Thereby, it once again gave women an honourable status and supplied proof that although woman had been rejected as evil and dangerous, she could also bring salvation and be an object of veneration.

We should remember that Jesus had no flesh and blood father and that his only link with men passes through his matrilineal filiation: as Jean Markale points out, Jesus is "the purest example of a gynaecocratic society whose only link with mankind, since he had no fleshly father, was through his mother's line . . . Joseph was exactly like the fathers of Oceanic societies, a foster-father and an emotional father, but no more."

The Virgin is fecundated like a Mother-Goddess, by a spirit that penetrates her. She is a free woman who not only is not the slave of a man, as are her contemporaries, but who furthermore does without one to bring God's child into the world.

And yet, if at first the cult of Mary constituted a revolution in paternalistic societies, an attempt to give the mother back her true role, the official Church lost no time in divesting the concept of all its meaning. It transformed the Virgin into a being whose feminine character was now only attested by the aspect of the mater dolorosa, sacrificial, passive, and "the slave of the son". Apostles and other "fathers" of the Church took it upon themselves to distinguish Mary from all her sisters, the better to indicate their essential kinship with Eve.

Saint Augustine was not the least of those responsible for this, when he wrote of women's evil nature: "an animal that is neither firm nor stable, full of hatred, spreading evil . . . she is the source of all arguments, quarrels and injustice"[16] – definitive condemnations, which were tirelessly repeated until the end of the Middle Ages . . .

Indeed, Christ's message about women was corrupted by his apostles, and the seeds of revolution were crushed. On this point, the religion of the father had won, and for a long time to come. The pressure of the patriarchal milieu was far too strong for the slightest change in the condition of women to be brought about, or even for a simple amelioration of the image of women to be granted. The God of the patriarchs continued to triumph among the very people who had followed Christ. The legend of Eve was to go on occulting the exemplary Mary for a long time.

Procreative Power: the Father-God

From prehistory to history, there has been a double image of father-hood.[17] Social fatherhood, which was more characteristic of matrilineal societies, was followed by the recognition of the biologi-cal father. The father, recognized as the genitor, established his own filiation. But the passage from the one to the other was accompanied by a genuine ideological revolution. The omnipotence of the father was substituted for that of the mother. It was then he who possessed the most important part of the procreative power.

The myths of the creation of the world, characteristic of patriar-chal societies, extended even further the father's advantage. Not only did he possess the power over the child that had formerly been the prerogative of the mother, he also became the creator of woman. This mythical theme is found frequently, and notably in three patri-archal societies as different as those of the nomadic Jews, Athenian democracy, and the New Zealand Maori.

For the entire Judeo-Christian civilization, Adam was created by a male God without the intervention of any feminine principle what-soever. After which, as Adam is bored, Jehovah puts him to sleep and makes Eve out of one of his ribs. Thus woman is doubly the child of the male. She has been created by a "God" out of the body of a "man". Symbolically, Adam's rib is the equivalent of the maternal womb. If God is Eve's creator, Adam is her mother, or more pre-cisely, her father/mother. Masculine "parthenogenesis" justifies the qualitative difference between Adam and Eve. Adam is the son of God, created in his image, but Eve is only the daughter of man[18] and, as such, less close to the Divine than her consort. For her, procreation will be a curse. Whereas Adam gave birth to her in his sleep, as in a dream, Eve will bring forth Adam's children in pain, as in a nightmare. Adam will keep the essential, spiritual role, in the image of God; Eve will have the contingent, material role. *He* will be the agent of the transmission of life; *she* – that of death.

In the new Olympian mythology, Zeus has dethroned the original goddess of the Earth. He even goes so far as to incorporate her procreative power. We should remember the famous myth of the birth of Athena, as recounted by Hesiod in his *Theogony*. Metis, Zeus's lover, was about to give birth to Athena when the all-powerful god devoured the mother and the baby she was carrying. The child was born from Zeus's head. The same adventure happened to Dionysus, son of Zeus and Semele. When Zeus caused his mother to be consumed and reduced to ashes, "the child of which she had been pregnant for seven months," says Lemprière, "was with difficulty saved from the flames and put in his father's thigh, where he remained the full time which he naturally was to have been in his mother's womb."

Athena, in *The Eumenides*, is "the daughter of a very powerful father". Aeschylus, like Homer, makes her belong only to her father, and owe everything to him. As "One never nursed in the dark cradle of the womb", and who can claim that "No mother gave me birth," Athena is the only important goddess in the pantheon and embodies all the masculine virtues: daring, will-power, courage. She watches over the warrior in battle and over every heroic action, but love and the feminine virtues are foreign to her. The daughter of an omnipotent god, Athena is herself more like a god of feminine appearance than a daughter of Demeter. She does not bear children.

Polynesia offers particularly fascinating mythical material which is very similar. For the Maori of New Zealand:

"In the dim and distant beginnings of the world, shrouded in the mists of time, the sky and the earth were not separated as they are today. *Rangi*, the Sky-Father, and *Papa*, the Earth-Mother, were so closely united in their amorous embrace that everything was indistinct . . . In those sombre days (in which nothing could germinate), the couple's children used to crouch down in the Earth-Mother's armpits . . . They numbered 70, *all of the male sex*, they became weary of this dark, cramped existence, and one of them, Tane, suggested that they should separate their parents."[19]

Such is the beginning of the creation of the world, in which Tane plays the chief role. The story goes that once he and his brothers were free from their parents they set out in search of the female element, in order to beget man. Finally, Tane "took a part of the body of the Earth-Mother and fashioned it into a woman, whom he quickened by giving her the kiss of life in her nostrils, her mouth, and her ears."

By this woman, Tane had daughters, the oldest of whom, Hine Titama, became his wife. He also had several daughters by her. But one day Hine Titama asked him who her father was. She guessed the truth, and was so affected by it that she chose to leave this world and became the great queen of the night. Serge Dunis rightly observes that the Maori myth tells how men arrogated to themselves the merits of the creative exploration of the world, the better to expel women from it and to align them on the side of death. As in the two preceding myths, it is the male God who is the Creator of women; she is the second, not to say secondary, element of creation.[20] Athena does not bear children; both Eve and Hine Titama introduce death into the universe: the former chooses to commit evil (the sin of the flesh?), the latter is disgusted by incest – a double illustration of the mortal danger represented by femininity.

Many patriarchal societies consider woman a necessary evil. Since they cannot do without her, men will do what they can to restrict her domain as much as possible, to reduce her powers to the minimum, and finally to impose on her an image of herself that is the reverse of theirs.

From that time on, the complementary representation of the sexes was beset by negativity. It was the function of man, God's creature, to embody Good. Woman, a demoniacal creature, would have Evil as her share. Greek philosophy was to translate this into: form and matter.

Philosophical Justification of Man's Superiority in Procreation

Long before philosophy became involved, we have seen Greek mythology dreaming aloud of a purely paternal heredity. As it happens, an exceptional institution did exist within the Greek family system, *Epikleros*, which came quite close to realizing this dream. Jean-Pierre Vernant observes that similar practices existed in India. "In Greece, as in India, the daughter of a man who had no male issue had to give her father a son in order to inherit the paternal *Kleros*. On the father's death, the daughter becomes a member of the *Epikleros*."[21] She must be married to the man closest to her father in degree of kinship, in order to perpetuate the line.

The child of this marriage will continue the line of the mother's father, not that of its own father. In this way, the grandfather achieves, both symbolically and institutionally, his dream of perpetuating his race without having recourse to a foreign wife.

However revealing this may be, this institution has always been an exception in the Greek matrimonial system and was not sufficient to satisfy the paternal *hubris*. Aeschylus made himself the echo of men's profound desire to shake off feminine domination once and for all by claiming the credit for their own posterity. In *The Eumenides*, he proclaims the new truths through Apollo's mouth:

"The mother is not the true parent of the child/Which is called hers. She is a nurse who tends the growth/Of young seed planted by its true parent, the male./So, if Fate spares the child, she keeps it, as one might/Keep for some friend a growing plant. And of this truth,/That father without mother may beget, we have/Present, as proof, the daughter of Olympian Zeus . . ."[22]

But Aeschylus's assertions have more to do with denial and incantation than with proof. Reference to myths could no longer persuade men who were coming to respect reason more and more. It was Aristotle, a century later, who undertook to "rationalize" the ideological change proclaimed by Aeschylus.

In order to do this, he used a combination of the weapons of metaphysics and of natural history, which he founded. At the same time he showed that the male has the essential part in generation, that he transmits Humanity, and that it is he who is the bearer of the divine principle. In generation, the male transmits form, but the female only contributes matter. He is the generative and motor principle, "the being who engenders in another,"[23] whereas she waits passively to be engendered. He is the artisan. She is the matter on which the artisan works.

It will be understood that it is the man who transmits the soul, the divine principle that renders the living being human.[24] As such, he is obviously superior to woman, whose matter is devoid of form and reason. Since man gives form to woman, it is easy to understand Aristotle's frequently repeated proposition: "It is man who engenders man."[25] He sometimes adds, as if to stress even more strongly the pre-eminence of the male: "Woman too is born of man."[26]

Aristotle completed his metaphysical theory with considerations of a biological order,[27] which said the same thing. It is the sperm that contributes the seed. And the female produces no seed, she merely provides the place of generation. The female, being devoid of seed, contributes nothing to generation but raw material (her menses), which are devoid of the heat necessary to the formation of life.

Here, the role of the mother is doubly devalued. Aristotle, like the other men of his time, was always bent on proving that "woman does not herself engender";[28] in other words, he was trying to put an end to the ancient belief in parthenogenesis. Moreover, if the female possesses the same soul as the male, why should she not be able to engender on her own? The answer is simple: the female does *not* possess the same soul as the male. The cognitive soul is transmitted *solely* by the male.

Despite all these metaphysico-biological justifications, it would not be fair to say that Aristotle quite simply substituted the idea of masculine "parthenogenesis" for the ancient belief in feminine procreation. Even if he plays with homonymy to keep reminding us that man engenders man, the philosopher knows very well that generation cannot take place without a feminine receptacle.

Not being able to eliminate the feminine principle completely, Aristotle applied himself to devaluing it in another way. Apart from the fact that the principle of matter introduces corruption – in the sense of decomposition – and death into the universe, it is also the cause of monstrosity. This is a very clear suggestion of the mother's responsibility for the monster.

Strictly speaking, monstrosity applies only to cases in which the being engendered is not of the same species as the generator.[29] Simple dissimilarity is enough to constitute a monstrosity in the broader sense: thus a female begotten instead of a male is a monster.[30] "She is a mutilated male",[31] the result of the failure of the male principle. It is as if the sperm had not been strong enough to "form" the menses properly.

However much Aristotle consoled himself with the thought that this monster, the female, is necessary in order to protect the difference between the sexes, he nevertheless presented her as a failure on the part of humanity.[32] With Aristotle, nothing remains of the mother's creative power or of feminine prestige. From this follows naturally the condition they will be accorded.

The same procedure is to be observed in India after the definitive adoption of the Laws of Manu,[33] which governed the behaviour of Hindu society for a long time. "Manu's code provided a long sought after resolution to the intellectual conflict generated by the 'seed and soil' theory. The question was – 'Which is hierarchically superior? – the soil which receives the seed, or the seed which makes the earth productive?' . . . The sage Manu summed it up this way: 'By the sacred tradition the woman is declared to be the soil, the man is declared to be the seed . . . On comparing the seed and the receptacle [of the seed] the seed is declared to be the more important; for the offspring of all created beings is marked by the characteristic of the seed.' "[34]

The *Koran* makes the same analogy between a woman and a ploughed field.[35] Woman, like the soil, is *merely* the receptacle of the seed which is entrusted to her. She plays a secondary role in conception, as opposed to man who is the creator because he receives his power from God. The prophet therefore recommends husbands to be pre-eminent over their wives,[36] because, as Camille Lacoste-Dujardin observes,[37] "male domination is indispensable to men's appropriation of the produce of feminine fecundity: male children". She notes that in Islamic law, women are "conscripted into a veritable patrilineal procreative service", and, in a more general fashion, that "it is a constant of Mediterranean patriarchal societies that they confiscate woman's creative power for man's benefit".

The father's appropriation of the procreative power is a theme that is in evidence far beyond the confines of the Mediterranean. Even nowadays, in many primitive societies of the patriarchal type, ethnologists hear theories or observe practices that bear striking witness to this profoundly-rooted desire in men.

For some, the mother's womb is likened to a boat, a mere temporary resting place for the foetus.[38] Others, like the inhabitants of Ross Island,[39] believed that the father lays an egg inside the woman, who is regarded, as by Aristotle, a a purely passive receptacle. Finally, the Montenegrins went even further and were said to deny any relationship between mother and child.

What they all have in common is that they assign the best role to the father. Sometimes, however, it seems that theories are not enough to appease the paternal torment. In that case, men will go to the lengths of physically enacting the role that belongs naturally to women.

When the Father Substitutes Himself for the Mother

This is perhaps the most fabulous myth . . .

Whether it is a question of Greek mythology or of the Amerindian world,[40] there are many stories of a pregnant man. Our thirteenth-century "chantefable", Aucassin and Nicolette, is another literary equivalent of these. And countless examples of ritual couvade[41] may be found in history and ethnology.

Diodorus of Sicily said of the Corsicans: "Their strangest custom is the one they observe when children are born. Indeed, when a woman gives birth, no one takes care of her. The man, on the other hand, takes to his bed for several days *as if he had pains all over his body.*"[42]

F. Michel wrote in 1857 that in the Basque region: "Immediately after giving birth, the women get up and go about their household tasks, while the men *take to their beds with the newborn babies*, and are congratulated by their neighbours."[43]

The ethno-psychoanalyst Geneviève Delaisi de Parseval has stressed the wide geographical extent of the phenomenon, pointing out that its traces can be found from the Mediterranean to the Baltic, and from the north of Japan to the whole of the American continent.[44]

There have been many, sometimes contradictory, interpretations of this phenomenon. For two American sociologists, Karen and Jeffrey Paige, who have studied more than a hundred birth rituals, these couvade rites are "one of the strategies to defend and prove paternal rights in societies in which the rights of the father are not institutionally established".[45]

According to Alfred Métraux, who has observed couvade among South American Indians, these various rituals are based on a belief in the existence of bonds between a father and his child that are more important then those between mother and child. This hypothesis is supported by the anthropologist P. Rivière, who studied couvade among the Trio Indians,[46] and maintains that the father nourishes his child spiritually in this way.

Lévi-Strauss rejects the analogy of the father and the mother: "The father does not play the role of the mother: he plays the role of the child."[47] This point of view is today shared by certain psychoanalysts, who see such rites as a way for the father to relive his own birth, to "abreact" archaic emotions.

If the identification of the father with the child was an obvious fact for Lévi-Strauss when he was observing South American Indians, this may perhaps still not say the last word about the ritual of couvade. As for his first disclaimer: "The father does not play the role of the mother", is not some doubt thrown upon it by recent work on couvade-like, non-ritual manifestations in Western industrial societies?

Several American, French and English studies have brought to light the existence of minor psychosomatic disorders in future fathers, especially first-time fathers, during their wives' pregnancies: insomnia, indigestion, marked increase in weight, dental extractions (particularly in the last months of the pregnancy), ENT troubles, and sties on the eye.

In his thesis on paternity, which Geneviève Delaisi de Parseval quotes, Dr Renoux made a survey of fifty "normal" fathers whose wives had given birth. Of them, twenty-two had followed the preparations and been present at the birth; the other twenty-eight had not taken part. However (with just one exception), all the somatic symptoms were found in the group of those who had not been involved in the preparations for the birth. It was as if close participation by the fathers in the different stages of motherhood had been able to appease their archaic feelings of distress, which could take various forms, ranging from a feeling of uselessness to aggressivity towards the unborn child, and going as far as doubt about paternity, as opposed to the certainty of maternity.

However that may be, in many men the approach of paternity mobilizes a defensive fantasy in which "we find at first the man's *envy* of the woman's capacity for carrying, giving birth, suckling; jealousy of her creative power, of her sensual pleasure, her mystery".[48] This conclusion by a specialist in fatherhood who combines analytical experience with ethnological knowledge, reinforces our conviction that couvade rites are a method of abolishing the distance between the father and the mother – a way of giving men the feeling that they share procreative power with women.

But couvade rites are not the only ones practised by men to reinforce their feeling of paternal power. In some societies, the initiation rites of the adolescent males conducted by the men constitute another method of compensation for the fundamental inferiority of the fathers.[49]

Among some of the Pacific tribes studied by Margaret Mead, the men take the male children away from the women on the pretext that they are incomplete. They consider that "women, it is true, make human beings, but only men can make men".[50] She adds that all these initiation rites are symbolic imitations of birth, and indeed of suckling.

In *The Golden Bough*, Frazer describes an initiation rite that can be considered representative:

"In the west of Ceram [an Indonesian island] boys at puberty are admitted to the Kakian association . . . The Kakian house is an oblong wooden shed, situated under the darkest trees in the depth of the forest . . . Thither the boys who are to be initiated are conducted blindfold, followed by their parents and relations . . . As soon as each boy has disappeared within the precincts, a dull chopping sound is heard, a fearful cry rings out, and a sword or spear, dripping with blood, is thrust through the roof of the shed. This is a token that the boy's head has been cut off, and that the devil has carried him away to the other world . . . During his stay in the Kakian house each boy . . . is warned by the chief, under pain of death . . . , never to reveal what has passed in the Kakian house . . . Meantime the mothers and sisters of the lads have gone home to weep and mourn. But in a day or two the men who acted as guardians and sponsors to the novices return to the village with the glad tidings that the devil, at the intercession of the priests, has restored the lads to life. The men who bring this news come in a fainting state and daubed with mud, like messengers freshly arrived from the nether world."[51]

Bruno Bettelheim adds: "One might equally well say, like persons who are totally exhausted after childbirth." He points out that "the dark, oblong hut might represent the womb to which the boys return to be reborn. That the ritual may be designed to imitate the act of parturition is also suggested by the behavior of the boys themselves, who pretend to be as disoriented as one might expect a newborn infant to be. When they return to their homes, they act as if they had forgotten how to walk . . . If food is given to them, they hold the plate upside down."

In actual fact, the boys know very well that they have not been born a second time and that it was the priest who played the role of the devil. But the main object is to detract from the women's importance, and to conclude a secret pact among the men never to reveal the truth. Bruno Bettelheim thinks that the men's secret is the symmetrical answer to the secret that surrounds the women's childbirth rituals.

In a superb book, Maurice Godelier[52] has described the secret of the initiation rites of the Baruyas of New Guinea. In this fiercely patriarchal society, the purpose of the immersion of a boy in an exclusively masculine world (the men's house) is also for him to be "reborn" as a man.

For the Baruya, a child is above all the product of a man's sperm. But once it has been enclosed within the woman, the sperm is fused with her liquids. If the man's sperm prevails over the woman's water, the child will be a boy; if not, it will be a girl.[53] Furthermore, the man does not content himself with fabricating the child with his sperm, he then nourishes it by repeated acts of coition, and makes it grow in the woman's womb.

The Baruya revealed to Godelier two secrets that they had long kept hidden from Whites. The first is that it is sperm that gives life its strength. For this reason they make women drink sperm when they have been weakened by their periods or by childbirth.[54]

"The second secret, which is even more sacred since no woman must know it, is that sperm gives men the power to enable the boys to be reborn outside their mothers' wombs, outside the feminine world, into the men's world, and by means of them alone. This most sacred secret is that as soon as they enter the men's house, the young initiates are nourished with the sperm of their elders, and that this ingestion is repeated for many years, with the aim of making them grow bigger and stronger than the women, superior to them, capable of dominating and guiding them."[55]

The answer to the question as to which of the men may take the boy's father's place in order to continue this nourishing work is that: "all married men are excluded ... for it would be the worst humiliation ... to treat the boy's mouth as a vagina and transfer all the pollution of the feminine sex into his mouth. Only young virgin men must give their sperm to the new initiates, who were obliged (under the greatest duress) to accept the penis offered them."

However, neither their relations in the maternal line nor those in the paternal line were allowed to give their sperm to the young initiates. We should not make the mistake of believing that these practices are to be explained by homosexuality. Godelier points out that on the one hand those who give sperm never take it, and on the other hand, and above all, "that the very idea of ejaculating into the anus of another man seemed to them both grotesque and repugnant".

The object of all these practices is to limit women's fecundating powers. While it is admitted that women can engender girls, they are denied the ability to create males. And even then, their power is limited by the assertion that the foetus only develops because of the masculine sperm, and that the milk with which they later suckle the child is only the result of the sperm.

Every Baruya representation of the reproductive process reveals the male obsession with short-circuiting the creative power of women, the better to establish that of men.[56] This obsession must be seen within the more general context of an extreme reluctance to admit all feminine creativity, in whatever domain. If the theories and behaviours of the Baruya surprise us, it is because they express, more brutally and more crudely than in other patriarchal societies, a fantasy of omnipotence which they often have in common.

From the Maori of New Zealand to the Roman *paterfamilias*, from the knight of the Middle Ages to the eighteenth-century peasant, many civilizations have been built on one simple idea: men must have all the power over women, because they are "essentially" better than women.

Absolute Power

Observing American society in 1948, Margaret Mead noted that its organization was patrinomial, patrilocal and, as a whole, patriarchal. Even if American fathers no longer resembled the traditional image of the all-powerful father, "the basic legal assumption" was still "that a woman as a minor is dependent upon her father, and thereafter upon her husband".[57]

It is the institution of marriage, ordained by the law of exogamy and the prohibition of incest, that is at the origin of this domination.

Georges Duby writes: "The rites of marriage are instituted to ensure an orderly distribution of the women among the men; to regulate competition between males for females; to officialize and socialize procreation. By designating a father, marriage adds another form of affiliation to the only self-evident one, through the mother ... Marriage establishes relations of kinship. It underlies the whole of society."[58]

To this definition, we will add another consequence of marriage: it is what gives woman the status of an object twice over. She is an object for the father who exchanges her. She remains an object for the husband who acquires her.

Her Father's Daughter

The economic vocabulary used by Claude Lévi-Strauss to describe the status of women in patriarchal societies is extremely revealing. In turn, they are called "objects of exchange", "benefits", or more simply "goods". He talks about "freezing women", of their "equivalence", or of their "rarity". How could the fact that they are merely objects among others at men's disposal be better put?

The exchange that constitutes the foundation of social relationships is "a total phenomenon . . . comprising food, manufactured objects, and that most precious category of goods, women".[59] Thus, in primitive Polynesian societies, a man who cannot pay for his boat will as soon give the seller women as land.

If, among all these goods, women have the privilege of being the most highly valued, it is for the double reason that they are at the same time "rare" and essential to the life of the group. Lévi-Strauss explains their scarcity by the men's natural tendency towards polygamy. In primitive societies, monogamy seems to predominate where the economic and technical level appears the most rudimentary. In fact, in all societies, including our own, the tendency is towards a multiplicity of wives, quite simply because in man, polygamous tendencies are natural and universal.[60]

Lévi-Strauss adds that "even if there were as many women as men, these women would not all be equally desirable", from both the erotic and the economic points of view. Since the most desirable women must form a minority, "the demand for women is in actual fact, or to all intents and purposes, always in a state of disequilibrium and tension".[61]

In this connection, we note Lévi-Strauss's indifference to the "natural" polyandry of women, who can copulate with extraordinary regularity and who are equipped to experience even more intense sexual pleasure than the human male.[62] Unlike men, the more orgasms a woman has, the more intense and frequent they become. This phenomenon, known as "satiation-in-insatiation", suggests that it is hard for a single man to satisfy a woman. If culture and repression had not intervened,[63] could we not say that polyandrous societies would be just as natural as polygamous societies?

But the essential problem that arises for human beings is not so much the satisfaction of their desires as that of their most elementary needs. Now, in order to feed and reproduce themselves and to live in peace, men have to exchange women. We know of Lévi-Strauss's surprise when, in a central Brazilian native village, he saw "a young man crouching for hours upon end in the corner of a hut, dismal, ill-cared for, fearfully thin, and seemingly in the most complete state of dejection . . . Intrigued . . . I finally asked who this person was, thinking that he suffered from some serious illness . . . I was told: 'He is a bachelor.' "[64]

This was a clear demonstration of the vital importance of marriage for every individual in these primitive societies. The wife's function there is not limited to sexual gratification. Her economic contribution is essential, since man and wife are employed in producing different foodstuffs. Only a couple can provide complete and regular nourishment.[65]

The women do not have only economic value for the men who exchange them. Their primary value is for making peace and alliances. If incest is everywhere prohibited, if one "freezes" the women in the bosom of the family, this is less for moral or biological reasons than for social ones. Everyone gives up his daughter or his sister, on condition that his neighbour does the same and that they can be mutually exchanged. In this way the natural hostility between the groups is transformed into relations of alliance. Everyone knows that by exchanging their sisters, brothers acquire brothers-in-law to go hunting with; their friendship networks are extended and, by these reciprocal gifts, they effect the transition "from anxiety to confidence".[66]

It is the women's job to establish peace between the men, but only as objects. In no case do they have the status of an active subject. Hence Lévi-Strauss's famous proposition, which is presented as a universal law of human societies:

"The total relationship of exchange which constitutes marriage is not established between a man and a woman, where each owes and receives something, but between two groups of men, and the woman figures only as one of the objects in the exchange, not as one of the partners between whom the exchange takes place. This remains true even when the girl's feelings are taken into consideration . . . In acquiescing to the proposed union, she precipitates or allows the exchange to take place; she cannot alter its nature. *This view must be kept in all strictness, even with regard to our own society, where marriage appears to be a contract between persons* . . . The relationship of reciprocity which is the basis of marriage is not established between men and women, but between men by means of women, who are merely the occasion of this relationship."[67]

Lévi-Strauss, as we know, illustrates his thesis with many examples taken from primitive societies. But the law he puts forward goes far beyond – as he himself says – the limits of ethnology. The historian Georges Duby has had occasion to verify its accuracy with regard to the society of the Middle Ages. He notes that in the twelfth century a whole *strategy of marriage* had been built up by the knights, who did their best to marry off all the available girls in their family, while limiting the marriages of their sons.

"By thus distributing the blood of his ancestors," the head of a family "was making alliances that would be reinforced in the next generation by the special relationships ensuing between the sons of these marriages and their mother's brothers. I return to northern France for an example. Hilduin of Ramerupt had through his wife inherited the comté of Roucy, and to strengthen his hold on it had married his widowed mother-in-law to his own brother. He arranged the marriages and remarriages of his seven daughters ... On the other hand, prudence required that someone in his position should allow only one son to take a lawful wife, unless for one of the others he could find a brotherless young woman, hence an heiress."[68]

William the Marshal acted no differently when, around the turn of the thirteenth century, he was trying to make some new friends. He distributed his daughters among the great families in his neighbourhood in order to consolidate peace with them. William was pleased that he had put his three oldest daughters *"to good use"*; in Georges Duby's terms, they were *"delivered up"* (livrées) to three sons of earls.[69]

As for the kings, they had already long been trafficking in their daughters. Charlemagne had exploited to the full the two forms of union that still existed in his day: concubinage (*Friedelehe*) and legitimate marriage (*Muntehe*).[70] The emperor did not marry off any of his daughters, for fear of creating too many claimants to the succession. He kept them at home with him in his *Munt*, his power. But he did lend them in *Friedelehe*, thus providing himself with grandsons whose rights were as nothing compared with those of grandsons born of lawful marriages. In this way peace was preserved and the inheritance protected.

In the Middle Ages, as still in the eighteenth century, the father had complete power over his children, whom he either married off as he pleased, or prevented from contracting a marriage. But the father's authority over his daughters was incomparably more oppressive than was his authority over his sons. Roman law, which held sway over much of France in the Middle Ages, made woman an eternal minor. When he married her off, the father transferred all his rights to her husband, and while she was not directly refused her share of the paternal inheritance, she was not allowed to have the disposal of it as she was subject to the authority of her husband.

Initially the object of her father, the new wife became the object of her husband until his death (if she survived him). On marriage, her husband acquired complete power over her person and her property . . . so long, that is, as her father had left her the right to her inheritance.[71]

Her Husband's Wife

In the eyes of her husband, a woman's status as an object was three-fold. She was at the same time an instrument of social promotion, a possible object of pleasure, and a womb to possess.

From the eleventh century on, the king and the great feudal princes distributed wives to the most loyal of their followers. Marriage, a means of making alliances, was above all an instrument of social promotion for ambitious young knights, loyal to their masters but having no money. "By taking or stealing a wife or receiving one at the hands of their lord," some knights "managed to escape from another man's house and found one of their own."[72]

This was the case with William the Marshal, who was born around 1145 and died in 1219. "When he felt in his limbs the onset of age . . . it seemed a matter of some urgency to obtain, while there was still time – while Henri II survived – a solid reward, one that would assure him a position and stable resources . . . His poverty . . . was a consequence of the fact that he was still a bachelor. Hence, what he wanted, at nearly fifty, was to cease to be so, to receive at last a wife who might be a rich heiress, to establish himself at once in her bed, in her house, in her seigneury. If, four years previously, he had rejected the daughter offered him by Robert de Béthune, this was perhaps because she brought to the marriage only income and not the land and seigneurial powers of which he dreamed."[73]

This was how the king came to offer William the daughter of his seneschal, who had died three years previously without a male heir. She was "the damsel of Lancaster", and she was not yet nubile. He must wait ... Two years later he asked for something better, and got it. "The damsel of Striguil brought him sixty-five and a half fiefs as a wedding present. With this fortune he crossed over to the right side, the side of the 'seigneurs'."

Everything indicates that the Marshal was very fond of his young wife, who was thirty years younger than he. But Georges Duby insists on the fact that in the twelfth century, women were less the objects of consideration than of diversion.

In this masculine world, in which only the males count, the wife's place remains marginal. She has not even the right to speak. If the ladies appeared at the start of a tourney, it was only to encourage the combatants to renewed valour, or "to distract the knights waiting to fight".

In contrast to what has been said about Courtly Love, Georges Duby thinks that "the love that the knights devoted to the chosen lady may have masked ... the essential: amorous exchanges between warriors".[74] All the young knights pay court to the wife ... in order to win the love of the seigneur. Love is first and foremost a feeling that men entertain. This loving friendship is present in the whole of the narrative from the Middle Ages, from which women are almost entirely absent.[75]

While women could be the objects of covetousness or distraction, a wife was above all a womb whose principal function was to provide children for her new House. Lord Raglan has opportunely reminded us that the word "father" seems to have only one meaning in all Aryan languages: "possessor".[76] Consequently, when he marries a woman, the husband takes possession of her womb, and of all the children it will shelter.[77]

But how can one ever be sure of a woman's fidelity? How can one prevent her from peopling the line with illegitimate children who carry the blood of another? For the main purpose of women's fidelity is to protect the man's inheritance. In masculine filiation, the son has to succeed his father, and he must be the son of the father and not of the mother. Consequently, the man may indulge in adventures with other women without endangering his line, but the opposite would be the denial of this filiation.

The obsession with female adultery makes the wife suspect, "an adversary. Men saw marriage as a sort of combat, a fierce battle calling for constant vigilance . . . The husband was afraid that he alone might not be equal to quenching her fires . . . He was afraid of treachery, of being hit below the belt."[78]

This terrible dread of women's treachery obtains in every human community, but patriarchal societies have invented many stratagems to enable a man to remain master of his wife's womb: the husband can keep her away from all other men; this is the *harem*: he can invent a mechanical system that prevents sexual relations; this is the *chastity belt*: he can remove her clitoris, to reduce her erotic urges; this is *clitoridectomy*.[79]

But when all this has proved insufficient, there is still repression. Female adultery – unlike male adultery – has always been severely punished. Depending on the civilization and the period, adulterous women have been stoned, tied into a sack and drowned, killed by their husbands, locked into a pillory, sent to a convent, or put in prison.

In France, it was not until 1974 that every specific punishment for female adultery was abolished.[80]

Marriage, the Foundation of the Patriarchal Society

Marriage is the universal response of human societies to the equally universal prohibition of incest. Now, whatever type of society is under consideration, it is always men, according to Lévi-Strauss, who exchange women, and not vice versa. Even if some south-east Asian tribes give the impression of the reverse, "this would not be to say that in such societies it is the women who exchange the men, but rather that men exchange other men *by means of* women".[81]

Lévi-Strauss seems to want to prove that through the universal phenomenon of the exchange of women by men, the patriarchal structure itself is, in the last resort, a given factor that is inherent in humanity. This is why he shows that regimes with matrilineal descent and matrilocal residence are very rare and deceptive exceptions.[82]

Generally speaking, there is an established correlation[83] between patrilineal institutions and the highest levels of culture, and between matrilineal descent and the most primitive societies. This observation merely reinforces Lévi-Strauss's conviction of the absolute priority of patrilineal over matrilineal institutions.

"Societies attaining this level of political organization tend to generalize the paternal right. *But it is because political authority, or simply social authority, always belongs to men, and because this masculine priority appears constant*, that it adapts itself to a bilineal or matrilineal form of descent in most primitive societies, or imposes its model on all aspects of social life, as is the case in more developed groups."[84]

Lévi-Strauss's hypothesis calls for several comments. In the first place, the relation between matrilineal descent, a more primitive character of a society and a lesser degree of political organization seems to us to show that this could have been the structure of the first societies in the Palaeolithic, and perhaps even of a large part of the Neolithic. On the other hand, the reverse correlation (more developed societies/primacy of political power/patrilineal societies) tends to prove the indestructibility of patriarchy in societies like our own.

In asserting that political power always belongs to men and that it is inseparable from patrilineal institutions, Claude Lévi-Strauss discounts the possibility of any overthrow of the patriarchal system. Indeed, in so far as he seems to equate the complexity of a society with patriarchy, every stage achieved towards greater complexity imprisons us more surely in this system. This is why he is able to conclude with a reflection in the form of a law:

"Behind the variations in the type of descent, the permanence of patrilocal residence attests to *the basic asymmetrical relationship between the sexes which is characteristic of human society*."[85]

In Lévi-Strauss's opinion, this "universal" asymmetry between the sexes, which operates to the detriment of women (they can never occupy either the same place or the same rank as men), is to be deduced "from the basic fact that it is men who exchange women and not vice versa".[86] And this very fact results from the prohibition of incest, which is the fundamental law of all human culture.

It seems that we have no way out of this. The universal prohibition of incest "naturally" has a discriminatory and hierarchical character. By making women play the part of commodities, "the prohibition of incest . . . stresses a social division and transforms the laws of kinship into co-ordinates of a 'motivated distinction' between men and women . . . Masculine equality depends on feminine submission."[87]

Nevertheless, such a system can last only on two conditions: the first is that marriage continues to mean an exchange of women; the second, itself a condition of the first, is that the asymmetry between the sexes is maintained, in other words that women continue to rank as objects. History and ethnology show clearly that every patriarchal society has expended infinite energy and ingenuity to enforce this asymmetry by fair means or foul. Some have not even hesitated to carry it to the extreme of making the One the reverse of the Other.

II

THE LOGIC OF OPPOSITES,
OR THE WAR BETWEEN THE SEXES

> Love – its means is war; its principle is mortal hatred
> between the sexes.
>
> NIETZSCHE, *Ecce Homo*

To keep itself going, the patriarchal system produced a new logic of
the relation between the sexes, out of all proportion to the previous
one. Not that it ever explicitly denied the complementarity of men
and women, but it pushed the assertion of otherness so far that it
almost negated the possible conditions for dualism.

Let us remind ourselves of some obvious facts: if the sexes are to
be considered complementary, we must see them as the two parts of
a whole. In other words, we must see them as participating equally in
the formation of a homogeneous unity: humanity.

A complement, in the primary sense of the term, is "a person or
thing that completes something". But it is impossible to fit the two
elements together without a minimal resemblance. Their differences
must not undermine their common nature; if they did, the two
would never be able to come together. This is what Aristophanes'
androgynal myth so charmingly showed: in the beginning, the whole
of humanity was constituted of a couple imbricated into each other
who formed the most beautiful totality imaginable. They were too
beautiful and too powerful for the jealous gods to bear, so they split
them down the middle into two parts. Separated one from the other,
man and woman now had only one desire: to reunite, to be together
again, to find the one in the other.

"Sexing" in no way excludes the idea of community, or desire and
love for one's moiety. That the One should have different attributes
(and attributions) from the Other, that each should do something
that the Other cannot do, should not be seen as opposition, but as a

mutual exchange that does not depreciate the One in order to ascribe more value to the Other. The androgynal myth reminds human beings that when the two sexes are united, they form such an image of completeness that the One separated from the Other becomes mutilated and incomplete.

Clearly, this lesson has not been learnt by the patriarchal ideology which has too often replaced the "symmetry" of the sexes by a radical asymmetry. Perhaps it was obliged to do so in order to establish its domination, without realizing that at the same time it was producing the seeds of its own death.

Absolute Patriarchy Threatens Complementarity

From Dissymmetry to Exclusion

Françoise Héritier notes that no society manages to make men and women absolutely symmetrical. This postulate seems to apply very accurately to patriarchal societies. Their creation myths and their many philosophical systems are built on a system of binary categories which opposes masculine to feminine as superior to inferior.[1]

In the eighteenth century, when society was recognized as having a greater influence on human nature, education was required to maintain complementarity in terms of opposition. When Rousseau, in his *Émile*, wanted to define the ideal couple, Émile and Sophie, he deliberately made Sophie Émile's complement.[2] But Rousseau and his contemporaries no longer trusted nature to make men and women complementary (the necessary condition for their mutual understanding). A sound, restrictive education was needed to prevent the "natural" or "ideal" characteristics of the One and the Other from becoming distorted. To prepare Sophie for her "vocation" of wife and mother, her character had to be *formed* to be gentle, she must be *trained* to accept constraint, *taught* that "dependence is women's natural state". This is not done without difficulty; it is as if her true nature protested at length before submitting to man's whims. The "training" of Émile and Sophie, and particularly that of Sophie, would seem to show that the nature of the two sexes is not so complementary as Rousseau hoped.

Even though they are the reverse of each other, Émile and Sophie remain linked by their common values and mutual love for a long time. Their conflicts do not undermine their parallel vision of humanity. The love that unites them in spite of, or because of, their dissimilarities does not allow the exclusion of the One by the Other. The dramas and developments that would tend to show that Sophie is not what we thought she was do not alter the fact that the One has meaning only in relation to the Other.

And yet, during the last three millennia in which patriarchal societies have flourished, the logic of opposites has often been transformed into a logic of exclusion. When dualism is taken to extreme hierarchical limits, the One – Good – becomes the enemy of the Other – Evil. The opposition, founded on a theology or a mythology, becomes so radical, so full of tension, that the idea of the similarity, of the resemblance of the sexes, is seriously threatened.

From the Indian civilization in the time of Manu to the culture of the Middle Ages, by way of the Muslim societies, we everywhere find the assertion that man and woman are implacable enemies. Countless texts speak of the war between the sexes and advise man to shun the woman he has sometimes been able to call his "companion".

The Mahabharata offers virulent support to Manu's androcentric arguments:

> "There is nothing that is more sinful than a woman. Verily, women are the roots of all evil." (38, 12.)

> "The destroyer, the god of the wind, death, the nether regions ... the sharpness of the razor, the dreadful poisons, the snakes and the fire – all these exist in a state of union with women." (38, 29.)[3]

Genesis, as we have seen, had made woman subordinate to man. The Fathers of the Church went further, and assimilated her to the serpent and to Satan. In the sermons of the Middle Ages (twelfth century), there was one constantly recurring theme that dominated everything: "Women were wicked, lewd as vipers and slippery as eels; not to mention inquisitive, indiscreet, and cantankerous."[4]

Such assertions invite men to distrust women and to treat them as they deserve, an attitude, Georges Duby notes, that was further justified by the "childish attempt" of the scholars of the time to press etymology into service. "*Vir*, the Latin word for a male, was said to be related to *virtus*, or strength, rectitude, whereas *mulier*, a woman, was supposed to be connected with *mollitia*: softness, volatility, evasiveness. Contempt for and mistrust of women were good arguments for keeping them subjugated and restrained."[5]

There is a unanimous answer to the question: What is the origin of woman's evil nature? It is: Her unbridled sensuality, which it is impossible for any one man to satisfy.

The Mahabharata again: "Women, o King, are fierce. They are gifted with fierce powers . . . They are never satisfied with one person of the opposite sex . . . Men should not love them . . . By acting otherwise a man is sure to meet with disaster."

The men and the priests of the Middle Ages thought no differently: women are by nature fornicators and insatiable. They were wary of widows, who were dangerous because unsatisfied, but also of the women's apartments, where they suspected them of the worst. In the twelfth century, Bishop Étienne of Fougères, in a sermon, recommended men to keep women "under strict constraint . . . Left to their own devices, their perversity would be unbounded: they would seek pleasure even among the servants, or with one another."[6]

The erotic religious language of the Muslim theologians, admirably analyzed by an academic, Fatna Aït Sabbah,[7] makes the reasons for men's suspicion even clearer. On the basis of two texts, one written in the twelfth century[8] and the other in the fifteenth,[9] and still very popular today,[10] the author reveals the unconscious origin of men's fear.

Both dreaded and desired, "omnisexual" woman is assimilated to a leech-vagina that is never satisfied. There is a consensus about the fact that women's desire far exceeds that of men:

"Some have declared that woman's desire is greater than man's . . . If one copulates night and day for years on end with the same woman, it seems that she never reaches satiation point. Her thirst for copulation is never quenched."

Copulation, then, has the opposite effect on each sex: women thrive on it, but it enfeebles men. It is not surprising, Fatna Aït Sabbah observes, that the only males equipped to face up to this "woman-crevice-leech" are not humans, but animals, and in particular the donkey or the bear, whose respective penises correspond better to female desires.

Confronted by this insatiable woman, a real man is totally condemned to live a life of failure. To fight against his fear of impotence, his obsession about the size of his penis and the way to lengthen it, the manuals of classical medicine devote whole chapters to recipes.[11]

But philtres, potions and advice can never suffice to re-establish the equilibrium between the sexes. The infinitude of women's desire renders them permanently dangerous. It is easy to imagine that omnisexual woman, driven by the animal force she holds between her thighs, can never become a pious Muslim whom the law obliges to be content with a quarter of a man.[12] She can only transgress the laws of Muslim life, namely: heterosexuality, fidelity, social homogeneity, virtue.

In a word, woman, "by nature", is a source of disorder, whom man must use all means to master. Driven by one single objective, the pursuit of orgasm, she is totally indifferent to social hierarchies (preferring the big phallus of a black slave to that of a man of her own rank!), and she is ill-suited to the two roles allotted her by Muslim society: those of wife and mother.

To maintain order, man must: "immobilize her, conceal her, keep her as much as possible away from the masculine sex". In other words, dominate her.

The texts of the Middle Ages made every effort to show that equality between man and woman was a heresy. Marriage, as the cornerstone of the social edifice, ought to reflect the hierarchy of the universe. Georges Duby describes a text written in the vernacular, *The Play of Adam*,[13] whose aim was to show that the relationship between husband and wife reflects at a lower level the primal, submissive relationship between the creature and his creator. Satan insinuated himself in order to break the hierarchy not only between

God and Adam, but also between Adam and Eve. It was because Adam regarded Eve as his equal that he believed her, and sinned.

Indeed, order was considered to imply not only respect for the hierarchy of the sexes, but also, indirectly, a difference in nature between the two, a difference that explains – better than hierarchy alone – the policy of "the two weights and two measures" constantly at work in patriarchal societies.

The best example, as we have seen, is the difference in treatment accorded to masculine and feminine adultery. In the eleventh century, Bishop Burchard of Worms compiled a collection of didactic texts, the *Decretum*,[14] which was immensely successful in France and throughout the Empire until the middle of the twelfth century. The Bishop decrees that "men and women are two different species".[15] Women are weak and easily led, and need to be judged differently from men. The *Decretum* insists above all on the need to take account of female perfidy. "If after a year or six months your wife says that you have not yet possessed her, and if you say she is your wife, you must be believed because you are the woman's head."[16]

Frivolity personified, chattering in church, forgetful of the dead, lecherous, lustful, women bear all the responsibility for abortion, infanticide and prostitution. The confessor must question women closely about the pleasures they may indulge in on their own or with other women or young children. Like the Muslim theologians, the Christian inquisitor fantasizes about her private world, "the women's quarters, the nursery, that strange but attractive world from which men were excluded and in which they imagined there took place perverse practices they were not allowed to enjoy".[17]

"Omnisexual" for some, "fornicators" for others, Bishop Burchard considered that as women were deceivers by nature, if a woman accused her husband of adultery and the man denied the charge, the man was the one to be believed. But in fact, Georges Duby remarks, "when did women ever come to the bishop for justice, asking to be rid of their husbands? The initiative always came from the men."[18]

As we see, the difference in the treatment of one sex and the other is always excused in terms of Manichaeism.

We still find the (very attenuated) traces of this in a patriarchal society as moribund as ours was in 1964. The list made by Anne-Marie Rocheblave-Spenlé, after a remarkable piece of sociological research,[19] of the masculine and feminine stereotypes current at the time, shows that the logic of opposites was still not dead yesterday.

TRAITS OF THE MASCULINE STEREOTYPE	TRAITS OF THE FEMININE STEREOTYPE
EMOTIONAL STABILITY	
Decided, firm, steady, calm.	Capricious, hysterical, sensitive, nervous, emotional, puerile, frivolous.
CONTROL MECHANISMS	
Disciplined, methodical, organized, rigid, likes organizing, discreet, outspoken.	Talkative, incoherent, affected, secretive, scatterbrained, sly.
AUTONOMY, DEPENDENCE	
Patriotic, likes risk, independent.	Need to confide, need to please, flirtatious, submissive.
DOMINANCE, SELF-ASSERTION	
Need of power, need of fame, ambitious, likes to be in charge, dominating, self-important, sure of himself, need of prestige, arriviste, need to assert himself.	Weak.
AGGRESSIVENESS	
Combative, cynical, likes a fight.	Sly.
LEVEL OF ACTIVITY	
Impetuous.	Passive.
ACQUISITION	
Egotistic, materialistic.	Inquisitive.
INTELLECTUAL QUALITIES, CREATIVITY	
Creative, lucid, objective, likes theoretical ideas. Natural disposition for science and mathematics. Sceptical, rational.	Intuitive.
AFFECTIVE TENDENCIES, SEXUALITY	
Obscene.	Affectionate, sympathetic, gentle, modest, likes clothes, need to have children, need of love.

On careful study of these stereotypes, a digest of ready-made opinions of men and women about themselves, we are struck by the eternal oppositions indicated by a *plus* or a *minus* sign.

Even if obscenity has become a male prerogative (at the same time losing the negative character it formerly had, when it was associated with women!), all the positive characteristics are on the men's side; active, creative and intelligent. The woman of the sixties, on the other hand, was still seen as the daughter of Eve and certainly not as a goddess: hysterical, frivolous, talkative, sly, flirtatious, passive, intuitive, affectionate, a mother . . . She is in every way the great-granddaughter of Rousseau's Sophie.

Such a picture could only justify the treatment that made woman into an object, and strengthen the Other in his conviction that he was "naturally" superior to her in every way.

The Common Consequences

In every kind of patriarchy – whether moderate or ruthless – we find a number of common features, whether unobtrusive or pronounced.

The first, as we have seen, is *the separation of the sexes*. But this separation has changed from what we imagine it to have been in the Palaeolithic Age – mutual respect based on a profound conviction of the necessity of the Other. In absolute patriarchies, separation is based on a hierarchy so radical that it seems to exclude all possibility of meeting and interaction. By dint of always thinking of the One and the Other in terms of the opposition of good and evil, of strong and weak, etc., one finally loses sight of what the two have in common. What possible relationship can there be between the chosen race and the accursed race? If, in spite of everything, the necessities of procreation (and production) keep them together, their relations are those of two heterogeneous, foreign, even enemy worlds. Their common humanity is consigned to oblivion, to the far-off days of the myths of origin.

Georges Balandier has described the relations between men and women in certain African patriarchal societies in terms of both togetherness and opposition. "Women are excluded from the most highly valued knowledge, relations and practices, they are relegated to the category of instruments and things, they are given inferior tasks, expected to be dependent . . . Woman is seen as 'The Other', rather than as man's complementary partner, and this otherness is expressed and reinforced by means of representational systems, symbols, imaginary constructions, behaviour models."[20]

This radical otherness excludes the interaction of the sexes that still obtained in ancient Greek society. At that time, young men and young girls exchanged their garments before entering adult society. Since then, nothing has been more disapproved of than for one sex to behave like the other. Not so long ago our society forbade little boys "to cry like a girl". As if tears, the expression of emotion, were feminine and not human. And conversely, women who wanted to "act the man" were severely stigmatized. The psychoanalyst Helene Deutsch could not find words cruel enough to describe the intellectual woman: sterile, a flatterer, unoriginal, and above all, suffering from a "masculinity complex"![21] If we try to extricate ourselves from *enforced dualism*, we run the risk of humiliation or madness. In either case, we represent a threat to patriarchal order, which thrives on oppositions and exclusions.

But by dint of defining woman as an antagonistic element, assigned to an oppositional relationship, she soon comes to be seen as the dangerous element, man's enemy. The ideology of the Lugbara of Africa, which quite simply represents woman as "the reverse" of man and an enemy of society, associates her with the work of aggressive magic and witchcraft, with the forces of change that erode the social order.[22]

It will already have become clear that the second feature common to patriarchal societies is a state of *latent war between the sexes*. In the erotic Muslim texts, women are only too often endowed with an acute intelligence that is dedicated to the "cold, calculated, and permanent destruction of the social system".[23] This devastating hostility justifies in advance the war men wage against them. Above all, it explains the real, secret terror wives have sometimes inspired in their husbands.

Georges Duby perceives in the eleventh-century chronicles men's dread that "the women might take some insidious revenge by way of adultery or murder". These chronicles "are full of princes who were supposed to have been poisoned by their wives, and of allusions to 'female intrigues', 'pernicious wiles', and spells of all kinds cooked up in the women's quarters. We can imagine a knight of the eleventh century lying trembling and suspicious in his bed every night, beside an Eve whose insatiable desire he may not be able to satisfy, who is certainly deceiving him, and who may be plotting to smother him under the bed cover while he sleeps."[24]

This graphic description is certainly not representative of all married life under a patriarchal regime. It is only the caricature of an extreme reversal of the relations between the sexes. There is a whole world between this type of relationship and the bourgeois happiness of the eighteenth century. The latter, though, does not nullify the significance of the former. On the contrary: the bourgeois ideal of a happy marriage is contemporaneous with the beginning of the long death-throes of patriarchy.

The interest of the Middle Ages and of Islamic societies lies in the fact that they demonstrate the patriarchal system at its most uncompromising, such as it can be deduced from its principles. At its beginning, men seized all the women's powers, but in so doing they lost their serenity and the women's friendship. Confidence gave way to mistrust. The more frightened men became of women, the more they tried to subjugate them and the more they feared their vengeance, a vicious circle from which the only way out may well be to put an end to the patriarchal system.

It would seem that in the Middle Ages – as in other patriarchal societies today – the social and religious institution of marriage is incompatible with love.[25] This is true both of the kind of loving friendship that one feels for one's kin (the wife entering her husband's house always remains a stranger), and of passionate love, which is only expressed outside marriage. But is not the very condition of passionate love the antagonism of the sexes? Does it not express a chronic state of war?

Desire and war go hand in hand, as the analogy between the two vocabularies demonstrates. From Antiquity, poets have employed warlike metaphors to describe the effects of passionate love. Eros is an *archer* who shoots *mortal shafts*. A woman *surrenders* to a man, who *conquers her*. Denis de Rougemont notes that "as from the twelfth and thirteenth centuries, the language of love is enriched by turns of phrase that do not only designate the elementary actions of the warrior, but are taken in very precise fashion from the art of the battles of the time".[26]

Summarizing the various expressions used, Denis de Rougemont records that from then on, the lover *lays siege* to his lady; he delivers *amorous attacks* on her virtue. He *closes in* on her; he *pursues* her, he tries to *conquer* the last *defences* of her modesty, and to *take them by surprise*. And finally, the lady *surrenders unconditionally* . . . Unfortunately, though, satisfied desire brings about the end of passionate love. Desire, then, does not merely imply otherness and war; if it is to last, it must never be satisfied. It is the antithesis of "sweet conjugal bliss", or quite simply the reverse side of the love that is defined by duration, connivance, resemblance and symbiosis.

Denis de Rougemont's masterly analysis of the myth of Tristan and Iseult[27] tends to show that the couple, who in Western thought incarnate the ideal of passionate love, are far more "in love with love" than in love with the Other. Their passion thrives on the obstacles that endlessly delay satisfaction. When the outside world no longer imposes obstacles on them, they invent them, almost wantonly. The lovers' separation "torments" and transfigures their desire.

Denis de Rougemont quotes the poem by Chrétien de Troyes in which Tristan declares: "With all other woes, mine cannot compare; I take pleasure in it; I rejoice in it; my woe is what I wish for and in my dolour is my health . . . I find such ease in this wish that I suffer agreeably, and such joy in my dolour that I am sick with delight." Is this not an avowal of the extreme egotism of desire? Tristan rejoices narcissistically in his woes, in not possessing Iseult, and seems indifferent to her symmetrical sufferings.

Does Tristan love Iseult? Is he loved by her? Denis de Rougemont answers these questions in the negative. "Everything goes to show that they would never have chosen one another were they acting freely." It was the love philtre that was the cause of their passion. When they visit the hermit Ogrin to make their confession, they do their best to prove that they are not guilty because they do not love each other.

TRISTAN: If she loves me, it is by the poison . . .
ISEULT: He loves me not, nor I him . . .[28]

It is some alien power that binds them together. Real friendship has no place in this unwanted passion. "What is still more striking, if moral friendship does at last appear, it is at the moment their passion declines. And the immediate consequence of their nascent friend-ship, far from being to knit them more closely together, is to make them feel that they have everything to gain from a separation."[29]

We know that their passion will lead them to death, which is the secret desire underlying lovers' passion. The absolute obstacle, death, is both the ultimate condition of passion and its annihilation. "The approach of death acts as a goad to their sensuality . . . It aggra-vates desire. Sometimes it even aggravates desire to the point of turning this into a wish to kill either the beloved or oneself, or to founder in a twin downrush."[30]

Otherness, antagonism, and desire, are the representative triad of the relation between the sexes: in the Middle Ages as in Muslim cul-ture, among the Baruya of New Guinea as in many African societies, and in general in all male-dominated societies. Even if we consider only their ideology and texts, we are obliged to observe that no basis exists for affectionate love, which is the surest bond between man and woman. This kind of love necessitates a different conception of the sexes, a different environment, one that consists of confidence, of a minimum of resemblance and, at the very least, of mutual respect.

The images of the woman "Sataness",[31] or of the "serpent woman", are not conducive to the development of such sentiments. Do not those particular cases that contradict ideology seem to be the exceptions that prove the rule, and to show the flexibility of human nature?

But the separation and the war between the sexes, which always end to the men's advantage, generate a third consequence which undermines their victory: the resurgence of the *feminine Other in the masculine imagination*.

Speaking of the social integration of the Lugbara woman (whose ideological situation is the reverse of that of the man), Georges Balandier writes that it is as if she were excluded from the present time: "She is relegated to the two extremes of the temporal scale: on the one hand to the time of the myths of origin, the time of begin-nings, of births, and on the other hand to the time of things-to-come (that of divination), the time of change, of disorder, and eventually of death."[32]

Birth and death are indeed the two events which haunt the human imagination, and which the unconscious and a great many myths associate with woman. She thus reappears as a threat to man where he feels the most defenceless, the most dependent.

The function of many myths of origin is to express men's fear, and to provide it with an antidote. This is the case with Baruya thought, which is on three implicit levels. On the one hand it recognizes woman's creative powers;[33] on the other hand it denigrates them, belittles their importance, or even abases them; and finally it transforms them into masculine powers, turning them against women, to subjugate them even further.

Among the many myths cited by Maurice Godelier, some express better than others the original pre-eminence of women and the arguments in favour of bringing them to heel. They declare that in the past, women possessed powers far superior to those of men: they created, they nourished, they invented the flutes on which they produced marvellous music, they invented the conditions for agriculture, the objects necessary for hunting, for exchanges . . . But man stole their flutes.[34] He took possession of the bow and arrows, because the women were killing at random and they held the bow the wrong way. Man put it back as it should be, and from then on he killed only the necessary game, and forbade women the use of the bow. Godelier notes that these myths do allow women an original and irreplaceable creativity, but as it was "disorganized, disproportionate and dangerous, men were obliged to intervene and put things back in place. This intervention and the violence it involved were justified, then, because they seemed to be the only way to establish order and proportion both in society and in the universe."[35]

But the many ideological justifications of the violence inflicted on women did not suffice to allay men's fears. Their superiority was not that of a group which possessed all the powers over another which had none. Their domination was all the more oppressive in that it was imposed on women who had real powers. Even if cases of feminine rebellion were extremely rare, men could still fear them.

Maurice Godelier[36] has observed a few cases of individual resistance: a Baruya woman can "forget" to give her husband anything to eat, refuse to make love with him, use witchcraft against him, collect the sperm flowing out of her vagina and throw it on the fire, at the same time secretly muttering a magic spell. If the man finds this out, he knows he is condemned to death and, in fact, it may well happen that he dies, either of fear, or by letting himself waste away.

Even though Godelier has never heard of any collective female resistance, any "feminine counter-model" opposed to the prevailing social order, even though each individual rebellion was severely punished, the Other nevertheless continued to haunt the masculine imagination. In particular, in the form of a witch who incarnates disorder, counter-culture, the devil.

Strength and Origin of the Dualism of Conflict

Men have two apparently contradictory fears, which seem to have no mythical or psychological equivalent in women. Even if each sex fears the other, the vagina seems to be more dreaded than the phallus. The phallus can pierce, wound, violate, but it is not an instrument of death. Although it possesses surprising properties, it is not surrounded by any terrifying mysteries. And while the symbolism of the unconscious sometimes assimilates it to a sword, a revolver or a serpent, the myths of origin usually identify it with strength and life.

The same does not apply to the vagina, which has given rise to an abundant and terrifying literature. Men fear it as the absolute Other, a danger even more threatening in that it eludes the gaze and its properties are mysterious. But this fear of the Other is not the only one characteristic of masculine psychology: a second fear is that of the confusion of the sexes. This fear is all the more tenacious and neurotic in that it cannot be dissociated from a fierce desire to possess the attributes of the Other.[37] This desire is overtly recognized in women, but severely repressed by the Western masculine unconscious.

100

The Fear of the Other

In the unconscious and in myths, the vagina is in turns represented as a devouring, devastating,[38] insatiable force, a "toothed"[39] cavern, "nightmarish",[40] and finally, mortal. This almost universal fear is linked to that of blood – of menstrual blood in the first place (and the Bible offers many illustrations of this), which is disturbing and unhealthy, since it is the object of an enormous amount of taboos, but also of the blood of defloration, which is said to bring bad luck.

To illustrate the totality of the anxieties caused by the feminine sex, we shall consider the mythology and practices of two primitive societies[41] which are still close to their ancestral traditions: the Baruya of New Guinea, and the Maori of New Zealand.

Maurice Godelier has observed that when the Baruya men think of menstrual blood, "their attitude towards it is almost hysterical, a mixture of disgust, repulsion, and above all, fear. For them, menstrual blood is an unclean substance which they rank with those other polluting and repugnant substances, urine and faecal matter. But it is above all a substance that debilitates women ... and would destroy men's strength if it were to enter into contact with their bodies."

This gives rise to a certain number of precautions and taboos that punctuate the life of the Baruyas. When a woman has her period, she takes refuge in a special house below the village. She is forbidden to prepare the food for her husband and family with her (impure) hands. When her period is over, she must purify herself before resuming conjugal life.

Apart from her menstrual blood, Maurice Godelier observes that woman represents a permanent danger for man: "The very configuration of her vagina, because of the inevitable fact that it is a crevice that can never completely retain the liquids that it secretes inside itself, or the sperm that the man deposits in it," means that it lets drops fall on the ground that then feed worms and serpents. These animals will seize upon these secretions and carry them away to "the unfathomable abyss that is the home of the evil, chthonian powers ... which use these substances to spread disease and death among human beings, in the crops, among the pigs ..."

Merely because of her sex, a woman permanently attracts the powers of evil. And without even realizing it, she seconds their nefarious effects on society. She is therefore doubly dangerous: "directly, through the flow of her menstrual blood, which menaces man's virility and consequently men's domination of society; and indirectly by the configuration of her vagina, which makes her the accomplice of undertakings that ruin the efforts of human beings to produce their material conditions of existence: beautiful gardens, nice fat pigs . . ."

The feminine sex is supremely dangerous. Man does not approach it without purifying rituals. Women are subject to many taboos. They must avoid stepping over any object lying on the ground, and in no case, under pain of death, must they step over the hearth in the home, even when the fire is out: their genitals would open and pollute the place where they cook the food that goes into the man's mouth.

Sexual relations are surrounded by numerous precautions and taboos in proportion to the fear they arouse: one must not make love when it is time to prepare the soil for cultivation, to plant and cut the sugar cane, to kill and eat the pig, before the man goes hunting, when one is helping to build a house, at the period of male or female initiations, etc.; nor in a garden, nor in the marshy areas where worms and serpents abound. One must observe total abstinence after the birth of a child, "until he has cut his first teeth".

Finally, during the embrace, the woman is forbidden to straddle her partner, for the liquids filling her vagina might spill on to the man's stomach. And whereas the woman sucks the man's penis (to nourish herself on the beneficial sperm), the man never puts his mouth anywhere near the woman's vagina, which oozes noxious liquids.

"It is very clear, then," Maurice Godelier concludes, "that for the Baruya, making love endangers the reproduction of both nature and society . . . Everything that follows is as if there were a profound contradiction between the sexual activities necessary to reproduction and all the other activities necessary to the reproduction of society."

The Baruya thus have several kinds of relationships with women which are determined by their sexual status. With women who come into prohibited categories – mother, sisters, aunts, girl cousins, nieces – men maintain positive relations of mutual aid and affection. On the other hand, they subject their wives, and secondarily their brothers' wives (from whom they inherit, if their brothers die), to an authority which – for their wives – is accompanied by varying degrees of repression and violence. A man exercises the most severe domination over the woman with whom he has sexual relations. Finally, the father's attitude towards his daughters is affectionate, although it becomes distant as soon as they become adolescent, that is to say sexually attractive.

With the Baruya, it is not so much the vaginal cavity that is feared, but rather the "poisons" it secretes. But in other societies, on the contrary, it is the cavern of the vagina that is the most frightening. The Maori myths explain the "reasons" for this.

As has been mentioned, the god Tane had committed incest with his daughter Hine-Titama who, when she discovered that this was so, was so distressed that she retired from the world of light to the realm of darkness. She had changed her name and taken that of Hine Nui Te Po,[42] the great queen of the night. In so doing, she made death possible.

It was into this new world that the demi-god Maui[43] was born prematurely into a family of four boys. As his mother, Taranga, wrapped him in the hair of her chignon[44] (tikitiki), he was called Maui Tikitiki a Taranga. Supposed to have pulled New Zealand up out of the Pacific Ocean, Maui is known for his exploits throughout Polynesia. He is reputed to be mischievous, inquisitive, and creative. He hoped to make man immortal by trying to assassinate Hine Nui Te Po. So he went off to the chthonian world where the Goddess of the Dead lived. He intended to take advantage of her in her sleep, to enter her body through her vagina, cut out her heart and then emerge through her mouth. Before setting out, he had advised the birds accompanying him not to make any noise, so as not to wake the goddess. But just when he was introducing his head into Hine Nui Te Po's vagina, one of these birds found the sight so comic that he couldn't stop laughing. The great queen of the night awoke with a start, pressed her thighs together, and the mischievous Maui died of strangulation. And it is only since this accident that death has existed in the world.

This story, which associates women with death, abounds in symbols. The female genital organs cause devastation. In physical love, the male sex organ, "Tiki", Dunis notes, is defeated by the dangers concealed in the vagina, which is called "the house of death and

103

misfortune". Even though the Maori also dread the maleficent power of menstrual blood, there is a profusion of expressions to refer to "the hole that destroys". The analogy between the mouth and the vagina makes a woman "a devourer of the vital principle, the favourite agent of death".

Dunis has observed that Tane, the god, had created humanity by committing incest yet without losing immortal life. But Maui, and men, died of it. "The myth is careful to distinguish between the innamorata, the sexual woman (Hine Titama), who is reserved for Tane, and the mother, in other words, death (Hine Nui Te Po), who is reserved for men."

The analogy between the mother and death, so frequent in myths and in our unconscious, indirectly implies the reverse analogy between man and life. Although the vagina gives life, it is also mortal, and this is the aspect that is stressed, while its lifegiving properties are forgotten.

Simone de Beauvoir has made an excellent summary of man's feeling of revolt against his carnal state: "He sees himself as a fallen god: his curse is to have fallen from a bright and ordered heaven into the chaotic shadows of his mother's womb . . . The contingency of all flesh . . . dooms him to death. This quivering jelly which grows in the womb (the womb, secret and sealed like the tomb) evokes too clearly the soft viscosity of carrion for him not to turn shuddering away . . . The slimy embryo begins the cycle that is completed in the putrefaction of death."[45]

She adds that "in most popular representations, Death is a woman, and it is for women to bewail the dead because death is their work . . . The Woman-Mother . . . is the chaos from which all have come and whither all must one day return." But in the societies in which men have appropriated the essential and positive part in procreation, all that remains for women to do is to play the negative role of destruction.

By attributing feminine features to death, certain cultures have taken otherness to its farthest extreme, an odious, terrorizing, and legitimately hateful otherness.[46]

The Fear of the Same

The confusion of the sexes, lack of sexual differentiation, seems to pose a dangerous threat to people's sense of identity. Ethnologists, and some psychoanalysts,[47] agree in thinking that little boys find it more difficult to acquire this sense than do little girls.

We all know that in the beginning, a baby does not see any difference between its mother's body and its own. Unlike his sister, who immediately identifies with her mother's sex, the male baby has to make a considerable effort to differentiate himself from his mother, to become aware of his own body and enter the world of men.

Margaret Mead observes that the little girl meets no such challenge. Even though to start with she is not very sure of her future maternal role, her doubts will vanish once she has had a child: "So the life of the female starts and ends with sureness, first with the simple identification with her mother, last with the sureness that the identification is true, and that she has made another human being."[48]

For the boy, however, "the gradient is reversed . . . He is forced to realize himself as different, as a creature unlike the mother, as a creature unlike the human beings who make babies in a direct, intelligible way, using their own bodies to make them. Instead, he must turn out from himself, enter and explore and produce in the outside world, find his own expression through the bodies of others." In other words: he must realize, and show, that he is a different creature from woman.

This unsureness of masculinity is further increased by the absence of any tangible physiological sign of the power to procreate. In all human societies, however primitive, everyone knows that as soon as she has started menstruating, a woman can have children. But the capacity of the male in this domain is not so apparent. Bruno Bettelheim thinks that the object of the wounds inflicted in masculine initiation is to show that men are as fertile as women. If they make their penises bleed, it is to show that they have the same power as women.

The difficulties of masculine identity are made even more acute by the male's deep-rooted envy of the female functions, which is no less widespread than penis envy in girls.[49] But unlike the latter, in most human societies the male's envy is profoundly repressed, because male homosexuality (with which, rightly or wrongly, it is thought to be linked), is always considered more repugnant than female homosexuality.

Men, then, have to fight harder than women to differentiate themselves from the Other and acquire the psychological sense of their sexual identity. Torn between the challenge of being a male and the forbidden envy of being the Other and possessing her powers, men have invented rites to help them in this task: circumcision – the pendant to female excision, but far more widespread – is one of the ways of fighting against original bisexuality.

Among many others, the creation myths of the Dogons (of Mali)[50] relate that in the beginning, every human being is provided with two souls of different sexes. In man, the female soul is in his prepuce. In woman, the male soul is in her clitoris. But this double soul is a danger for the social (and psychological) order. A man must be male and a woman female. Only circumcision and excision can put things right.

In the Dogons' eyes, the "uncircumcised" are interested in nothing but disorder and trouble. They are marginal to the group, because "nothing in them is fixed". So long as a child still has its prepuce or clitoris its masculinity and femininity are of equal strength, and if this indecision about its sex were to continue, a human being would never feel the urge to procreate. What is more, an individual cannot behave "normally" under twofold direction. So the child must be freed from an evil force and helped to belong definitely to one sex. The *section* of a piece of skin is the condition of psychological and physical *sexing*.

George Groddeck, who has thought deeply about human bisexuality, has interpreted the circumcision of the Jews not only as a desire to eliminate every trace of femininity (the prepuce is assimilated to the vagina, in which the female glans is located), but also as a sign of submission to God, who alone can incarnate bisexuality. Groddeck thinks that the plural *Elohim*, which designates God, is explained if we take it that the legend saw God as bisexual.[51]

In his commentary, Roger Lewinter insists that "circumcision is really the emblem of the human agreement by which the human being fully accepts his finitude in relation to the infinite: his *sexing* in relation to what is sexless or cannot be sexed. God, who is *bisexing* or Elohim, a single plurality, in contrast to the human being who is a dual unity."[52]

Circumcision, the symbolic renunciation of bisexuality, is therefore the emblem of the unisexual human. By disregarding female excision, the Jews have shown that women do not have the same status as men. Only men sign the pact of humanity with God and constitute the chosen people.

But apart from the metaphysico-mystical aspect of circumcision, many psychoanalysts, such as Theodor Reik,[53] Géza Roheim,[54] and Bruno Bettelheim, have shown that circumcision detaches a boy from his mother. It admits him (much earlier in the Jewish than in the Muslim rite) into the community of men, and thus reinforces his masculinity. Others insist on the fantasy of male "rebirth" that it occasions. Herman Nunberg wrote in 1949: "Through circumcision, the glans penis is liberated; it emerges like a child coming out of its mother's womb; in other words, after circumcision, a new penis is born that resembles a retracted phallus. As in the unconscious system, or in primitive thought, the part is taken for the whole, in this case it is the whole body that is identified with the new phallus: the child is born; the initiated, circumcised boy is reborn without a prepuce, and is thus a man."

In most societies, the sexes are separated later than they are among the Jews. Circumcision can be carried out as late as adolescence, and in societies where circumcision is unknown, boys undergo initiation rites between the beginning and end of adolescence.

Boys' initiation rites, which we have already mentioned from the point of view of the father, have not merely the one function of taking over women's procreative powers. They also aim to establish boys' virility; in other words, to complete the psychological work of male identification.

Maurice Godelier has insisted at length on the different amounts of energy expended by the Baruya society in their making of a complete adult man or woman. The Baruya consider that it takes ten years of sexual segregation, four great ceremonies each lasting several weeks, to detach a boy from the feminine world and make him into a real man. On the other hand, girls' initiation needs something less than a fortnight to turn them into women. "The few days the girls spend with the women interrupt, but do not interfere with, their daily life"[55] and its regular tasks.

In this way, Baruya wisdom indicates that it is infinitely more difficult to acquire a masculine sense of identity than a feminine one. From birth, the male child's masculinity is fed on his mother's femininity, and for him to become free from it not only will he have to be kept away from all feminine contact for a long time, he will also have to be reborn by men until he is ready to be married. For him to be able to take a wife in his turn, the young Baruya must have abandoned all his original femininity with his childhood, and be confident of his obvious superiority to women, which cannot appear at the beginning of his life.

It is only much later that a man rediscovers his mother. When he himself has several children, when he can bring her some game he has hunted, he can make her a double offering: "With his first gift he releases himself from the prohibition of speaking to her, which has been weighing on him since he has been initiated; with the second, he is finally allowed to eat in her presence . . . without danger . . . So we find a tremendous ambivalence in his relations with his mother. She is the first woman on the path of life, protection, gentleness, affection; and yet the boy has had to learn to live without her and against her in order to become a man. Between a married man and his old mother there is an attitude of reserve and cautious affection, which is punctuated by long silences, whereas the links between a mother and her married daughters are all laughter, mutual aid, quarrels, presents, consideration."

Even when he is married and the father of a family, the Baruya man still observes a certain distance from his mother, as if he wanted to avoid the slightest (unconscious) temptation to revert to his original, childish state of dependence, passivity and femininity. As with the Jews, according to Groddeck, the essential content of male Baruya repression is bisexuality. Unlike the Jews, though, it is not circumcision that helps the Baruya to avoid it but a long, long detour in the men's house.

Whatever the culture he belongs to, a little boy is always subject to a threefold fear: of losing his male attributes, of not being a complete man, and of reverting to the passivity of a babe in arms. The aim of circumcision and initiation is to drive these fears back into the depths of the unconscious. But the dreams of adult men disclose that these fears are never entirely dead, because they are part and parcel of the powerful desire for bisexuality.

Fear of the Other, coupled with fear of the Same, explains the conflict dualism of the sexes psychologically. This dualism reinforces the sense of gender identity and justifies the repression of the Other, objectively in social relations, and subjectively inside oneself. If the interaction of the sexes causes anxiety, particularly in men, one can understand their aggressivity towards women and the process of sexual segregation that leads to conflict. It is as if they preferred hierarchy, even at the cost of war, to peace seen as a source of chaos, disorder and lack of differentiation. Sex equality runs the risk of provoking comparisons and changing submissive women, imprisoned in their otherness, into competitors.

Serge Dunis thinks that "misogyny is not a disease, but a policy that systematically discredits women, the better to establish the creative powers of men". Being less convinced of men's psychological strength than he is, we are inclined to believe that it is indeed first of all a disease, which later controls a policy. The great thing is to discover when and how this disease began, or whether it is inherent in the masculine condition. The distant past seems to show that relations of complementarity between the sexes were indeed possible, and perhaps more serene than those that have obtained for the last three or four thousand years. But this does not prove the absence of all fear of women on men's part, and vice versa. However, more evenly-balanced powers protected the One from the oppression of the Other, and for that very reason reduced the threat of a revolt or of conflict. On the other hand, the moment one sex possesses all the powers – and this can only be the masculine sex, which relies on its permanent physical superiority – it reigns in the terror that its powers will be stolen from it by the Other, and that it in its turn will be reduced to nothingness.

This is perhaps the origin of the masculine obsession with women's maleficent powers, all the more to be feared in that they are officially denied but secretly desired.

The Ultimate Consequences

By means of segregation and exclusion, some patriarchal societies, "sicker" than others, have reduced to absurdity the idea of a humanity common to both sexes. In such systems humanity is not one; there are two heterogeneous humanities, the good, masculine one, and the bad, feminine one, and they are opposed as nature is to culture. In different periods and civilizations, woman has been identified either with dangerous nature or guilty culture. But whatever the chosen system, the aim has always been to justify its oppression.

For Islam, omnisexual woman embodies a natural disorder that is opposed to a hierarchical, patriarchal culture. Fatna Aït Sabbah writes: "When she listens to the muscles quivering between her legs, a woman erodes the social hierarchy, opens her vagina to the big phallus of low-class men, of poor men, of those whose place is at the bottom of the social ladder, thereby reversing the system of values."

In the twentieth-century Fascist regimes, woman was also assimilated to nature, but this time she was ordered not to go outside it.

In Nazi ideology, woman is an animal who procreates, and whose universe is limited to the family, as opposed to man, who is the architect of the macrocosm. Rita Thalmann points out that the word "woman" (*Frau*) is not even to be found in the index to *Mein Kampf*, but the archaic, biological and pejorative term: *Weib*.[56]

One of the vestal virgins of National Socialism, Guida Diehl, was able to write that the feminine sphere is defined by nature (motherhood), as opposed to that of man (dominated by reason), which extends over the whole of the State and the community. By virtue of this conception, the Nazis drove women out from posts of responsibility in the different sectors of public life[57] and instituted the *numerus clausus* in higher education.[58] In this, they were treated like the Jews and the enemies of the ruling powers. But unlike the latter, whom it wanted to sterilize and exterminate, the IIIrd Reich ordered women to place their bodies at the disposal of the regeneration of the Germanic race. "Zoo technicians were put in charge of the racial reproduction of the German State. Heinrich Himmler, a former student of agronomy at the Munich Technical College, was to transfer his experience of aviculture to the breeding of a warrior caste."

At the Congress of Nuremberg in 1934, Hitler called for a veritable maternal mobilization which was to take place within a racial perspective. While those women who did not have the requisite genetic qualities were sterilized, prison sentences were reintroduced for anyone who took any part in an abortion, and measures were taken to reward good, prolific mothers.[59]

Pushing the logic of feminine animality to its extreme, the Nazis created the famous *Lebensborn*, a veritable SS stud farm. Wives, girlfriends, fiancées of SS men were invited to these "reception centres" in order to reproduce themselves as quickly as possible. German women were reduced to the status of fillies. The more murderous the war became, the greater the demographic obsession became: on 8 May 1942 Himmler gave the order to plan a great *Lebensborn* centre capable of accommodating 400,000 women. As men became less and less available, the Nazi leaders decided that certain selected men would be allowed to have two wives, and even that the whole idea of illegitimate children would be abolished. "Every German woman must be able to give birth as she pleases, if the Reich is not to lack the divisions necessary to the survival of our people in twenty years' time."

Nazi ideology, in the lineage of misogynous thinkers from Schopenhauer to Otto Weininger,[60] returned to the thesis of a masculine/feminine bipolarity similar to that of mind and matter, reason and instinct, light and darkness.

We do not need to add that the manly values were said to embody order and the creative forces, whereas the feminine values were synonymous with chaos and degenerescence. Women's place was certainly on the side of nature, but a constant watch had to be kept to ensure that they remained there and did not introduce disorder and anarchy into the culture. In Germany, then, a country in which there had been powerful movements in favour of female emancipation since the beginning of the century, in which women were eligible for election and had the vote thanks to the Constitution of the Weimar Republic, the men of the Third Reich had every reason to fear that women had a malign desire to emerge from their natural condition.

In other patriarchal ideologies, the reverse schema asserts itself. Man is closer to nature than is woman, it is said, and nature is good, whereas woman is suspected of unleashing "cultural" catastrophes.

111

This was the case with Eve, who gave birth to culture as the punishment for her sin. To a lesser extent, it is also that of the Baruya women. It will be remembered that according to their myths of origin, it was women who created the flute, the bow, etc., but they did not use them properly. For the Baruya, men's superiority comes from their familiarity with the world of the forest, of hunting,[61] whereas women are confined within the "civilized" space of the gardens, the village. According to Maurice Godelier, if these young women are dominated, it is because they belong far more to the side of culture than to that of nature. "Baruya women do not gain in prestige from having – by imagination, by thought – made agriculture possible."

Whichever way we look, women are excluded from the good side of humanity and are said to deserve the treatment inflicted on them. Sometimes assimilated to a kind of sub-humanity because of their resemblance to the animals, sometimes to the diabolical side of humanity because of their connivance with disorder, women are no longer seen in a complementary relationship. Co-operation and brotherly affection have no place in a situation where the Other is the implacable enemy one must beware of. In the patriarchal system, men have more experience of desire, fear, passion, than of the loving friendship that thrives on equality, confidence, and the possibility of identifying oneself with the Other. When an Indian, Islamic, medieval or Baruya couple is united by a feeling of this sort, it is less representative of the usual state of affairs in that society than of a kind of individual "deviation". It constitutes something of a challenge to the society's basic values.[62] It is the exception that confirms the rule of the society. But it also proves the possibility of a different type of relationship between man and woman.

Before concluding this chapter, there is one remaining question, to which the answer is not easy. If there were places and periods in which women had prestige and certain powers, how and why did they allow themselves to be dispossessed of them?

Some have pointed out that this was precisely the proof that women had never dominated men, or been in privileged situations. "It is hard to see why," Françoise Héritier writes, "if they had been politically, economically and ideologically dominant in one place, women should have been incapable of adapting to social transformations . . . In every case, the levelling in question seems to have taken place through the worsening, not the gradual reversal, of a situation."[63]

If it does indeed seem unlikely that women were ever all-powerful, as men were later, many indications are still extant of their ideological supremacy, as well as of their control of the economy over a long period.

Certainly, this positive status enjoyed in former times in some regions of the world does not constitute a universal fact. It would be absurd to think that the relationship between men and women obeys something like a law of the three estates, applicable at all times and in all places. But it would be no less dangerous to believe – especially when we observe the present evolution of Western societies – that masculine superiority is itself a universal law of culture.

It is true that women have allowed themselves to be dispossessed and oppressed without objecting too violently. At least, no trace of any rebellion remains. To explain this change of status, which was slower and more gradual than people like to imagine, it seems necessary to come back to humanity's essential bisexuality, which makes man and woman beings who are at the same time active and passive, aggressive and submissive, manly and feminine. By gradually surrendering their ascendancy, women have been freed of the responsibilities incumbent upon it. In exchange, they have gained the pleasures of passivity, and perhaps even the satisfaction of secret masochistic desires.

Men, on the contrary, have been able to give free rein to their aggressive, dominating and active instincts. So much so that they have sometimes broken the treaty of alliance they had with their feminine counterparts.

It is not surprising, then, that women one day decided to remind men of what they have in common – humanity. Sated with passivity, weary of their submission, imprisoned in their inferior status, they realized that the repression of a large part of their desires and ambitions could be brought to an end.

This realization on the part of Western women was the beginning of another war, which lasted for centuries. Even today, its wounds are not yet healed.

III

THE DEATH OF THE PATRIARCHY

Patriarchy is not a simple system of sexual oppression. It is also the expression of a political system which, in our society, has enlisted the support of a theology. According to whether this theology was authoritarian or tolerant, respectful of the individual or not, during the course of history patriarchy has shown different faces, ranging from the most terrible to the tolerable. There is no doubt, for example, that in the eighteenth century the Catholic monarchies exercised power more harshly than did the great Protestant countries, nor that the keyword of the former was submission, while that of the latter was tolerance.

The relationship between man and woman is part of a general power-system that controls the relations of men among themselves. This explains why in the beginning the first attacks on patriarchy were made by men and not by women. Before thinking about destroying the power of the father over the family, the absolute political power of the sovereign had to be abolished and its religious foundations undermined. This is the way every Western society has evolved, through revolutions and reforms, right up to the twentieth century. But if men have been determined to build a new society based on equality and liberty, their project, at first political and later economic and social, has been confined to themselves, because they wanted to be its sole beneficiaries.

Men have fought to obtain rights from which they were careful to exclude women. Was there any need for women to vote, to be educated, or to have equal protection to men at their place of work? Equality stopped at the frontiers of sex, for while most men wanted to free themselves from political patriarchy, they wanted at all costs to maintain patriarchy in the family. Hence the constantly-repeated warning, in the nineteenth century, by conservatives and the Church: in fighting for more liberty and equality you are attacking paternal authority and undermining the foundations of the family.

There is no denying that the battle fought by democrats over two centuries was the prime cause of the fall of the patriarchal system. But it was not its sufficient reason. It was women, making common cause with the most fair-minded of the men, who laboriously brought the work to its conclusion. It took them nearly two centuries to get their fathers and husbands to admit that they were "Men" like everyone else: that they should have the same rights as their partners, and share the same duties.

Once this obvious fact has been recognized, it becomes fraught with consequences, not only because it puts an end to a relationship between the sexes that is several thousand years old, but above all because it inaugurates the deal of a new hand, which obliges us to rethink everyone's specific characteristics. Democratic values were fatal to the king, to God-the-Father, and to the Father-God. At the same time they rendered the traditional definitions of the sexes obsolete, and they are still perplexing and worrying a large part of the world.

The Death Throes

Exclusion and hierarchy were slowly beginning to decline when the new ideal of liberty, equality and fraternity imposed itself all over the West. Even if women were its ultimate beneficiaries, the ideological upheaval introduced by the French Revolution, the most decisive of all revolutions in the Western world, dealt a mortal blow to every power imposed by the grace of God, and by the same token to every idea of the natural superiority of the One to the Other.

The French Revolution: Parricide and Deicide

At the end of the seventeenth century and the beginning of the eighteenth, the theoreticians of absolute monarchy tried to find legal justification for the authority of the king by linking it to that of God and of the father. Thus Bossuet,[1] collecting and systematizing the lesson of Saint Paul (*Nulla potestas nisi a Deo*),[2] reinforced the power of the one by that of the two others. Comparing the sovereign to the father of a family, he made monarchy a natural right. To render this even more indisputable, he raised political authority into a divine right. God, he said, is the perfect model of paternity. And the king is the image of God on earth, the father of his subjects. The simple father of a family is therefore a substitute for the divine, royal image in relation to his children. Everyone gained in some way in these successive analogies. The father in magnificence and authority, the king in goodness and saintliness. God himself was brought closer to his creatures.

Bossuet advised obedience to the great, who are linked by their common origin. But this cunning argument was not without danger. With God, the king and the father so closely linked, the fate of the one governed that of the other two. Hence by killing the king, the revolutionaries struck a decisive blow against the power both of God and of the father: "The act of killing the king is a simulacrum of the death of the father."[3]

As the philosopher Jean Lacroix has well shown, democracy is incompatible with the paternal power of former days. All emancipation is first of all liberation from the father. Popular sovereignty is born of parricide. By killing the king-father, the people, long kept down by being treated as minors, gain the autonomy of the adult. To achieve this end they had to guillotine the sovereign in public, to make everyone fully aware of the change in the State.[4] Once the deed had been done, the reversal of values became effective. The triptych Liberty, Equality, and Fraternity was substituted for the old one: Submission, Hierarchy and Paternity. In a republic, brotherly friendship between citizens replaces the feeling of respect that unites sons to their father. Vertical links yield to horizontal links, the only ones compatible with the egalitarian ideal.

Jean Lacroix was right to stress the fact that modern democracy is "a search for fraternity accompanied by a refusal of paternity". Revolutionary fraternity, sealed by royal parricide, gives a different meaning to the notion of the sacred. "The idea of the sacred that arises from participation in a superior reality is replaced by that which stems from the fellowship of equals."[5]

It will have become clear that the rejection of the king and the father is here, even more profoundly, the rejection of all transcendence. The rebellion could not spare God, the universal Father of the human race. The 1789 revolutionaries, who were passionately trying to promote the concept of Humanity associated with the values of equality, liberty and fraternity, were bound, somewhere along the line, to meet God, intimately linked with the old values. The philosophers of the nineteenth century, among them Feuerbach, Proudhon, Marx and Nietzsche, drawing the inferences of the French Revolution, proclaimed the death of God, as this appeared to be the necessary condition for the liberation of humanity.[6]

Going farther than the philosophers of the nineteenth century, Lacroix stresses that if humanity wanted to rid itself of God, it was primarily because it saw him as the symbol of the father. Man asserts himself against the "king of kings, the supreme enunciator of age-old prohibitions which have always stood in his way. Even if God were love he would still repudiate him, for he seems only able to love like a father... Man rejects this perpetual judgment, he wants God's grace and Salvation no more than he fears the punishments postponed until after the end of history."[7]

From then on, Theology was to yield its place to Anthropology.

But at the end of the eighteenth century, the rejection of divine transcendence, or rather the assertion of the primacy of the individual, was not yet expressed in these terms. Without talking about "the death of God", they patiently built a State free of all religious influence. Starting with the French Revolution, a slow but profound movement of secularization developed in the Western world, breaking with a tradition that went back more than ten centuries.

Until the schism brought about in the sixteenth century by the Reformation, which shattered the Christian establishment, all European nations had three features in common: the indisputed place of the Catholic Church, a religious State, and a theory of social order drawn up by theologians.[8] But whereas the Protestant Reformation, the first attempt to secularize the State, constituted a revolt only against ecclesiastical constraints, the French Revolution declared itself to be a refusal of God. From the end of the seventeenth century, the Protestant countries (England and Holland) had begun the process of laicizing the State. By developing the spirit of freedom of thought, by tolerating a diversity of faiths and sects, by recognizing that the right of the State did not extend over the individual conscience, the Protestants finally defended God's cause better than the Catholic countries did.

In the latter, the process of secularization came later, but was more radical. Between 1789 and 1799, the French Revolution brutally shattered the framework of the Christian era and replaced the *Civitas Dei* by the *Civitas Humana*. By proclaiming the religious neutrality of the State, by laicizing the public services and by later separating itself definitively from the Church, the French Republic became a model of laicism for modern Christian States.

In the nineteenth century, Italy and Germany also tried to impose civil marriage, but it was only in the twentieth century that laicism became a general principle of modern States. International declarations were all lay. While the separation of Church and State is written into the First Amendment of the American Constitution (1787), and while Article 10 of the French Declaration of the Rights of Man proclaims freedom of opinion, it was not until 10 December 1948 that an international decision – by a deliberate omission – ratified the principle of laicism. In fact, the First Article of the Universal Declaration of the Rights of Man declares that "all human beings are free and equal in law. They are endowed with reason and must act towards each other in a spirit of brotherhood."

In the debates preceding the vote, a minority of countries[9] had expressed the wish that the name of God should be mentioned, and suggested that the text should remind men that they were created in his image. But this motion was opposed by the representatives of the USSR and of France. Finally, "God found himself being refused rights in the United Nations, to which he appeared to be the greatest common divisor."

By asserting the transcendence of Man, the new "Tables of the Law", introduced in 1789 and declared "sacred and inviolable", made Man into a god. From then on, men were going to legislate for themselves. There was going to be no more submission to the all-powerful father who alone decides what is good or bad for his children. The ideology of the Rights of Man became, at least in theory, a veritable religion, and sanctified the Republic of brothers, whose similarities were more important than their differences. Their common humanity made everyone equal, independently of their specific religious, racial, economic or social character. It remained to be seen, though, whether a specific sexual character was not a major handicap.

Rights of Man or Rights of Men?

Although the men of the French Revolution never publicly deliberated this point, there was one great question that was not even asked: were women Men like everyone else, and were they also to benefit from the sacred rights that had just been proclaimed? In other, and more brutal, words: were women not by nature apart from humanity?

In the absence of any political debate on the subject, the problem had been raised by "intellectuals", well before the start of the Revolution. The precursor was Poulain de la Barre who, in a book[10] that was ignored at the time (1673), put forward one of the most revolutionary of all propositions: the equality of the sexes. For this disciple of Descartes, equality is to be total because men and women, endowed with the same reasoning power, are similar in almost every respect. Feminine nature is so intrinsic a part of human nature that Poulain dreamed of seeing women having access to all occupations in society: professors of medicine or of theology, ministers of the Church,"généralles" [sic] in the army, or présidentes of Parliament. By reducing the difference between the sexes to the minimum, Poulain wove bonds of fraternity between men and women and restored women to the bosom of humanity.

Unfortunately, the men of the eighteenth century, who had not read Poulain, were much more timorous. None of those who expressed an opinion on the nature of women went as far as the great seventeenth-century unknown. The debate on the feminine question brought to light three points of view. Some descendants of

Poulain de la Barre stressed the similarity of the sexes and militated for their equality. Others, agreeing with this principle, insisted above all on their necessary complementarity. Finally, the majority, following Rousseau, went on thinking of femininity in terms of an irreducible difference. By accentuating this difference, they justified in advance the inequality in Émile and Sophie's education, in their social and even political life.

If we leave aside the polemical and political aspect of the equality of the sexes, the philosophical debate, which is still being carried on by present-day feminists, consists in knowing whether to stress the identity or the difference, whether to give priority to the concept of human nature or to that of feminine nature.

Diderot, in whom many women could recognize themselves today, argued the case for equality within difference. Making a pretext of the publication of a little pamphlet on women by Thomas,[11] he wrote a short essay on the subject.[12] Diderot singles out the fair sex for the strength of their feelings: "It is above all in the passion of love, in their transports of jealousy, in their fits of maternal tenderness, in their superstition, in the manner in which they experience skin-deep and popular emotions, that women astonish us. I have seen women carry love, jealousy, superstition and anger to excesses that man never feels."

The reason for such violent transports, which Diderot considered foreign to men, is of an anatomico-physiological order. Woman "has within her an organ that is liable to terrible spasms, which dominates her and stirs up phantasms of all kinds in her imagination." It is not surprising, then, that she can pass from hysteria to ecstasy, from revelation to prophecy. Slaves of their uterus and of their fiery imagination, women are "most extraordinary children" who inspire Diderot with tenderness and pity. He pities them for being what they are – not only doomed to the pains and dangers of childbirth, but also to "long and dangerous illnesses" when they are past childbearing age.

But the natural differences between the sexes perceived by Diderot incline him to defend the cause of women, in order that "the cruelty of the civil laws laid down against them in almost every country" should not be added to the cruelty of nature. Diderot demands that they should no longer be treated like "idiot children", that they should be decently educated,[13] and, finally, that their particular genius should be recognized: "When they have genius . . . it is of a more original stamp than ours."

In concluding this several-page-long essay, Diderot probably thought he had made out a good case in favour of women, since he went on to write: "If I had been a legislator . . . I would have emancipated you, I would have set you above the law; you would have been sacred wherever you happened to be."

Put on a pedestal thus, what more could women have asked?

But Diderot's old friend, Madame d'Épinay, did not see things in the same light. Followed shortly afterwards by Condorcet, she thought that the resemblance between the sexes is more important than what separates them, and that simple equality might well be worth more than a pedestal. She too criticized the essay of poor Thomas, and was one of the first to decry those who "continually attribute to nature what we have clearly acquired from education or institutions."[14] In her opinion, men and women have the same nature and the same constitution. The mother of three children, she did not attach the same importance to the uterus as did Diderot. On the contrary, with calm audacity she asserted the very modern idea that "even the weakness of our organs is certainly a function of our education and the consequence of the condition in society that we have been assigned."

Madame d'Épinay observes that both sexes are subject to the same defects, the same virtues, and the same vices. Two centuries before Simone de Beauvoir, she thought like her that one is not born a woman, one becomes one, and that feminine characteristics are not so "natural" as people like to make out. Physical strength, moral courage and intellectual ability would be identical in man and woman if society and education had not taken it upon themselves to differentiate them. However, having no expectation that any revolution would produce real equality, Madame d'Épinay concluded: "It would take several generations to return us to what nature made us. We might perhaps gain thereby, but men would lose too much."

Condorcet was one of the rare politicians[15] to militate for the equality of the sexes using the same arguments as Madame d'Épinay, and also because the contrary seemed to him an intolerable injustice.[16] He demanded that "the rights of half the *human race* should no longer be forgotten by every legislator,[17] that women should be allowed to vote and to be eligible for every office. Less audacious than Poulain, he nevertheless thought that women would not cover themselves with ridicule if they wished to command an army or preside over a court of law. Anticipating the traditional objections concerning the insuperable obstacles posed by pregnancies, childbirth and nursing, Condorcet retorted that men suffering from a cold were not forbidden to vote or to assume their responsibilities. As for the alleged incapacity of women to create, he replied, not without humour, that he did not believe in it, and that if only men capable of inventing were admitted to office, there would be many vacant places, even in the academies . . .

Since he also thought that "there is no difference between women and men that is not the product of education," in 1792 Condorcet put forward a remarkable draft decree that radically modified the education of women. He demanded a common syllabus for both sexes, whose "aim was to teach individuals of the *human race* what it would be useful for them to know in order to enjoy their rights and fulfil their duties".[18]

Unlike the immense majority of men, Condorcet considered women to be the legitimate "*competitors*" of men in many offices and professions, including those connected with the sciences, and he therefore concluded that there was an absolute necessity for a similar training. Whereas Talleyrand, a year earlier, in a debate on Education in the Constituent Assembly (September 1791) had reminded his audience that the exclusion of women from public employment was a way of increasing "the happiness of the couple" for both sexes, and exhorted them not to make "*rivals* out of their life companions", Condorcet supported the opposite idea. "Lack of education would introduce an inequality into families which would be against their happiness . . . because equality is everywhere, but above all in families, the foremost element in felicity, in peace, and in the virtues."

The argument in favour of happiness through the equality of the sexes was rejected by the men of the Assembly, who were more susceptible to the Rousseauist arguments of Talleyrand than to the revolutionary ideas of a Condorcet. Condorcet's plan got absolutely nowhere. While it was a great inspiration to the revolutionaries of

1880, the education of women up to then had run counter to his ideas. By settling the problem of women's education in this way, the men of the Revolution had put off the debate instigated by Poulain de la Barre for a long time to come. Women were not individuals like other people. Their femininity remained an insuperable obstacle to their integration into humanity.

Undeniably, women were the rejects of the Revolution. And while the revolutionary ideal placed strict equality above natural differences, sex remained the ultimate criterion of discrimination. The Jews were emancipated by the decree of 27 September 1791, Negro slavery was abolished on 4 February 1794, but, in spite of some people's efforts, the condition of women remained unchanged. The Rights of Man, those natural rights attributed to the human being, were not allowed to them.

Olympe de Gouges' 1791 *Declaration of the Rights of Woman and Citizeness*[19] remained a dead letter, as did the draft plan for a Civil Code put forward by Cambacérès,[20] which declared the full legal competence of the young married woman, the entire equality of spouses, and granted them both absolutely identical rights in a joint estate. The Convention opposed the women's vote, forbade them to enter into any association, and sent them back to their homes, on the pretext, expressed by Amar, that "each sex is marked out for its own appropriate type of occupation; its action is circumscribed by a circle it cannot go beyond, for nature, which imposes its limits on man, gives imperious orders and accepts no law."

Napoleon's Civil Code ratified the inequality of the sexes in the name of their necessary complementarity. To men: the rights; to women: the duties. The emperor intervened personally to restore the full authority of the husband,[21] whch had been slightly undermined at the end of the eighteenth century. He insisted that, on the day of her marriage, the wife should explicitly recognize that she owed obedience to her husband. In her thesis already mentioned, Françoise Picq puts this very well: "The Civil Code is the code of the rights of the strongest, and guarantees those of the husband and the father . . . It organizes the downward levelling of the condition of women."

Women's Long March

It took more than a century and a half[22] for the totality of women in the West to acquire their rights as human beings: civil rights, rights to education, to which the right to choose motherhood must be added.

When it came to granting civil rights to women, once again the Protestant nations were in advance of the Catholic countries. It was the United States that set the example to the Western world. Even though American women had to wait more than a century before they obtained a constitutional amendment, the wives of the "pilgrims", blessed with greater authority than European women, began to fight for the right immediately after the War of Independence. When this question was referred to them, the federal Congress in Philadelphia, representing thirteen States, decided to leave each State free to choose whether or not to write women's suffrage into their Constitution. None of them did. After half a century of silence, women took up the struggle again in 1840, in conjunction with the movement for the abolition of slavery. In 1848 they organized the Woman's Rights Convention, then in 1850 the National Woman Suffrage Convention, which bore no fruit until after the Civil War (1861–5). Three years after the abolition of slavery (1866), the State of Wyoming was the first to grant women the vote, followed a year later by Utah (1870). At the end of the nineteenth century there were suffrage associations in thirty-six States,[23] but it was not until 1919 that a constitutional amendment was passed, recognizing the right of every woman to vote. It was ratified in 1920.

Germany[24] and England[25] followed suit at the same period. It is true that since the beginning of the century there had been continual agitation in both countries, whose suffragettes were in permanent contact. The English suffragettes had benefited from the valuable help of the philosopher and MP John Stuart Mill,[26] and the Germans from that of August Bebel.[27] But it was above all thanks to the action of Clara Zetkin and her paper *Die Gleichheit* (*Equality*), founded in 1892, that the socialist party agreed to include the political, economic and social equality of women in its programme.

French women, as we know, were the worst off. They had to wait until the end of the Second World War for an ordinance of General de Gaulle's provisional government to grant them (21 April 1944) the right to vote, and unrestricted eligibility.[28]

It must be admitted that the French suffragette movement had few followers in the nineteenth century, and that the women who carried on the struggle were extremely isolated. Apart from Jeanne Deroin, who was a pioneer (she stood for parliament in 1849), it was not until 1870–80 that the right to vote was again fought for. It was Hubertine Auclert – who had become famous by writing to the prefect in March 1881: "I don't vote, I don't pay (my taxes)" – who rekindled the debate, even though she remained isolated within the feminist movement. The movement was too much influenced by socialism, and didn't separate women's claims sufficiently from the general political context. Apart from a few militants like Marguerite Durand, Madeleine Pelletier and Nelly Roussel, the feminists saw their salvation as lying within the men's fight for liberty. They were wrong. In 1936, Léon Blum's government made three women Under-Secretaries of State,[29] but omitted to reopen the question of women's suffrage. Finally, when this right was eventually granted them by General de Gaulle, no specific action by women had been necessary to obtain it. A woman deputy even went so far as to say that "Frenchwomen patiently waited for the right to vote."[30]

In general, the great battles that have punctuated the history of the emancipation of women have not been fought in the same way in France, a Latin country, and in the great Anglo-Saxon nations. Feminists are seen in a very bad light in France, which has mocked them in turn as "précieuses", "femmes savantes", "pétroleuses", "bas-bleus", and "cervelines".[31] The Latin mentality finds it hard to accept women who make their own claims, instead of waiting for them to be granted as a favour. In contrast to the United States, where the "pilgrims" played an important part in the foundation of the democracy, the republic was created without women, almost against them. The noisy manifestations of the English suffragettes[32] at the beginning of the century shocked the temperament of the French; the powerful Swedish, Norwegian and Finnish associations had no equivalent in France.[33] As Rilke wrote: "From the north comes the light." We might explain this, with Tocqueville, by the Protestant influence.[34]

In contrast to the education of French girls, that of the Americans, in 1840, surprised Tocqueville by its absence of timidity or false modesty. A girl was taught early to know how to direct her thoughts and words,[35] for the Americans "have seen that within the bosom of a democracy, individual independence could be very great ... paternal authority weak, and the husband's power contested."

From 1826, all the American States had primary and junior schools for girls like those for boys. Thanks to feminine agitation and to the entry of women into the teaching profession, girls were able to lay claim to higher education in universities established by private foundations. In 1848, New England opened the first faculty of medicine for women; between 1865 and 1885 the great women's colleges and universities were founded: Vassar, Wellesley, Smith, Radcliffe, and Bryn Mawr. By the end of the nineteenth century, every profession was open to women.

So far as Frenchwomen are concerned, here too it was not so much the claims of the women themselves that triumphed over the old conservative attitudes, it was rather the action of the anti-clerical republicans. It was because girls' education was in general given over to nuns, that men like Victor Duruy,[36] Camille Sée[37] and Jules Ferry fought to remove them from anti-republican clerical influence. In 1870, Jules Ferry explained this clearly: "There is a barrier between woman and man . . . An undeclared struggle between the bygone society, the *Ancien Régime*, (which woman perpetuates), and the society that proceeds from the French revolution . . . Whoever controls woman, controls everything, in the first place because he controls the child, and then because he controls the husband."

Once liberated from religious education, French girls had to wait until the early 1920s for a decree that finally put the secondary education of girls on the same footing as that of boys, and led to the equivalence of their *baccalauréats*. For if, in principle, the faculties of medicine, of letters and of the sciences had been open to women since the Second Empire, in reality only a handful of girls – a few hundred – had any secondary education during the 1880s.

In order to be the equals of men, women still had to acquire one ultimate right: the right to dispose of their own bodies, or more precisely to obtain the means whereby motherhood could be planned.

At the end of the nineteenth century, women's voices were raised in France,[38] England,[39] the Netherlands[40] and Germany,[41] at the same time against "double sexual standards" and for "motherhood by choice". Supported by the Neo-Malthusian organizations, which tried to popularize every method of having sexual relations without risk of pregnancy, women fought less for sexual liberty, which was frowned on in this century of moral restoration, than to avoid the repeated confinements that wreaked havoc with their lives and health, and caused children to be born although even their minimal well-being could not be guaranteed.

Around 1920, these claims began to be met. In the United States, Margaret Sanger, a nurse, revolted by the death of her mother while giving birth to her eleventh child, and after having come across the European Neo-Malthusian movements, opened the first American birth-control clinic in 1917. The first English clinic was opened by Marie Stopes (1880–1958) in 1921, and the first German one was started in Frankfurt-am-Main in 1924.

Unfortunately, France, as a good Latin country, did not follow suit. In the absence of any real popular support for the fight for planned motherhood, the Neo-Malthusians found themselves progressively isolated in the face of more and more numerous attacks by the upholders of the moral order and those favouring an increase in the birth rate. The medical and ecclesiastical hierarchies insisted that a woman who refuses to have children "no longer deserves her rights; she no longer exists ... If she remains voluntarily sterile, she is no better than a prostitute."

Just after the First World War, the opponents of planned motherhood managed to introduce a real judicial straitjacket. This was constituted in two stages: the law of 1920, which put birth-control propaganda on the same footing as incitement to abortion and suppressed all information on contraception and all practice of it, and the law of 1923 which, by sending cases of abortion to a court of summary jurisdiction, put an end to the indulgence of some Assize Court juries. Thanks to the vigilance of the police, various kinds of contraceptives disappeared from the pharmacies overnight, and militant Neo-Malthusians were prosecuted.[42]

Whereas in the thirties, the partisans of birth control were tolerated and even encouraged in the Scandinavian countries, America and England,[43] France, profoundly marked by Catholic ideology, continued to condemn all methods of contraception. On this point, there was no appreciable change in the condition of Frenchwomen until the sixties.

Begun in the eighteenth century in the democratically-inclined countries, patriarchy's death throes lasted almost two hundred years, not without experiencing moments of extreme remission in some countries. The dictatorships that devoured Europe between the two wars, and even afterwards in Franco's Spain, were so many deliberate attempts to reinforce patriarchy. We have seen how things were under the Hitler regime, but the situation of Italian women under Mussolini and Spanish women under Franco was not much better.[44] The ideology of the prolific mother, requisitioned in order to procreate and obey, was much the same in Berlin, Madrid and Rome. According to economic or ideological requirements, women were used as cheap labour or sent home to fulfil their vocation of mothers and housewives. Whether brood mares or lumpen-proletariat, they had no right to any great respect.

In the East, too, patriarchy gained a new lease of life during the thirties and forties. Whereas the young Soviet Union had voted laws to liberate women[45] and remove from men all prerogatives over members of their family,[46] the experiment failed. Russian society underwent a sexual counter-revolution that made it more and more like other European countries. Under Stalin, it extolled the traditional family with as much zeal as Nazi Germany. All Lenin's liberating laws were abandoned, and repressive ones substituted.[47]

After the Second World War, and with Western Europe's return to democracy, the fight for the equality of the sexes was still only semi-successful. In principle, women enjoyed the same rights as men, but in fact, continuing customs and practices made their lot quite different. Patriarchy still existed, because the ideology of complementarity was still very much alive. Woman's destiny continued to be played out in the home, because of her duties as a mother. A woman was only "respectable", and "fulfilled" as a function of her status of mother and housewife.[48]

In the sixties, a revolution of a different kind swept through the Western world and completed that of the eighteenth century. Once again, it was procreation that was at the centre of the debates. The question was no longer, as formerly, to decide who played the essential part in the work of procreation,[49] but rather how to control one's fertility so as only to become a mother by choice.

The Coup de Grâce

In most Western democracies, the patriarchal system has received the *coup de grâce* in the last two decades. A minute dot on the line of human evolution, the nineteen-eighties have transformed the relations between men and women in a large part of the world, although we have still not fully realized the fact.

Speaking of the beginnings of *homo sapiens*, Edgar Morin could write in 1973 that "the male group appropriated the government and control of society and *imposed on women and the young a political domination that has still not ceased*".[50] In this end of the second millennium, this assumption is no longer obvious. The power of the father and husband is becoming extinct. Men's ideological, social and political domination has been seriously eroded.

The death of patriarchy is the result of a double upheaval: the father has lost his prestige, and Eve has dealt herself a new hand. The eighteenth and nineteenth centuries dispossessed the father of his divine sponsorship, the twentieth century will finally deprive him of his moral authority and the exclusivity of his economic power. Françoise Héritier has defined patriarchy as the control of women's fertility, and the sexual division of labour. If this is so, then the last twenty years have been marked by a double feminine conquest: the control of their own fertility, and a share in the economic world.

They have stopped being *objects*.

The Moral Defeat of Western Man

The twentieth century has sounded the death knell of male values in the West. At first, it seemed as if it was the very nature of the Second

World War that was responsible for our traditional values being re-examined. The fact that one of the most civilized peoples in the world had allowed itself to be engulfed in such destructive madness provoked a multiplicity of questions. The Nazis' policies exalted and concretized male values and took them to tragic extremes: might became right; aggressivity, violence and sadism were officially normalized. Not for a very long time had the supremacy of the (white, Aryan) male been asserted with such passion.

During this war, which marks a decisive turning point in the history of the West, manliness showed its ugliest – most murderous – face. In contrast to previous wars, death was not only dealt on the battlefields. It was organized, systematically and rationally, to be used against civilians who did not conform to the Nazi norms. (Prisoners of war were better treated than the civilians deported to the camps.) During this period of madness, none of the positive aspects of manliness could be expressed. Pity, respect for international agreements, and above all the protection of women and children, were excluded from this genocidal war. While it may be true that wars always constitute parentheses in the observation of the Rights of Man, Europe had never known such a betrayal of the ideals she had been establishing for two centuries. By shattering the concept of humanity, the war waged by the Nazis provoked a genuine horror of all the "values" in whose name it had been fought. When the survivors were able to assess the full extent of the human disaster, they turned against all ideas of racism or discrimination. Violence and the use of force were stigmatized as being Absolute Evil. Whether we like it or not, it was the archaic, manly values that people were thus putting in the dock. In the post-war democracies, the Fascist slogan "¡Viva el muerte!" and the fascination exercised by death were no longer current. The warrior had become suspect, and respect for the Other once again became a sacred value.

The decolonization of the fifties and sixties was one of the consequences of the re-establishment of human values. After having denounced all forms of oppression, it became more and more difficult to justify the maintenance of some peoples under the guardianship of others. Decolonization completed the democratic process initiated by the French Revolution. Whatever their race or culture, the peoples of the twentieth century wanted to benefit – sometimes at the cost of terrible wars of liberation followed by fratricidal combat – from the ideals the Westerners had built up for themselves. While they rarely managed to create free States which respected their citizens' equality, at least they were no longer subjected to the laws of the white man.

It is within this context that we must place the movements for female emancipation that appeared in all Western countries at the end of the sixties. Beguiled during their adolescence by the themes of the right of peoples to run their own lives, young women also began to search for their identity. The most radical among them developed the themes of interior colonization. In France, they said that they were exploited just as much as the members of the former colonies had been by the white man. In the USA, they compared their lot to that of the black community. There, under the aegis of Betty Friedan,[51] or in France, in a voluntarily anonymous and unorganized[52] fashion, militant feminists drew up a list of the various kinds of exploitation of which they were the victims: sexual, domestic, economic, social and political. Indefatigably, they set forth their grievances against men, as if they felt an irresistible need to release words that had been stifled since the beginning of time.

In 1972, the MLF (the Movement for Women's Liberation) organized a conference in Paris: *Days of denunciation of crimes against women*, in which anonymous evidence came flooding in from all kinds of witnesses. Some complained that they were shut in, and subjected to discrimination in many ways; others told of rape or abortion. All expressed their oppression and their resentment. At first, these cries were greeted with guffaws and insults. But the men who had militated for decolonization were the first to be concerned by the women's challenge. They felt the same guilt as they had done previously about the colonized peoples. Before, it was the white man who had been challenged. Now, it was simply man as such who was under cross-examination, and there was no way of putting any distance between himself and his accuser. Some men espoused the women's cause, but most felt an inexpressible unease. They understood, or refused to understand, that in the more or less long term, the women's struggle represented "a total reversal of their values, of their laws, in a word, of the whole of their civilization".[53]

The re-examination of men by women was reinforced by that of fathers by sons. At the end of the sixties, women and the young, at the same time challenging the husband and the father, objectively formed "a new alliance". Young Westerners no longer wanted to identify themselves with their fathers. Although their fathers had no blood on their hands, the values they stood for seemed both derisory and deadly. Their insatiable consumerism, love of possessions and gadgets, allied to the economic war, the arms race, and the unprecedented exploitation of nature, constituted an absurd, mediocre and unethical model in the eyes of their sons. Young people rejected the traditional manly values *en bloc*, and adopted more feminine values. Denying all idea of authority or natural superiority, they preached non-violence in all its forms. The Vietnam war, which rightly or wrongly they saw as a resurgence of the old Western imperialism – and hence of patriarchal authoritarianism – was universally reviled by the new generation of the sixties and seventies. Young Westerners, who never wanted to hear another word about war,[54] preferred life at any price,[55] militated in favour of respecting nature, and displayed their mistrust of the progress being made in science and technology, since it could threaten the environment.

In challenging all their fathers' values, the sons unconsciously moved closer to those of their mothers, who are traditionally anti-war, non-competitive, and have no experience of power – other than over their families – or of acting the oppressor. This reversal of alliances did indeed take place, and put an end to the millenarian prestige of the father and the husband. But in reality, the new alliance was based on a misunderstanding. At the very moment when young men were turning their backs on the manly stereotypes and adopting more feminine behaviour, women themselves were abandoning some of their millenarian attitudes and taking possession of domains that had previously been the preserve of men. This generation of sons, which had often associated itself with the women's campaign, realized too late that it had been swindled. The ones who had drawn closer to the traditional values of their mothers found it difficult to accept that women were just then distancing themselves from such values. For while these men were trying to build a less aggressive world in which competition would be less fierce, women were now turning out to be formidable competitors. They were no longer merely tenderness and devotion, they were also ambition and egotism. The disarray of the fathers became that of the sons – and so it remains.

Eve Deals Herself a New Hand

In the space of twenty years, the relations between men and women have become radically modified. By setting out to conquer the outside world, Eve has put an end to the sexual division of labour. By fighting for the right to contraception and abortion, she has taken sole control of her own reproduction. Finally, with her body liberated, mistress of her own life, she is no longer an object of exchange between men. In this way, the three pillars of patriarchy have been annihilated in less than two decades in the major part of the Western world.

In 1906, Frenchwomen made up thirty-nine per cent of the working population.[56] This proportion continued to decrease over some forty years. It was not until 1975 that the figures returned to the same level, not only in France, but in most industrial countries[57] with the exception of Japan. This upward trend is relatively recent, then, but it seems to have started an irresistible movement. Despite the economic crisis rife throughout the Western world, there were more women on the labour market every year. In 1985, it was estimated that there were almost ten million Frenchwomen gainfully employed.

But there is an even more important phenomenon: the number of working mothers has increased considerably. In the USA, there has been a tenfold increase since 1940.[58] This development is identical throughout the Western world, even if not quite at the same rate in countries where the Catholic influence is strong, such as Italy and Spain, or in those with few crèches.

Studies of French women show that more and more of them are working[59] when they have two children,[60] or a baby.[61] In the aggregate, more than fifty per cent of children below the age of sixteen have a working mother, as against 36.8 per cent in 1975.

All these figures bear witness to a considerable revolution. By taking possession of the outside world, women are putting an end to the sexual division of roles and to the millenarian opposition between the home life to which they were formerly restricted, and the professional life which automatically belonged to men. Whereas in patriarchal societies a woman was primarily a mother, responsible for the health and happiness of her family, the new society, by spreading confusion as to what is woman's true role, strikes a blow at one of the most ancient masculine characteristics.

Every day, most jobs lose a little of their sexual character. Nineteenth-century mechanization began the devaluation of man's strength. Twentieth-century technology has finally rendered it useless, in the same way as it has made women's delicate skills unnecessary. In the age of the computer, no one any longer bothers to make a distinction between male and female jobs.

The other factor in the "desexualization" of labour is the effort Western societies have made to give a common and identical education to boys and girls. Since 1972, when three of France's great higher educational establishments opened their doors to women, co-education has been in force all the way up the scholastic ladder. Even if the results still seem disappointing to those of us who are in the greatest hurry,[62] it is noteworthy that in twenty years the number of women in managerial positions has quadrupled, and that at present, of every hundred jobs vacant, forty-six are given to women.[63] In the United States, women in such positions are still in a minority, but those who leave a large firm to set up their own small business are already five times as numerous as men who do the same. In quoting these figures, Brigitte Ouvry-Vial notes that "While the spirit of enterprise is a constant in French history, the very marked advance in the number of women in this domain is a novelty. Between 1970 and 1979 their number increased by fifty-six per cent; today, there are more than two and a half million of them."[64]

Very gradually, the most privileged women are catching up professionally with the most privileged men. For such women, work has now acquired an entirely different meaning from what it had for the women of the beginning of the century. At that time, only hard, repetitive work was open to them. Exploited even worse than men, and paid less,[65] women constituted a particularly pliable reserve labour force. It is true that this sort of boring, despised work[66] served only to make up the shortfall in the family finances, and that the women who engaged in it were viewed with something like contempt. Almost until the First World War, women's work – and especially work that had to be done outside the home – was looked on with suspicion by bourgeois society. It was seen as social and economic failure. Indeed, it was thought that the fact of a woman working away from home revealed her husband's incapacity to provide for the household needs and, worse still, to give his children a good mother.

The meaning of women's work is very different today. While it is true that many women work only for economic reasons and are prepared to do any kind of job without getting the slightest satisfaction out of it, merely to bring a second wage into the household,[67] their condition is no different from that of the most underprivileged men. Nevertheless, we cannot restrict ourselves to this one motivation. At the other end of the social scale, women consider the practice of a profession necessary for two reasons unheard of at the beginning of the century: work is the condition of their autonomy, and it also provides them with a sense of personal fulfilment that they no longer find in the home. Here too, like the most privileged men, they have discovered that the outside world is the only place where they can fulfil their ambitions. For them, work is no longer the symbol of failure, but on the contrary the clearest sign of their social, economic, and even personal success.

Between these two extremes there is a very large category of working women who are paid a modest wage for doing jobs in which they are not necessarily vitally interested and who, experts have calculated, are working for virtually nothing.[68] Such women are a favourite target for the *natalistes*, who advise them to stop work and have children, but they show more clearly than some others the dismay that can be felt at having to stay at home. If they do not find the monotony and fatigue of work any more congenial than running a house, they nevertheless find compensations at work: friendships and a more stimulating social life that enable them to escape unbearable solitude. Confrontation with the outside world takes woman out of her "natural" domain.

Not long ago, Edgar Morin regretted that feminine culture was incomplete, because it had no access to men's culture.[69] But that is no longer the case today, because they now share adult masculine culture with men. By becoming men's competitors in what used to be an exclusively masculine domain, women are divesting them of the exclusive glory derived from the mastery of the world. Some men are already complaining that women have acquired "the toughness of the hunter".[70]

The second stage in women's emancipation concerns their control of their own fertility, and hence, their sexual liberty. The acquisition of this right was the result of a long war (it lasted almost a hundred years) fought by women in association with all those men who believed in liberty.[71] The battle for the separation of sexuality and procreation had begun in the West by the end of the nineteenth century. But *natalist* politics are a natural result of wars, so it was not until the sixties or seventies that this essential claim was met. It was made possible only by the conjunction of biochemical discoveries and a profound change in the mentality of every Western country.

It will be remembered that in the United States, the birth-control pioneer Margaret Sanger fought for the diffusion of the diaphragm, which for a long time was one of the most efficient methods of contraception. But as it came up against certain bodily taboos, it was not always readily accepted. In 1951, Margaret Sanger took the problem to Dr Gregory Pincus (1903–67), a renowned biochemist, and he agreed[72] to undertake research into the production of an oral contraceptive. Thanks to the work of the chemist Russell Marker, who in the forties had discovered the possibility of extracting progesterone from a plant, thanks also to a greater knowledge of the phenomena of fertilization and of the feminine cycle, Pincus's work, carried out in collaboration with Drs Chang and Rock,[73] culminated in a product that inhibited ovulation. The first Pill was tested as an agent to combat sterility, and then in 1956, in Puerto Rico, as a contraceptive. In 1960, the first oral contraceptive went on sale in the USA without having given rise to any great controversy between the feminists and the authorities.

The same was not the case in France. Between the first article on the Pill, written by Madame Weill-Hallé in 1961, and Dr Neuwirth's law authorizing it on 28 December 1967, there was a period of six years of desperate militancy on the part of the French movement for family planning, which had been blocked by the 1920 law that forbade Frenchwomen to use the diaphragm, and hence deprived them of all possibility of contraception. The political Right, the French doctors' governing body and the Catholic Church were against it, while the Left, the intellectuals and the majority of women hoped that the 1920 law would be repealed. The traditionalists were terrified of female libertinage,[74] fearing that they would no longer be able to control the sexuality of their daughters and wives; others spoke of unwanted pregnancies and their resulting misery. In the end, the law authorizing contraception was passed, partly with the idea that it would check the clandestine abortions that were so injurious to women's health.

But at the same time as the French government was giving the green light to contraception, abortion was being legalized in England (1967).[75] And the American feminists had already joined battle. Despite the fact that contraception had long been available, hundreds of women were dying every year as a result of illegal backstreet abortions. The feminists put together dossiers that revealed the extent of the tragedy. There was talk of a million legal and illegal abortions a year, and of 350,000 women suffering from post-operational complications, the poorest of whom were the most affected. The situation was more or less the same throughout Western Europe, and the feminist movements in all these countries took much the same kind of action: demonstrations, petitions, show trials of women who had had abortions, etc.

After some impassioned debates, abortion was legalized in the USA in 1973, in West Germany in 1974, and in France in 1975.[76] In the years that followed, most of the other Western countries passed similar laws.[77] Some countries, such as Belgium, Canada, Switzerland, although still officially forbidding it, more or less tolerated it. Others, such as Spain and Greece, have restrictive laws that permit abortion in certain circumstances. To date, two eminently Catholic countries are the only ones that remain really hostile to it: Portugal[78] and Ireland.[79]

The consequences of this development are considerable, and still incalculable. When women acquired the right to refuse to become mothers against their will, they welcomed this new freedom as an intimate, personal acquisition. No one realized that contraception, backed up by the right to abortion, could so radically revolutionize the relations between the sexes, and even the whole of society. To free women from the obligation to have children was to shatter the millenarian equation "woman=mother" that had seemed eternal, because so firmly anchored in the deepest depths of biological nature. What seemed to be an exclusively feminine right and a decisive step towards the equality of the sexes, was in reality the beginning of a new era that goes far beyond the exclusively feminine domain.

When women first won the right to contraception, men immediately lost all control over women's sexuality. "Those societies in which one of the requisite cornerstones . . . was *coercive* suppression of women's inordinate sexuality"[80] were deprived of one of their most valuable *raisons d'être*. However, if women were in fact unfaithful to their husbands, then men would be less likely to have to accept bastards. Infidelity had become as easy for women as for men, but at least it no longer threatened the lineage. It was now only respect and love that kept women faithful. Mutual confidence was substituted for supervision and repression. In this way, equality had finally been re-established between the One and the Other.

But female contraception struck the final blow against the patriarchal family, giving the control of procreation to the other side. From then on, it was no longer the man who determined it, by practising withdrawal, but the woman who chose whether or not to have a child by a particular man. The tables had been completely turned, and the father deprived of one of his essential powers. Everything now depended on the woman, and nothing could be done against her wishes. Not only could she refuse a man the child he wanted, she could also have one he did not want, and indeed reduce him to his biological role of inseminator, and he might never know that he was a father.

From this point of view, one inequality has been substituted for another, although it is true that the one now weighing on men is far less onerous than that which formerly victimized women.

The legalization of abortion has guaranteed woman's exclusive power over procreation. The right of life and death over the child has also changed sides. Not so long ago, at a difficult birth, the doctor would ask the father to choose between the life of the child and that of the mother. It was the custom for the father to choose the mother, but his patriarchal right allowed him the possibility of not so choosing. Today, the situation is reversed, and the woman takes precedence over the unborn child and the father. In this respect, the right to have an abortion – even more than the right to contraception – has produced a radically new ethic: the woman's rights come before those of the foetus and before her duties as a mother. The twentieth century has decided that an existent individual takes priority over a potential human being. Motherhood is no longer sacred, and woman has finally become a simple human being.

There is no doubt that such an upheaval is in itself sufficient to bring about a fundamental reappraisal of patriarchy. Not only is woman no longer seen solely as a mother, the role in which nature and society had imprisoned her, but her absolute control over her procreativity reverses the millenarian balance of power between man and woman, and gives her a completely new hand to play. From now on, a man can only be a father if a woman allows it: if he wants a child, he has to ask her for one. Formerly, men controlled women's fertility. At present, it is women who decide whether men shall be fathers.

This revolution, combined with the blurring of the traditional sexual roles due to women's desire to share economic power with men, has put an end to the patriarchal system which only a short time ago was believed to be universal and eternal. The ultimate proof of this change resides in the fact that on the eve of the third millennium, Western men no longer exchange women.

Only a few decades ago, marriage was at the same time a symbol of security, respectability, and fertility. Today, it has lost these three essential characteristics.

In poor societies, yesterday as today, marriage stands first and foremost for economic security. As Evelyne Sullerot says: it is a "life assurance".[81] She points out that the rejection of marriage has spread in the richest countries in the world: Sweden, Switzerland, the United States, Denmark, England and France. Conversely, in some countries like the USSR, where in theory morals could be free, the housing shortage has made the cohabitation of young people practically non-existent.

Formerly, in our societies, it was above all women who sought economic security through marriage. Finding a husband sometimes became an obsession.[82] Girls of marriageable age still lived with their parents, even though the most fortunate among them might go to university "to broaden their minds", and others might take a little job while waiting to get married. But in just a few years, the extraordinary increase in the number of women wage-earners[83] has made an important contribution to changing women's mentalities. Apart from getting into the habit of working outside the home, "they have often achieved, or considerably increased, their financial independence. For many, work provides them with a secure income. As much as, or more than, marriage . . ." Material security, then, is no longer what women are looking for in marriage; they are becoming more and more able to provide for their own economic needs.

Marriage is no longer seen as the condition of feminine respectability. The best proof of this is the extraordinary advancement of the single woman. What progress has been made in the last century! We have only to think of the former state of permanent inferiority of a young woman, anxious to find a husband and probably deeply distressed, in case she failed, at the prospect of finding herself in the detestable situation of being an "old maid", whereas the old bachelor used merely to provoke an ironic smile. This is no longer the case today, because marriage has officially lost the sacred and divine character that rendered it indissoluble. The considerable loss of influence of religion has made possible the development of two new practices formerly unknown: divorce and cohabitation.

Until somewhere around 1965, the number of divorces in France remained relatively stable: about 30,000 to 35,000 a year. Since 1967, this number has regularly increased, and by 1984 it had reached the record number of 130,000. This phenomenon is found throughout Western Europe,[84] and is particularly marked in the Nordic countries (Sweden and Denmark) and in the United States. In 1979, there was one divorce for every 2.6 marriages in three industrial countries as different as the USA, the USSR[85] and Sweden.

Not only has divorce become common with extraordinary rapidity, but the proof that marriage is no longer where feminine respectability lies may be seen in the fact that wherever divorce exists, it is always women who form the majority of petitioners. In France, of every hundred petitions for divorce, sixty-four come from women, which shows that the conjugal state is sometimes less enviable than that of celibacy.

At the same time as the rise in the divorce rate, in the last ten years or more there has been a growing disaffection with marriage. It no longer constitutes the obligatory detour in the life of the couple or even in the institution of the family. Whereas in 1972, France celebrated 417,000 marriages, in 1985 there were no more than 273,000. Taking into account the increase in the population between these two dates, this number represents the lowest marriage rate since the last war. Not only has the prestige of marriage never been so low, but young couples are no longer in a hurry to get married in order to have a regular sex life, since society more readily accepts that they should live together without being married. For many, marriage is no longer a moral, social or economic imperative, and some even mistrust it as a convention that can undermine the affection resulting in the foundation of a family. The generations that followed the revolution of 1968 could therefore sing with Georges Brassens: "I have the honour not to ask you for your hand."

The considerable spread of cohabitation (formerly called concubinage) in all Western countries constitutes, with divorce, the second factor in the depreciation of marriage. It is no longer indissoluble, but has become contingent. It can be postponed indefinitely, and can be dispensed with even when a family is to be founded. The proportion of unmarried couples has more than doubled within ten years. There were 411,000 in 1975, and a million in the 1985 census. The increase is especially marked among the young: the number of unmarried couples living together in which the man is under 35 has more than tripled, going from 165,000 to 589,000.

The phenomenon is most widespread in the big towns. Paris beats the national record with 30.3 per cent of couples cohabiting as against 7.4 per cent in rural communities. In 1985, the census confirmed that in Paris and its suburbs, among childless couples in which the man is under 35, the unmarried are in the majority.

While young couples are more willing to marry when they want a child or have already conceived one,[86] more and more children are being born outside wedlock, since their parents see this as no reason to go through "the simple formality" that marriage has become. Children are being born to couples who cohabit, who recognize the child jointly,[87] but who do not marry. The number of children born outside wedlock virtually doubled between 1976[88] (63,400) and 1982

(113,400). In 1985, they represented sixteen per cent of births as against six per cent in 1966 and 8.6 per cent in 1976. According to the demographer Michel L. Lévy, the only difference between married and unmarried couples, apart from the moral aspect, is mainly of a legal and administrative order. All things considered, couples have realized that it is more advantageous to cohabit than to marry.

Not so long ago, marriage altered a girl's civil and social status. She was addressed as "Madame", and she changed her surname and first name. Rose Dupont became Madame Yves Durand. One of the characteristics of the patriarchal family was that it constituted a group of individuals who answered to the same name. It was a disgrace for a child not to bear its father's name and for its mother to have to declare it under her "maiden" name. In just a few years, public feeling on this subject has completely changed. The law allows both spouses to keep the use of his or her own name, and women no longer fight to use that of their husband. To the extent to which a name forms an integral part of an individual's personality, to change it is felt as an alienation, a loss of identity. It implies disengagement, separation from one's original family; the adoption of a new patronymic is a symbolic manifestation that women are changing their family, that they "belong" to a different father, in other words that they are indeed the "objects" described by Lévi-Strauss. This condition is rejected by the present-day generations.

The new attitudes to marriage show that it is no longer an essentially religious, social or economic affair, but above all a private affair that commits two individuals and no longer two families. Since the end of the eighteenth century, marriage for love[89] has continued to gain ground until it has become the unique motivation for twentieth century marriage. Parents have gradually been excluded from matrimonial choices. "The new marriage model has made the autonomy of the couple into a dogma. Every attempt on the part of the parents to interfere is now seen as an attack on personal liberty. Concubinage merely perpetuates this state of affairs, merely strengthens its development: it is marriage itself that is now being called into question. Parents are no longer in a position to urge their children to marry. They have to give up AND give in."[90]

While in concubinage, relations linking the child to its consanguineous line (particularly to the feminine line) are still maintained, on the other hand it has been observed that the relations between in-laws have become less close. "The parents of the two partners rarely meet . . . The links between parents and 'pseudo-children-in-law' have been noticeably weakened."

Everyone feels freer to have selective, optional relations with the other. The situation is not noticeably different with married couples. Often, the two original families only meet just before the wedding, or even on the day itself, and do not frequent each other afterwards. "The couple of today does not make alliances between families. It no longer unites two parentelas."[91]

The institution of marriage, therefore, has lost the greater part of its traditional meanings. Present-day society is no longer character-ized by the asymmetry of the sexes, and men no longer exchange women in order to gain brothers-in-law. The system described by Lévi-Strauss, which was perfectly adapted to patriarchal societies, is no longer applicable to the Western societies of the end of the sec-ond millennium. Lévi-Strauss, it will be remembered, asserted that women have neither the same place nor the same rank in human society as men, because it is men who exchange women, and not vice versa.[92] Today, women are no longer "objects of exchange", indeed, marriage has lost its character of an exchange between families, of "the men's transactions". Lévi-Strauss thought that "the perma-nence of patrilocal residence attests to the basic asymmetrical relationship between the sexes which is characteristic of human soci-ety."[93] But the increase in the number of unmarried and divorced women[94] modifies both the regimes of filiation and of residence.

All this inclines us to think that today "human society" is not necessarily identified with the patriarchal mode of organization. Western societies have undermined the foundations of patriarchy, which has thereby been relativized from both the spatial and tempo-ral points of view. It can no longer claim to be the universal social and family system.

On the other hand, the new types of bond uniting men and women dismiss the famous "reciprocity between men by means of women". We are regarding less and less favourably the vast system of social exchange that gave the law of exogamy all its positive charac-ter, namely the prohibition of incest. As women no longer have exchange value or peace value, the necessary prohibition of incest has lost one of its most valuable justifications. After the biological explanations of the interdiction of incest[95] – we know today that endogamous marriages are no more disastrous than the others – the social advantage of the necessary alliances has now also disappeared. But humanity has still not come to the end of its arguments against something that inspires it with horror: the maintenance of the taboo is now justified in a different way. It is no longer spoken of in terms of biology or anthropology, but of psychoanalysis. It is madness that is now seen as the ultimate rampart against incest. Sexual relations between brothers and sisters, and especially between parents and children, have been declared pathological and a source of calamity.

But for the first time, some people are openly daring to claim the right to incest,[96] and others are doing what they can to make it less dramatic. For instance, Wardell Pomeroy, co-author of the famous Kinsey Report on the sexual behaviour of the Americans, calmly asserts that "it is time to recognize that incest is not necessarily a perversion or a form of mental illness, but that it may sometimes be beneficial". For his part, the American sexologist James W. Ramey considers that "our present-day attitude to incest is identical to the reactions and fears provoked by masturbation a century ago".[97]

There is nothing to prevent us from thinking that the acts of the former and the theories of the latter are perverse, and therefore "abnormal". But one cannot help feeling somewhat bewildered at the idea that the madness argument is in its turn being beleaguered. Now that the prohibitions are carrying less and less weight and that the temptation to defy them is becoming greater, the universal taboo against incest may well become a dead letter. It is hard to imagine the consequences of the ultimate triumph of individualism, of the lack of distinction between the generations, of the end of exogamic practices.

The twentieth century has put an end to the principle of inequality that used to preside over the relations between men and women. In the West, it has terminated a long stage of humanity that began more than 4,000 years ago. It is probable that men would have preferred to settle for equality within difference, in other words, for a return to an authentic complementarity of roles and functions. Unfortunately for them, however, the experience of our societies proves that complementarity is rarely synonymous with equality, and difference is soon transformed into asymmetry. The days of the primitive separation of the sexes have gone, and the time has come for them to share everything.

The fight for equality has so effectively blurred the differences that it has once again called each side's role into question. The schema of complementarity is giving way to that of resemblance, so long feared by men. Some men see this change as "the great historical defeat of the masculine sex",[98] as if they feared the establishment of a feminine power similar to that which they have exercised for so long.

In reality, there is absolutely no question of substituting a pseudo-matriarchy for yesterday's patriarchy. Everything is against it: the egalitarian ideology still prevalent in the West, and women's refusal to confine the exercise of their power to motherhood.

Resemblance does not lend itself to the domination of the One by the Other. On the contrary, it leads to peace between the sexes.

PART THREE

The One Is the Other

"Mon enfant, ma soeur
songe à la douceur
d'aller là-bas vivre ensemble!
. . . au pays qui te ressemble!

BAUDELAIRE

"The time of the androgyne approaches . . ."

APOLLINAIRE

To assert that the One *is* the Other – is that not to be needlessly provocative? Anatomy, stamped with the seal of the universal, is there to challenge us. However far their evolution may have led them towards greater resemblance, men and women are fundamentally differentiated by their sexual equipment. Far from being identical, they naturally complete each other.

Leaving aside the subtleties of Platonic dialectics as in *Parmenides*, we know very well that the verb "to be" does not only refer to a relation of identity. To say that the One is the Other does not here mean that the One is the same as the Other, but that the One *participates in* the Other and that they are at the same time similar and dissimilar.

While anatomy has scarcely changed in the course of the centuries and millennia, history and ethnology show that societies have very different ideas about its importance. Some, like the Mundugumor, tend to minimize the consequences of the difference; others, on the contrary, exaggerate them. According to time and place, men and women see themselves as more different than similar, or vice versa. But this is recent evidence, which has not so far received sufficient thought.

Today, by refusing to allow anatomy to weigh with us so heavily, Western societies give more importance to the similarity between the sexes than was possible for any previous society. By increasing our control over the phenomena of life, by separating social roles and functions from their physiological roots, by finally becoming aware of our physical and psychological bisexuality, so long denied, we are reducing the otherness of the sexes to the strict minimum. For the moment, the only remaining difference is the irrefutable fact that women carry men's babies, and not the reverse. And

149

while motherhood remains the irreducible sign of feminine sexual identity, men are beginning to question themselves about their own.[1] What characteristics do they still possess that are not shared by women?

Being unable to answer this question, men and women are more and more tending towards a single model. At the very moment when they are in control of their fertility and hold the essential power of procreation, women are showing in many ways that they no longer intend to confine their destiny to motherhood. Nor do they intend to use their new powers as a means of blackmailing men or getting them under their thumb. By distancing themselves from motherhood, women are taking an implicit step towards their male companions. Nature's ascendancy retreats and, with it, the difference separating the sexes.

The relationship that unites them is once again changing. In the far distant past there seems to have been a period of relative equilibrium due to the separation of roles and powers. Woman worked the miracle of life. Man dared to defy death. Both had their specific prestige, as can still be seen in paleolithic and prehistoric art. The equilibrium that was founded on a complementary approach to sexual functions was upset by ecological, economic and ideological upheavals. What in former days constituted the glory and specific character of women was credited to men who, as absolute masters of the external world, eliminated the goddesses in favour of gods, and claimed for themselves the prestige of human procreation. Reduced to the marginal status of womb and housewife, for a very long time women lost every kind of participation in transcendence. Complementarity became no more than a snare wherever the One was made the reverse of the Other, as if they no longer belonged to the same species.

This negative complementarity was the source of a kind of war between the sexes. It inclined yesterday's losers to throw out all similar schemas. Having learned from experience that complementarity carries with it the germs of inequality and oppression, they were determined to undermine its foundations.

But the equality, which is now coming about, engenders a resemblance that puts an end to this war. Now that the protagonists like to think of themselves as the "whole" of humanity, each side is in a better position to understand the Other, which has become its shadow. The feelings uniting this couple of mutants can only change their nature. Strangeness disappears and becomes "familiarity". We may perhaps lose something of our passion and desire thereby, but we shall gain the sort of tenderness and co-operation that can unite the members of a single family: the mother and her child, the brother and sister . . . In short, all those who have laid down their arms.

I

THE RESEMBLANCE BETWEEN
THE SEXES

The new model now developing is alarming for more than one reason. As actors in a revolution that has scarcely begun, we have lost our old reference points but are not yet sure of our new ones. Cut off from our roots, which still belong to the old world, we have been overtaken by the formidable change in civilization that we have brought about. This change arouses contradictory feelings in us, which make us uncomfortable. We find it both too rapid and too slow; we want to break with the old civilization, yet we fear the new one; in short, we know what we no longer are, but we cannot see clearly what we would like to be.

We all see that the relation between man and woman cannot be upset with impunity. At the crossroads of nature and culture, it is not merely the "paradigm"[2] of every society, it also influences our most intimate being. We wanted to modify the power relationships within our society, but we find ourselves in the process of changing our "nature" – or at least we are seeing hitherto unknown aspects of it. Our most primordial certainties have been shaken, and are transforming things that seemed obvious into problems.

At a time when social reference points are vanishing, when sexual roles are becoming flexible, when women may choose not to become mothers, the specific difference between the One and the Other is becoming more and more difficult to pin down. The growing revelation of our bisexual nature is completing the process of disorientation. Apart from the irreducible chromosomal difference (XX for women, XY for men), we are now reduced to making distinctions between the "more" and the "less". Certainly, the One has more male hormones and the Other more female ones,[3] but both sexes produce feminine and masculine hormones.[4] Men have greater muscular strength than women, and greater aggressivity,[5] but these differences vary enormously from one individual to another.

Indeed, if we are definitely differentiated by our hereditary genetic material, which is responsible for the sex of the reproductive cells,[6] mental and physical pathology, as well as various cases of intersexuality, oblige us to admit that although the law recognizes two sexes, there does exist a varying number of intermediary types between the well-defined female and the well-defined male.[7] This leads Professor Baulieu to think that there is both "a great initial similarity and a certain flexibility in the differentiation between the sexes". In other words, that "there are no fixed borderlines between the masculine and the feminine."

Apart from the similarity of roles that we have mentioned, there is also a physiological flexibility that until recently we could not even have suspected. These resemblances, this interaction, do not of course make us identical, but they do lead to a new way of thinking about the sexes, and this is all the more difficult and dangerous in that there has never been any model anywhere on which to base it.

A Vertiginous Mutation

The resemblance between the sexes is such an innovation that it may legitimately be envisaged in terms of a mutation. Up till now, all known societies have always assigned different roles and tasks to men and women. Even though their attribution has always varied in every possible way from one society to another, "the binary concept of the division of roles nevertheless seemed so universal that it might almost be considered as one of the facts of life of our species."[8]

By putting an end to this universal schema of complementarity, our civilization may well have begun to modify some of the "essential" features of the human species. While it is much too soon to be able to measure all the consequences - and in particular, those of a biological and genetic order - of a change that may go on operating over several generations, or even centuries, it is nevertheless possible to perceive that in our part of the world the twentieth century has inaugurated something that looks like a new era.

Some lucid people will remember that great events arrive "on doves' feet", and that true mutations are imperceptible to the view of the individual. Others, more pessimistic, will imagine that a war or a particularly acute crisis could very well put an end to such a social evolution. Others again – the moralists – will simply see this change, so contrary to the natural order, as a manifestation of decadence similar to so many others known to history. And they will trust Nature to return to the straight and narrow path from which she ought never to have strayed.

Who, today, could completely ignore these objections? Each has its share of truth. The first invites prudence by reminding us that any mutation is perceived only once it is complete, and concerns us more than the other two, which implicitly deny all thought of change. The second states a truth that has often been borne out by history, although today it concerns the short term rather than the long term. While it is true, for example, that the Nazi and Fascist experiments put a brutal end to democracy, the ideologies of the rights of man and the liberation of women, these three aspirations of Western humanity took on a new and better lease of life, as if they were irreversible, when those terrible regimes disappeared.

We would be more inclined to regard these events as a temporary halt in evolution rather than as a transcendent punishment for any sort of violation of nature, which is sometimes seen as a moral transgression. Palaeontology, evolutionary theories and history exist to remind us that nature and humanity have never stopped evolving and that morality, too, is subject to change.

While we are aware of the hazards of this proposition and of its gratuitousness – would not some people even consider it imaginary? – we are nevertheless prepared to wager in favour of mutation. There are two reasons for this: such aspirations and behaviour are something totally new, and there is the strong feeling that roles and places are no longer pre-ordained from on high.

A Great "First" in the History of Humanity

In order to get a better idea of the extent of the change we are now living through, let us return for a moment to the observations of the anthropologists. All, without exception, declare that the division of labour is specific to humanity. The techno-economic relations of man and woman are always and everywhere strictly complementary, they say, unlike the animal world, in which there is no sexual specialization in the search for food.

However far back in time we go, hominid fossils are the proof of the sexual division of labour: the woman immobilized by her childbearing, the man a nomad, explorer and hunter. Edgar Morin has pointed out that "the men's and women's groups each developed their own sociability, their own culture, and their own psychology", to the point of forming two different societies which were in some periods more, in others less, complementary. It is also true that this relation has been fundamentally reproduced up till our times, appearing to be a universal phenomenon, and hence specific to humanity.

But now that the opposition of the sexes is vanishing, let us again recall Margaret Mead's decisive statement: "We *always* find the patterning [the differentiation of the sexual roles]. We know of no culture that has said, articulately, that there is no difference between men and women except in the way they contribute to the creation of the next generation."[9]

What are we doing today, though, if not saying that men and women resemble each other except in the domain of procreation?

That wise woman Margaret Mead also perceived that one of the specific characteristics of human societies lay in a certain contribution by men to the education of their children. She observed that the specifically human aspect of the family does not lie in the man's protection of his wife and children (which is also to be found among the primates), but in his nurturing behaviour. "In every known human society . . . the young male learns that . . . he must provide food for some female and her young." In spite of exceptions,[10] "every known human society rests firmly on the learned nurturing behaviour of men."

Whatever the needs – which are different according to social customs – for which men must provide, even so this behaviour, "learned" and "fragile", as Margaret Mead herself says, lasted everywhere until yesterday. Today, it has lost the general character that made it one of the foundations of human societies. While women have always taken a greater or smaller share in providing for their own and their children's needs, a man's contribution was still indispensable, and its absence cruelly felt. Men alone had access to certain techniques and activities that complemented those of women, but this is no longer the case in the West. Not only are women becoming more and more capable of providing for their own needs without men's help, but the new types of family that have appeared within the last twenty years show that women are also capable of providing for the needs of their children. This is borne out by the single mothers who want no involvement with the father, and by the more numerous cases of divorced women who receive derisory sums in alimony – when they receive anything at all.

It is true that all societies still oblige fathers to share the responsibility for their children. But their contribution is no longer "qualitatively" distinguished from that of the mother – both of them work and earn money – and the father's participation is seen at least as much as a moral duty as an economic necessity.[11] It is as if society had to take it upon itself to remind the father of his responsibilities as a "provider", which he might otherwise tend to forget.

Finally, Françoise Héritier observed that in all known societies "men have created a reserved domain for themselves which is inaccessible to women, and symmetrical to biological reproduction, which is inaccessible to men. This domain is that of some specialized technical knowledge reserved for the exclusive use of the male. This still necessitates an apprenticeship that is either genuinely or falsely sophisticated. Nothing in women's physical constitution explains why she should be denied access to it."[12] But here too, the reference points are disappearing. The notion of a reserved masculine domain has become virtually non-existent – so much so that we should be hard put to it today to cite a single activity specific to man and totally unknown to women.

On the contrary; our society is energetically engaged in encouraging both sexes to take on roles and functions in domains which were formerly thought irreducibly specific to one sex or the other.

War and Mothering

Ever since *homo sapiens*, there have always been two activities that were the respective prerogatives of man and woman: hunting and war are masculine, mothering is feminine. But the new habits are working on our "inward eye", and more and more our resemblances seem greater than our differences. This is influencing our behaviour, both in relation to war and to our care of babies. Women are becoming more manly, and men are becoming more feminine.

The explicit rejection of the model of man as warrior has certainly contributed to the modification of the sense of masculine identity, and also to modifying the way women regard their companions.[13] But the very way we regard war has been greatly modified in just a few decades. The reasons for our new perception, which no longer excludes women from this mortal activity, are more deeply rooted in the world of our imagination than in our day-to-day experience. But that probably only makes them stronger. All modern armies have women in their ranks. Even if they are not supposed to fight the enemy face to face, we have a picture of women in uniform, weapon in hand, marching in step with men. Their femininity obscured, we see them as no different from their male counterparts.

Other images in our minds give credit to the possibility of the woman warrior. In the first place, there are the wars of national liberation waged by Third-World countries. These "ghost armies" often called on women to plant bombs and kill. Even the Islamic countries have not hesitated to enrol women to fight side by side with men. The "good cause" takes precedence for a moment over millenarian prejudices. Then, people were amazed at the considerable participation of women in the Italian and German terrorist movements of the nineteen seventies. They represented more than fifty per cent of the Red Army Fraction,[14] and almost as many in the Red Brigades. More than their male political friends, these women were accused of perversity and inhumanity, but they made a mark on the collective imagination. Even if the community rejects them in horror, these young women – for the most part from well-to-do families[15] – have provided the absurd proof that the desire for death and violence is not specific to men. Women can torture and kill with neither restraint nor pity, and this time for "a bad cause". It may perhaps be said that such aberrant behaviour is in fact the reverse of the norm, but whatever the reasons for women taking up arms, we now know for certain that they too are capable of a potential aggressivity that shatters their traditional image. And while all periods have had murderesses, we now know that they can take part in an organized war or throw grenades with the same determination as men. We can try to repress the horror we feel at such images, but we can no longer efface them.

The threat of a world nuclear war still further emphasizes the blurring of sexual roles. If we try to imagine a war of this type, we see that it no longer has any place at all for the combatant. Whether men or women, we see ourselves as immediate victims, deprived of any means of defence. Courage, strength, endurance, would no longer be of any use. Confronted with the atomic bomb, the difference between the sexes has lost all its meaning: we would all be victims, and we might just as well all be killers. Pressing a button and unleashing a nuclear war has nothing to do with sex, but rather with the ethics and character of a Head of State whose sex is of no importance.

We can refuse to allow ourselves to be sidetracked by these fantasies, and continue to think of war in traditional terms, that's to say as a specifically masculine activity. That does not make the possibility of the other war any less real, but it profoundly modifies our representation of millenarian masculine culture.

This culture has been thrown into equal confusion by a new approach to fatherhood, which tends to show that mothering is no longer the exclusive business of women. Even though a good deal has already been written on what some people ironically call a new "fashion", the slow evolution of paternal behaviour seems to us the most essential factor in the blurring of roles, and hence of the resemblance of the sexes.

For the last fifteen or so years, the demarcation line between the domain of motherhood and that of fatherhood has gradually been disappearing in most Western societies. Men have begun to learn at first hand what it means to be a parent, and to do for their children what women have done since time immemorial. With the new kind of fatherhood, they are affirming their "nurturing ego", and thus a femininity of whose very existence they were often unaware.

James Levine, who has studied the new fatherhood in the United States, has observed that the progressive disappearance of the frontier between motherhood and fatherhood manifests itself in different domains.[16] In the legal sphere, the nineteen seventies and eighties have marked an important step forward. Several American states[17] have authorized joint custody of children in divorce cases, and the percentage of fathers who have custody of their children has steadily grown in the last decade. In France, fathers are given custody of their children in between nine and eleven per cent of such cases. This figure has remained stationary for several years, mainly because of the weight of the stereotypes and the mentality of the judges. But fathers have pressed their claims so energetically that the courts have begun to take note of the equality of the paternal and maternal functions.[18]

In the scientific domain, people are becoming more and more interested in the "new fathers". Only twenty years ago, fathers constituted an almost non-existent species in the eyes of behavioural specialists, but today, in the USA and other Western countries, research on fatherhood is rapidly coming to the fore.[19] Its general tendency is the re-examination of the assumptions about the supposed differences in the capacity of mothers and fathers to care for their young.

This assumption is now disappearing from the popular child-care manuals that have sprung up in spectacular fashion in the last ten years. In 1974, both the bible of the American baby, Dr Spock's *Baby and Child Care*, and that of the French mother-to-be, Laurence Pernoud's *Nine Months to Motherhood*,[20] still treated fathers as if they had little interest in, and talent or responsibility for, bringing up children. Mothers were advised not to force their hand and to respect "a so-called disgust typical of males".[21]

Somewhere around 1975-7, the new fathers went ahead of the child-care manuals and forced the advice-givers to revise their opinions. "Dr Spock puts forward a New Testament with chapters and verses entirely recast," writes James Levine. "This is his prescription for the new fatherhood: the father should share with the mother the everyday care of the child from the moment it is born . . . This is the natural (spontaneous) way for the father to get to know the child, just as it is for the mother."

In the behavioural sphere, single men are adopting children in more than half the American states; the cinema, photography and newspapers pay tribute to the physical contacts between fathers and their babies, but the phenomenon of the new fatherhood is still rare. Yet we should not regard it as a passing fashion, because it both responds to a demand on the part of young mothers, and throws light on new aspects of the masculine unconscious. Moreover, it takes several generations for a social revolution to be brought about.

Numerous studies have already been made on the new fathers. These show that they are young, play a part in their wives' pregnancies and confinements, feed, change, and bathe their babies with all the necessary tenderness. Such men show the complex and ambivalent reactions to their offspring that had so far been thought to apply only to the mother.

For the first time, an interest is being taken in the experiences of men who are expecting a baby. People talk, without irony, of a "pregnant man", or of a *"primipère"*,[22] and are beginning to see that such a father also reacts with his body to the imminent arrival of the baby. Geneviève Delaisi de Parseval is undoubtedly right when she predicts that in a few years' time, the couvade will become commonplace and typical among Western men.

Without going into details of the couvade syndrome once again, let us consider the conclusions to be drawn from the in-depth study of twelve normal first-time fathers made by the ethno-psychoanalyst Geneviève Delaisi de Parseval. In the first place, she notices an *"extraordinary similarity of the fantasies of men and women with regard to procreation"*, fantasies which bring about the same modification of the libido when the first child is born. The only difference is that for the woman, the fact of " 'becoming-a-mother' may perhaps tend to reflect her relation – real or fantasized – with her own mother, whereas 'becoming-a-father' is played out more between the man and his father."[23]

Where procreation is concerned, then, *men and women have similar psychological reactions, because they have the same two sources of parenthood in common*: their biological bisexuality, and their dependence on their mother. Geneviève Delaisi de Parseval, taking up the theory of the American psychoanalyst Therese Benedek,[24] thinks that in order to understand the sources of parenthood, it is better to stress the importance of the pregenital elements rather than the Oedipal elements that are classically advanced. "Becoming-a-mother", like "becoming-a-father", makes both women and men regress to the phase of oral dependence. In other terms, "men and women start off with the same psychological baggage (both conscious and unconscious) and in this sense are human beings before becoming sexed beings." These notions are confirmed by the paediatrician Dr Michael Yogman, who succeeded Dr Brazelton at the Harvard Medical School and who admits to having been "struck by the resemblance that exists on the psychological level between fathers and mothers, from the point of view of the experience of pregnancy and of the care given to the very young".[25]

The new father discovers that the foetus is perceptible through its movements. When the father caresses the mother's stomach, the child feels it and responds with movements[26] which arouse paternal feelings much earlier. At eight months, the foetus can hear sounds coming from outside, and the father will feel less embarrassed at talking to it than would have been the case in former generations. But apart from touching it and talking to it, the father-to-be can make visual contact with the child (ultrasound), and aural contact (listening to its heart beats), so that present-day fatherhood really does precede birth.

When he is present at the birth, the father can cut the umbilical cord, place the child on its mother's stomach, and then give it its first bath. In these moments, the father experiences emotions and a sensual joy that have so far been reserved for the mother. When we see him thus caring for his newborn, we observe an ease, a gentleness and a tenderness that could never have been suspected in the traditional father. Masculine sign language becomes feminized during these tête-à-têtes which our civilizations had previously thought were the monopoly of women. This is surely the moment in his life when a man's psychological bisexuality can be most strongly expressed, a sort of return to his own childhood, in which he identifies himself both with the child he once was and with his mother.

The new fathers are certainly not yet in the majority, but our collective imagination has adopted them, too. Almost fifteen years ago, advertising, which likes to reflect social reality and our fantasies rather than to anticipate them, began to take note of our new parental desires. In 1971, the Publicis agency launched a publicity campaign for *Prénatal* (a firm which makes maternity clothes) which was aimed exclusively at the father-to-be, and was illustrated by whole-page photographs of smiling, virile young men. The "pre-papa" campaign, whose slogan was "It takes two to expect a child", was a tremendous success;[27] it moved people and raised a smile. This advertisement surprised, but it did not shock. It corresponded to a new feeling. It might even be said that a consensus was taking shape that men should take their part in women's affairs – that the true father should finally be born.

The Ideology and Politics of Resemblance

Until about the nineteen sixties, the difference seemed to be so profoundly rooted in nature that people considered it legitimate for men and women not to do the same jobs or have the same rights. The sexes were brought up differently, so that they should be better prepared for their separate destinies. Everywhere, from school to factory, from kitchen to living room, from lavatories to clubs, special places were assigned to each sex which reinforced their separation and their difference.

The feminist movements of the seventies aimed at putting an end to this division of the world. Their linguistic militancy was just as important as their organized action. Without directly challenging the differences, two new terms became current, and cast shame on everyone who championed them. "Sexism",[28] and "sexual discrimination" became charges that were as morally reprehensible as those of "racism" and "racial discrimination."[29]

It is true that a certain number of talented feminists[30] protested against the resemblance model, which they saw as a threat to femininity. Fearing that women would conform to the masculine model and fail to appreciate their own resources, they tried to show that such a development ran the risk of constituting men's ultimate triumph. They therefore applied themselves to the task of defining and ascribing value to feminine characteristics: they discovered the existence of a feminine type of writing and thought, of a feminine unconscious. In short, they reintroduced the idea of a specifically feminine nature and culture, whose authenticity and value men must be made to recognize. While completely in agreement with the egalitarian claims, these feminists wanted to preserve their differences come what may, as, incidentally, was the case at the same period with all the militants in the minority cultures (Jews, blacks, emigrés, regionalists, etc.), whose slogan was "equality within difference".

No one dared dispute this claim, hard though it would be to achieve, but all were agreed that they must first fight for equality. Differences, the source of so many past misfortunes, would come later. From the nineteen seventies on, under constant pressure from the feminists, a genuine political consensus emerged in favour of removing the traces of sexual discrimination that marred the different spheres of private and public life. From 1974 until the present day, governments in France, whether of the Right or the Left, have gone to great lengths to bring about equal opportunity. The family code was modified, co-education was made compulsory in schools and universities, and all professions were gradually opened to everyone, regardless of sex.[31] The law of July 1983 reinforced professional equality by making discriminatory job advertisements subject to a fine.[32] School textbooks have had the dust removed from the sexual stereotypes which sowed the seeds of sexism in children's unconscious minds. And finally, in every domain open to the legislator, politicians have tried to enforce equal opportunity and equal pay. For this purpose they have deliberately done all they could to establish the model of sexual resemblance, even though the law cannot guarantee a change in private behaviour.

The fact that a considerable proportion of Western conservatives have sought to oppose this development has not prevented the spread of the ideology of resemblance and the desire to complete the egalitarian programme of the French Revolution. The governing classes[33] have not always acted with enthusiasm, but even so the feminists' accusations rang in the ears of democrats as an unendurable cry for justice. The political will has often been ahead of the popular will, which does not easily submit to the demands of new models. Nevertheless, although people were slow to follow the spirit of the law, this particular model seems to be approved by the majority of the public. Equality and equal opportunity for women are the watchwords of the younger generations, whatever the remaining distance between theory and practice.

The various French surveys on task-sharing show not only the very rapid evolution of opinion, but also that resistance to the new model does not come only from men. In 1971, Nicole Tabard undertook an important survey of nearly 2,000 families for the *Caisse Nationale des Allocations Familiales* (department of family allowances), which was published in 1974. Entitled *Needs and Aspirations of Families*, it gives the best picture we have of French opinion at that time. She observed that women's work was the subject on which there was the greatest disagreement between husband and wife. Asked to choose which of three models of the family they thought the ideal, the answers were as follows:

	Men	*Women*
Husband and wife, equally engrossed in their jobs, share the household chores	7.4%	14.5%
The wife, less absorbed in her profession, does most of the work in the home	24.8%	30.7%
Only the man has a profession and the wife stays at home	67.8%	54.8%

In 1971, while men were far more opposed to women's work than their wives – an observation verified in all social groups – the majority of women still wanted to keep the traditional division of labour. A few years later, surveys on role-sharing showed a considerable evolution of opinion, particularly among the younger generations. Louis Roussel and Odile Bourguignon[34] asked young people between eighteen and thirty the question: "It is often said that the roles of men and women in the education of their children and in married life are becoming interchangeable. Do you think this opinion is true or false?"[35]

	Married		*Unmarried*		*Cohabiting*		*Total*	
	M	W	M	W	M	W	M	W
True	71	72	70	71	75	78	71	74
False	21	18	17	16	12	15	18	17
Don't know	8	10	13	8	13	7	11	9

Those who answered "true" were asked a second question, which involved them personally: "Is this change really good? Good in principle but too extreme? Or rather dangerous?"

	Married		Unmarried		Cohabiting		Total	
	M	W	M	W	M	W	M	W
Really good	74	81	72	77	70	85	73	80
Good in principle but too extreme	16	15	15	14	18	6	16	14
Or rather dangerous	4	2	7	4	7	1	5	3
Don't know	6	2	6	5	5	8	6	3

It was observed that couples cohabiting in the Paris region replied "really good" far more frequently than the rest, as this was the opinion of 88 per cent of men and 92 per cent of women. A total of 55 per cent of those asked recognized the existence of a change, and positively appreciated it. Furthermore, the divergence between the sexes is so slight that we can legitimately speak of an ideological consensus[36] with regard to the equality of the sexes and the interchangeability of roles. This did not stop Louis Roussel from observing shrewdly: "In our society at the moment, it is difficult not to come out in favour of a more equal distribution of labour. But this doesn't prove that all men are capable of changing babies' nappies."

We shall see further on how difficult it is for deeds to follow words. But for the moment, let us consider the parallel development of male and female opinions, both of which are overwhelmingly in favour of the new model of the interchangeability of sexual roles. If the resemblance model is still not fully integrated, it is at least desired by most members of our society, who seem to want to be divided in other ways than by sex. In this connection, it is only right to pay homage to Evelyne Sullerot who as early as 1965, well before the upheavals we have been describing, perceived that resemblance was the model of the future, and that our societies were evolving "towards the differentiation of individuals and groups according to more subtle divisions than that of sex."[37]

The Advent of the Androgyne

Etymologically, "androgyne" means "man/woman"; but the dictionary definition is more restrictive. After saying that an androgyne is an individual that has both male and female sexual characteristics, it limits its scope by referring to morphology[38] and to the Hermaphroditus of legend who was supposed to have a human body that preserved the characteristics of both sexes. In biological and medical terms, the hermaphrodite is an abnormal individual, a monster. This is probably one of the reasons why talk of the androgynous frightens people.

In actual fact, we are all androgynous, because human beings are bisexual, on several levels and to different degrees. Masculine and feminine are intertwined in us all, even if most cultures have been pleased to describe us as all of one piece, and to want us to be so. The norm laid down was one of contrast and opposition. Education is expected to stifle our ambiguities and teach us to repress the other part of ourselves. The ideal is to produce unisexed human beings: a "virile" man, a "feminine" woman. But the adjectives reveal what people want to hide: a whole series of possible intermediate stages between the two ideal types. In fact, our training is only partially successful, and the adult self always enshrines an indestructible part of the Other.

The resemblance model helps us to take account of our androgynous nature. Today, we are quite willing to admit that it is through the recognition of their bisexuality that individuals achieve fulfilment.[39] But does not this "recognition" mean that we are accepting a previously unknown truth? It is therefore not so much the "advent" of an androgynous nature that we are becoming aware of but more its "return", in the same sense in which psychoanalysts speak of "the return of the repressed".

The Dual Creature

The complementary model was centred on the dualism of creatures. For harmony to reign, the One had to be different from the Other, but it was also necessary for the One to be powerless without the Other. Resemblance, or lack of differentiation, would have seemed contrary to the wishes of the Creator. Why two kinds of creature, if they are almost alike?

If God (or nature) – who does nothing without a purpose – created two different types of being, it was not simply to introduce richness and diversity into creation, it was also to give each a consciousness of limits, which differentiates creature from Creator. When solitary, the human being is sterile, incomplete. Happiness and completion only come from reunion with the Other. All theology, aiming to justify the dualism of the sexes, reasons thus. Two creatures are necessary to make a creator, otherwise God's status and predominance are threatened.

If men and women are more similar than different, if both recognize that they possess a large part of the Other, will they not feel liberated from the need to be two? Will they not be tempted to succumb to the fantasy of being all-powerful?

These questions cause disquiet. They make us think of megalomania, of solipsism, of the dissolution of family and social ties, and finally of the death of humanity. How can we refuse to obey the necessity of dualism? Two they are, therefore two they must remain, with their differences and their ties of mutual dependence, which alone ensure the reproduction of the species, social order, and happiness.

The most evocative illustration of the dualism of creatures will always remain the myth of the androgyne related by Aristophanes in Plato's *The Symposium*.[40] Originally, he says, man's constitution was different from what it is now. Each human being was a rounded whole, with double back and flanks forming a complete circle; it had four hands and an equal number of legs, and two identically similar faces... It had two organs of generation and everything else to correspond. There were three sexes then, not, as with us, two, male and female. The third partook of the nature of both the others: this was the androgyne, which now has vanished – the name alone remains, and that solely as a term of abuse.

The androgynes' strength and vigour made them very formidable, and their pride was overweening; they attacked the gods who, to punish them, cut them in two . . . It is from this distant epoch, then, that we may date the innate love which human beings feel for one another, the love which restores us to our ancient state by attempting to weld two beings into one and to heal the wounds which humanity suffered. Desire, born from this severance, is the very source of love, of the feeling of completeness, which, when fulfilled, deprives desire of its *raison d'être*.

If we consider the three mythical species described by Aristophanes, what are we other than one of the two halves of the androgyne?[41] And what is half an androgyne made of? According to Plato, it was constituted of two heterogeneous halves, one completely feminine, the other completely masculine, joined at the centre. When Zeus separated them, he produced two creatures who were distinct and complementary, but who had lost all trace of their dual nature. The androgynous species had disappeared, because it was understood that henceforth the feminine creature was a stranger to her former companion, and he to her.

The resemblance model may inspire a different interpretation of the myth. We could suppose that the two separated halves were not heterogeneous, but that both were the result of the fusion of the masculine and the feminine, like the mixture of substances operated by the alchemist. The intimate union resulting from their interpenetration would explain why the splitting of the androgyne did not give rise to two specifically different human beings, but to two different kinds of androgynous creatures, who would both simply be the reflection of the original one. It is true that this original one, sufficient unto himself, had no need of an Other. The divine punishment was dependence. The two new androgynes were endowed with complementary sexual characteristics, which inclined them to reunite.

The fact remains that these former accomplices are less foreign to one another than has often been said. They have in common their archaic memory, which precedes the split and their apprenticeship to the differences. The dualism of creatures is beyond question, but the time has come to perceive each creature as a dual being endowed with all the characteristics of humanity. The difference between the sexes does not exclude the interiorization of this dualism in every one of us. Although we are visibly two different beings, we have an intimate knowledge of the Other.

We demanded equality of the sexes, without realizing just how far it would reveal our androgynous structure, born in the night of myths. This new picture of ourselves implies, in its turn, a radical change in our philosophical approach. These days we want less of the "clear and distinct", and more of "the philosophy of combined bodies" so dear to Michel Serres. The logic of separation is giving place to that of interaction, combination and complicity, which is very difficult to assimilate for those who have been brought up on Cartesianism.[42] This problem is made still more arduous by the imperious necessity not to ignore the difference.

Our resemblance is not so much the effect of a neutralization of the sexual, but more the effect of the bisexuality common to both sexes.[43] The history of the individual shows evidence of this both on the physical and the psychological level. At the moment of birth and during the first years of childhood, the sex of an individual is only recognizable by the external genital organs. "This means that the whole body is still undifferentiated, that it is oriented neither in one direction nor the other. It is potentially bisexual, not only because it may acquire the characteristics of one sex or the other, but also because each sex shows the rudiments of the characteristics that are more pronounced in the other."[44]

It is not until puberty that morphological bisexuality is partially ousted, owing to a new surge of sexualization (differences in pilosity and body shape). On the other hand, as they get older, men and women become less and less differentiated. Old people follow the opposite path from that of babies, and end as they began: apparently desexualized.

The relation between sex and bisexuality, which goes on evolving through all the ages of life, is made even more problematical by our double hormonal structure. Hormones, as we have seen, involve a double sexual potentiality, and maintain, as Suzanne Lilar writes, "a sort of vacillation between the sexes . . . an oscillation. The inconsistency of the sexual characteristics determined by the hormones, their lability, their changeability, constitute an encouragement to regard sex as a temporary equilibrium that is always subject to revision."

Suzanne Lilar asks the question: What can we retain of this dance in which bisexuality gives place to sex only in order to step into its place or alongside of it once again? "Certainly nothing that resembles the traditional conception of a clear and definite 'section' of the species into two halves, but on the contrary, that of a division which is never so radical or so definitive that it cannot be accompanied by a tendency to reconstitute its union."

Psychologically, "sexing" is even less clear than it appears to be physically. It was one of Freud's great merits that he put forward the notion of "unconscious bisexuality", however much the idea dismayed him.[45] Referred to throughout his works from 1899 to 1938, psychological bisexuality has an ambiguous, even contradictory, status from one text to the next. Reluctant to "denaturalize" bisexuality, Freud sometimes maintains[46] that there is a close link between the constitutional and the psychological, and at other times points out the relative independence between psychological and biological bisexuality.[47]

Two different attitudes result from Freud's uncertainty as to how to classify biological bisexuality. In contrast to theoreticians like Jung, Groddeck and Ferenczi, who assign it a "fundamental" and positive place in every human being, Freud never stopped oscillating between two contradictory positions:

"He often sees bisexuality as an original, universal disposition, distinctly morbid when it is pronounced, whose natural destiny is its gradual reduction in the course of libidinal development. When this is complete, bisexuality 'normally' consists of no more than a few discreet personal traits, in desires whose aims are inhibited, or in inclinations towards socialization and sublimation . . . In the great majority of cases, the psychosexual identity becomes integrated into one specific sex: this implies the successful repression of the initial bisexuality . . . Freud sometimes shows that the differential integration of sexuality, far from excluding active psychological bisexuality and from demanding the total success of its repression, may go hand in hand with an authentic bisexual fulfilment,[48] if not in so far as the choice of objects and erotic realization are concerned, at least with regard to personal psychological characteristics and functioning."[49]

Unfortunately, the second aspect of the Freudian theory has not received its due place in his work. The first aspect is what is still regarded as the more important. In one of his last articles, *Analysis terminated and analysis interminable*,[50] Freud rethinks bisexuality in pathological terms. In the last resort, it is bisexuality that is the source of every request for analysis, since men cannot bear their femininity, nor women their lack of a penis.

For a long time, the psychoanalytic Vulgate accepted only this aspect of Freud's theory: the original bisexuality characteristic of the pre-genital stage had to give way progressively – owing to the Oedipean conflict and its resolution – to an unambiguous psychological "sexing". The little boy identifies himself with his father, the little girl with her mother, and the adolescent completes the process of psychosexual distinction by passing through a phase of claiming his own sexual identity. So a satisfactory psychological evolution involves the effective repression of bisexuality, which thereby loses any kind of positive status.[51]

If psychoanalysts have for long kept bisexuality at a respectful distance, outside the ideal of normality, it was to a great extent because they could not remain indifferent to the dominant social model. So long as this model was complementarity, that was what they identified with "normality",[52] taking it upon themselves to resist the bisexual irregularities that stuck out here or there. No one would dream of blaming the specialists of the unconscious for being, like everyone, sensitive to the dominant ideology. But we may be surprised at their extreme reluctance to admit it. Perhaps they have too often believed that the unconscious was a hypostasis that was totally insensitive to the environment and impervious to cultural upheavals.

In the last fifteen years, many psychoanalysts have changed their minds. Among them, Robert Stoller, in the United States, Léon Kreisler and Christian David in France, have done considerable work on bisexuality, and have acknowledged the influence of the environment on the human unconscious and on psychoanalysis in general. Christian David, so far as we know, is one of the first to have dared to write that "if some analysts are showing a new interest in bisexuality, *the immediate reason for it must no doubt be attributed to recent socio-cultural changes* . . . There has been such a rapid and spectacular evolution . . . that we are today obliged to pay more attention to bisexuality, not merely because it is in the street and everywhere, because the status of women, of the couple, and of homosexuality is being reconsidered, but also, it seems, because the whole dialectical equilibrium between the masculine and the feminine is in jeopardy. Now, *despite the timelessness of the unconscious, it is not* – at least in certain of its aspects – *impervious to modifications in the surroundings,* and certainly reacts to the new promptings of the outside world."[53]

While it is true, David concludes, that changes in models do not bring about a corresponding change in psychosexual dispositions, he recognizes that we are here on the borders of the individual and the social, that the way in which psychoanalysts formulate problems depends on the transformation of society, and that psychoanalysis is not an empire within an empire. This is why, considering the undeniable "socio-cultural crisis of sexual identity", he rejects the tendency of some analysts to equate bisexuality with morbidity or immaturity, and on the contrary attempts to re-evaluate it, particularly in the light of the second aspect of the Freudian theory.

While he acknowledges that "the antagonistic development of psychological bisexuality is often a sign of damage or disorganization," he thinks that besides these teratological and destructive forms, analysis can uncover a regenerative, restorative and creative effect of the work of bisexualization, and that the bisexual dynamic leads to psychosexual positions as far removed from *"neutraquisme"* (the desire to belong to neither sex) as it is from *"ultraquisme"* (the desire to belong to both sexes at the same time). On the other hand, the notion of psychological bisexuality seems the only way to overcome the difficulties linked to the absolute primacy of the phallus and the castration complex.[54] Finally, "the fact of carrying within ourselves a replica of the other sex as a psychological potential in no way precludes the recognition of each sex . . . *Bisexuality – and this is one of its paradoxes – is a source of strangeness, and can also be seen as a way of access to a strange person.* A sufficient bisexual integration, a developed bisexualization, is the only thing that can enable us to understand that there can be a sexual otherness in every one of us, without this otherness necessarily presupposing actual opposition."[55]

Christian David invites us to welcome the idea of "sexual mediation", in order to break down barriers, to stop being prisoners of the logic of enumeration, and to avoid obsessively determining the parameters of a built-in sexual identity. Men and women resemble each other in that they are both, the one and the other, "the conjunction of othernesses".

In the light of this analysis, we must modify the earlier psychological schema. The construction of the sense of sexual identity always follows the original bisexuality, but psychological evolution no longer stops there. When gender identity is well integrated, human beings can discover, as a further possibility of development, the advantages of their bisexuality. It is their bisexuality, for example, that enables men to "mother" without complexes, and women to use their masculine impulses in a positive fashion.

All things considered, if we wanted to illustrate the new man/woman relationship, we could borrow from Georges Balandier[56] an image characteristic of some African myths: She and He are *twins of opposite sexes*".

The Difficulties of Masculine Identity

It is quite clear that women are better than men at living with their bisexuality. Confident of their femininity, they use and demonstrate their masculinity without hesitation. Finding no difficulty in alternating between masculine and feminine roles according to the periods of their lives or to the moments of the day, they do not feel that their bisexuality is a threat to their feminine identity: on the contrary, they experience otherness as the condition of a richer and less predetermined life. On the whole, women seem satisfied with their new condition and accept the idea of being men's "twins". What they complain of is not that they regret the former model, but that their partners are evolving more slowly, resisting, or even regressing. The women who complain about being responsible for everything are not expressing the wish to return to the sexual division of roles, but the wish that all tasks should be equally shared. Women want men to live with their own otherness as well as they do themselves, and to agree to be their twins.

Recent years seem to have shown that only a minority of men are reacting to the new model. As a general rule – in this first stage of an evolution that has only barely begun – men show in various ways that they have no wish to be women's twins. To understand their reluctance, it seems necessary to go beyond the limits of the feminist claims that tax men with ill will. It is immaterial whether men claim to be reluctant or full of goodwill, for the problem lies deep in their unconscious. The fact that the best-intentioned of them have so much difficulty in reconciling theory and practice reveals a kind of resistance that cannot be overcome by mere discussion.

We saw earlier that it is easier for an individual to come to terms with his bisexuality when he has acquired a strong sense of his sexual identity. And it seems that this is always harder for little boys than for little girls to acquire,[57] and that the resemblance model characteristic of our societies makes this acquisition even more risky. Men's problem, then, is more psychological and social than moral and political.

Margaret Mead was one of the first to reveal this in the light of her anthropological experience. Her analysis supports that of the American psychoanalyst Robert Stoller, famous for his work on transsexuals. Her study of seven Pacific Island peoples[58] convinced her that suckling, which attaches the baby to the female breast, dominates the psychological evolution of every human being. For a girl, "it lays the basis for an identification with her own sex that is simple and uncomplicated, something that exists, requires no elaboration, can be accepted simply."[59] But for the boy, breast-feeding is a reversal of the future roles; the mother inserts and he receives. Before he is a man he has to accomplish a change from this passivity. "So the female child's earliest experience is one of closeness to her own nature. Mother and female child together fit one pattern ... The little boy, however, learns that he must begin to differentiate himself from this person closest to him; that unless he does so, he will have no being at all." So from the very start of her life, a girl can accept herself as she is, whereas a boy is required to make an effort to acquire his sexual identity.[60] She learns to *be*; he learns to *react*, in order to enter the world of men. She knows that her femininity will attain its apogee when she bears a child, whereas he will always lack so obvious a certainty. In paternity, the role of the male is specified as "a single copulatory act that was successful ... Paternity remains, with all our modern biological knowledge, as inferential as it ever was."

This, Margaret Mead notes, is why "the recurrent problem of civilization is to define the male role satisfactorily enough – whether it be to build gardens or raise cattle, kill game or kill enemies, build bridges or handle bank-shares – so that the male may in the course of his life reach a solid sense of irreversible achievement."[61]

By depriving men of the comfort of differentiated sexual models, our societies make it even more difficult for them to acquire a sense of their identity. Feeling insufficiently rooted in their own sex, men fear that if they were to do traditionally feminine jobs, that might awaken homosexual tendencies in them. Robert Stoller has given a very good account of this fear, which is infinitely more deep-seated in men than in women.

Unlike Freud, Stoller[62] does not think that the male child's first relationship with his mother is heterosexual. On the contrary, he believes that heterosexuality is only achieved after immense effort and not without pain. Money's work[63] has taught us that the little boy has to fight hard to free himself from the original symbiosis fusing him with his mother. He must stop identifying himself with her in order to rid himself of her femininity.[64]

The study of transsexuals shows that excessive symbiosis leads to extreme femininity. The more a mother prolongs this symbiosis, the more the core of gender identity is infiltrated by femininity. *Transsexualism occurs at the extreme limit of such a continuum.* When a boy is able to detach himself from his mother, from his femininity, then he can develop his later gender identity: masculinity. And only then will he be able to see his mother as a separate, heterosexual object whom he might desire. According to Stoller, masculinity is not present at birth – it is even latently threatened by the experience of felicity experienced with the mother.

Consequently, the development of the core of gender identity is not the same in males and females. Males experience a conflict that females are spared. As the male always carries with him the urgent need to regress to his original state of union with his mother, he is permanently on the defensive against the feminine. Homosexual drives, therefore, are experienced in a different way by men and women. In Stoller's view, women are "the strong sex", "the first sex", and it is quite possible that their homosexuality may be an advantage to them. Indeed, the development of the mother–daughter relationship of the first months – in a normal symbiosis – only increases the child's sense of identity.[65] Women adapt better than men to the kind of homosexual experience that Stoller calls "a fragment of acting-out on the path to maturity".

On the other hand, as the sense of being male is less deeply rooted in men, they feel homosexuality to be a mortal threat to their identity, and are both terrified and captivated by the attraction of a union with the maternal femineity.

Finally, Stoller reverses Freud's proposition: it is femininity, not masculinity, that comes first. As Simone de Beauvoir might have said: "One is not born a man, one becomes one."

By depriving male children of the social reference points of their masculinity, we have magnified a natural difficulty that for many males becomes the source of a real malaise. And we have to recognize the fact that when one sex suffers, the other also suffers. Men's difficulties with their identity and their bisexuality find their echo in their relationships with women. If women complain more openly about men than men dare to about women, it is nevertheless men who are the victims of an evolution which they have not sought. While readily acknowledging the legitimacy of women's egalitarian claims, many men feel them to be an unbearable threat to their masculinity. The resemblance between the sexes secretly horrifies them, because they see it as the loss of their specific character[66] and a tendency towards an excessive femininization of humanity. This is a fantasy that is certainly linked to the dreaded desire of the original maternal omnipotence, of which Robert Stoller wrote.

Some people may think that this masculine unease is only a transient effect of our mutation and that with time, with an even more bisexual education and a modicum of good will, the problem will be solved to women's satisfaction. This is not exactly our own point of view. The malaise being expressed comes from the depths of the unconscious and will not be remedied until we agree that the resemblance model, which brings adult men and women closer together, must give children of both sexes full latitude to settle calmly into their sexual difference. The necessary scholastic co-education, or the sharing of household duties, does not exclude identity claims, which we would be very wrong to try to suppress. Whatever their ideological prejudices, teachers know that at a certain age, children in the same class divide into two groups according to sex, observe each other, mutually display false indifference, or do battle, until the time when they once again come together in a single group. After that, adolescents unite according to their personal affinities and no longer simply according to sex. Neither the most feminist of mothers nor the fathers who are most at their ease in their bisexuality will ever be able to prevent their children from passing through a phase – sometimes a very short phase – of claiming their gender identity. During this phase, the respect and help of the parent of the same sex are called for. This means that the father has a considerable role to play in relation to his son, and that he will not be able to carry it out properly unless he has solved his own identity problems. Once again, the androgynous model towards which we are tending is no substitute for the acquisition by everyone – and particularly by men – of a solid assurance of his or her sexual character. It is only when this has been acquired that men and women can follow a common path.

Points of View on the Resemblance between the Sexes

Three attitudes are currently encountered: scepticism, pessimism, and optimism. The first is found more frequently in men than in women, for the reasons we have just seen. It is a scepticism tinged with rejection that we may outline as follows: You women may copy us if you like, but don't count on us to do the same, or to help you invade our territory. We shall resist, and hope that you will finally get tired of doing everything yourselves. The scepticism of many anthropologists is less strong; their opinion is based on the observation of societies which are known to have rejected the reality or the validity of the new Western model. If, they say, we have everywhere and always observed the existence of complementary and asymmetrical relations between the sexes, there is an extreme likelihood that this model has a supra-cultural necessity. Resemblance is an ideological snare, a feminist illusion which they are not ready to give up. The anthropologists' doubt is compounded by pessimism in the conditional tense. If we admit the possibility of this model that is unlike every other, we are afraid that something that is so contrary to nature may be a sign of pathology or degenerescence, one more threat to the realization of human happiness. The resemblance between the sexes seems to be a transgression both of the (paternal) law and of (human) nature, and this seems absolutely unthinkable to everyone who has been rocked in his cradle to the rhythm of Lévi-Strauss's principles.

In addition to these pessimistic theoreticians, there are the feminists we have already mentioned who consider that resemblance between the sexes constitutes the suppression of the feminine to the advantage of the masculine.[67] And more generally, a further addition is to be found in all those who only see the difference as an enrichment, and resemblance as an impoverishing move to uniformity. Since the complementary, tensional relation between men and women, according to Georges Balandier, is "the raw material on the basis – and model – of which social relationships can be conceived and formed . . . the union of similar human beings seems to be the zero state of social relations, a non-relation, and in a way the reverse of the union of differences that shows its fecundity in the exemplary character attributed to the masculine/feminine relationship."[68]

Then there are the optimists who, since Marcel Mauss, believe that "division by sex is a fundamental division that has burdened all societies to an unsuspected degree";[69] the people who are afraid that when the emphasis is put on the differences, a fundamental part of the human essence is eclipsed. Edgar Morin sees the feminization of men and the masculinization of women as a step on the way to humanization, as this means that both sexes experience the complete cycle of humanity. Observing that in their progress towards adulthood, men have for long repressed their feminine, juvenile culture, he notes that in modern societies, "feminine aspects are appearing in men . . . men are becoming of an unstable complexity, capable of passing from the merciless hardness of the hunter-warrior to the gentleness, kindness and pity of the maternal-feminine part that they still preserve in their inner selves . . . In our opinion, there is no doubt that men 'become humanized' when they develop their genetic and cultural femininity."[70]

And finally, there are the optimists like Serge Dunis who believe that the sacrifice of bisexuality resembles "the destruction of the individual,"[71] and as such is the source of a fundamental lack of comprehension between the sexes. Observing this lack of comprehension among the Maori of New Zealand, Serge Dunis quite naturally deduces that "in order to be authentic, the couple must first of all exist in both the individuals of whom it is composed."

Whether realistic or optimistic, this proposition seems destined to be the model for the societies of tomorrow. One can only hope that they will find it acceptable!

The Retreat of "Nature"

Without entering the interminable polemic that opposes the partisans of environment to those of heredity, the "cultural whole" to the "rock of nature", since the nineteenth century everyone has agreed that species evolve as a function of ecological modifications (Lamarck), and of the living environment (Darwin). Despite this theoretical agreement, many people still resist the fact that all man's hereditary characteristics are also subject to change. People are always ready to speak of human "nature" as if it were a universal, eternal, fixed and unalterable entity. The reason for this is that the scale of physical mutations does not lie within the space of a single man's life, or even within that of several generations. The transformation of the primate into *homo sapiens*[72] has to be evaluated in terms of millions of years, and seems so distant as not to concern us any more. Furthermore, we are irresistibly tempted to think that we have now left mutations behind us, and that our present state constitutes the culmination of humanity. From that stage, any possible change is envisaged as degenerescence, a fatal disruption of the fine balance we are supposed to have achieved.

Even though most of the social sciences have for the last few decades seriously attacked the concept of nature, and in particular that of human nature, it still remains one of their recognized criteria: the anatomy that distinguishes us, the needs[73] that unite us, not to mention certain feelings such as women's maternal instinct or our common aversion to incest. Of all these real or presumed determinisms, our firmest anchorage seems to be our bodies. A man's body is *designed to penetrate*, to exert his strength, etc; a woman's is *designed to receive*, to bear children. Is this not the inevitable origin of our psychological and social destiny?

It nevertheless seems that for some time now, our apprehension of the body has been evolving. The importance we attribute to it is no longer of the same order. The *reasons* for our interest in it have changed.

The Disputed Predominance of the Biological

It all began some thirty years ago[74] in the USA with the studies made by two psychiatrists, John Money and J. L. Hampson, on intersexual children.[75] They confirm an essential fact: the possible absence of any parallelism between the somatic sex and the psychological sex. These studies have proved decisive because of the abundance of the material studied (76 cases), their scientific rigour, and a more precise approach to psychosexuality.

The crucial experiment was this:[76] two children are born with the adreno-genital syndrome; they are both female on the genetic level, on the level of the gonads and of endocrinology, and their internal sexual structures are normal, although their external genital organs are masculinized. If, at birth, one of these children is correctly designated as a girl and the other wrongly labelled a boy, because of the apparently male genital organs, when these children have reached the age of five, the one who was unequivocally thought to be a girl does not doubt that she really *is* a girl, and the one who was thought to be a boy *knows* he is a boy. What determined their sense of identity, therefore, was not their (biological) sex but the experiences they had lived through after their birth, a process that began with society's authoritarian, arbitrary labelling of the young child as male or female.

This leads to the necessary distinction between biological "sex", and "gender",[77] which relates to the psychological make-up inherent in the sex to which subjects feel they belong, and which impels them to play a masculine or feminine role. The terms "sex" and "gender" indicate the division between somato-biological sexuality and psychological sexuality, and the possibility of their divergent evolution. "Whereas common sense sees *sex* and *gender* as being practically synonymous, and closely connected in everyday life," Stoller's work on hermaphroditism, transvestism and transsexualism "confirms the fact that the two domains are not in a symmetrical relationship, but may follow totally independent paths."[78]

Stoller also considers that gender identity establishes itself very early, certainly before the end of the second year, and perhaps by the end of the first year, hence before the phallic stage, and that once established it is indelible and remains unchanged, whatever misadventures the individual may suffer.

In the third place, the work of Money and Stoller confirms the primacy of the psychological factor in the determination of sexual orientation. The sense of sexual identity is essentially culturally determined, i.e. learnt after birth. "This process of apprenticeship comes from the social milieu . . . But the knowledge comes through the mother, so that what actually reaches the child is the mother's interpretation of society's attitudes. Later, the father, the brothers and sisters . . . influence the development of the child's identity."

Everything begins at birth, when the doctor declares the child's sex and it is officially registered. Parents and society then consider it a boy or a girl. It is not some innate force that tells the baby that he is of the male sex and will become masculine. It is what his parents teach him, and they could equally well teach him something else. From the moment they know they have a boy, they start on a process which, depending on their idea of masculinity, will make them encourage some kinds of behaviour and discourage others. The choice of name, the style of clothes, the way the child is carried, the kind of games, etc., constitute the greater part of the child's training[79] in the development of its gender identity. In most cases, what our society considers masculinity will be encouraged, and by about the end of his first year the little boy's behaviour has a distinctly masculine character.

In the case of the transsexual little boy, mother and son remain attached to each other: the mother lives in such close symbiosis with him that she treats him as a part of her body, and feels him to be such. A common feature of mothers of transsexuals[80] is that each feels total oneness with her child, who lives in permanent bodily contact

with her. He is allowed to see her naked and in intimate circumstances. He sleeps in her bed "as if there were no limits between their
bodies". This contact responds to a need in the mother, and gives
her intense, never-satisfied pleasure.[81] She tries to reduce any
unpleasant tension in her child and never denies him anything.

When such mothers are analysed they present an almost depressive sense of inadequacy, a strong element of homosexuality, and a
confusion of their own identity with that of their child. Moreover,
they are married to men who are totally absent and towards whom
they feel genuine contempt. The little boy is unaware of the existence of his father, who does nothing (when by chance he happens to
be there) to make contact with his son. His complicity in the continuing feminization of the child is obvious. He does nothing to stop
his transvestism, etc. Because of the particular nature of these
families, the necessary traumatism of the Oedipus conflict[82] is
denied to the little boy: not having adequately singled out his
mother as a desired sexual object, he does not have to lose a battle
against a more powerful masculine rival. Deprived thus of the
Oedipean sense of frustration, he will feel no desire to find another
woman with whom to reduce the tension that the conflict should
produce in the little boy.

Stoller's work drastically modifies some of the principles of
Freudian theory. His study of intersexual children[83] gives the lie to
the idea that the biological is the foundation of the psychological.
The genesis of hermaphroditic identity is due to environmental conditions, and in particular to the uncertainty of the parents as to the
sex of their child, an uncertainty echoed and incorporated in the
organization of the ego. However, if the parents adopt the opposite
attitude, the child will acquire a strong sense of psychologically
indelible sexual identity. The roots of masculinity or femininity,
therefore, are the result of the behaviour of the parents, and not the
expression of some unknown instinct.

On the other hand, while Stoller agrees with Karen Horney,
Ernest Jones and Gregory Zilboorg in thinking that feminine
psychosexuality comes first and appears before the phallic stage,
unlike them, he maintains as a clinical fact that woman's sense of
being feminine develops independently of her perception of her
genital organs. He totally rejects the discussions on the primacy of

the vagina or the clitoris in the determination of feminine psychosexuality.[84] Neither the absence of a vagina or of internal genital organs, nor the presence of a peniform genital bud, nor the absence of a clitoris, prevents the constitution of a feminine sexuality, provided that the people amongst whom the child lives have no doubt about her femininity.

In so far as the little boy is concerned, Stoller maintains two new theses, supported by clinical evidence. In the first place, the sense of being male becomes definitely fixed well before the classic phallic stage (between the ages of three and five). Then, while the penis contributes to the reinforcement of this sense it is not essential, as is shown by the observation of two boys who were able to develop a masculine identity despite congenital penile aplasia. Both managed to create a fantasy penis for themselves. Stoller thinks that the sources of this fantasizing are less an instinctual force than the influence of outside pressures. Without denying the influence of forces of a biological order, his many clinical studies lead him to believe that postnatal psychological factors concerned with relationships can obliterate the biological tendencies and finally control the direction of identity.

Thus the whole of Money's and Stoller's work tends to show that it is environmental determinants that override biological factors, and not the reverse. Their theses have not been uncontested by the partisans of "nature", who see them as the ultimate phase in the pervading culturalism. There are two major reservations that have frequently been voiced.[85] The first is that cases of hermaphroditism or sexual ambiguity are too exceptional to justify extrapolating conclusions from them to the whole of the human population. The second reservation calls into question the analysis of hermaphrodites. "It is wrong to assume that the environmental factors are the predominant ones unless a systematic separation of the two sets of factors is somehow achieved and it is shown that the other factors are less important."[86] For the moment, this is impossible.

In their turn, these objections give rise to two remarks. Stoller does not identify the normal and the pathological, but, like Freud, uses the latter in order to understand the former better. On the other hand, the absence of a "systematic separation" between the biological and the environmental factors does not invalidate the import of his experiments, although they may later be revised. So far, no one has been able to prove Stoller wrong, *pace* certain socio-biologists. After all, even if the studies of cases as exceptional as hermaphrodites and transsexuals are treated with scepticism, there are other aspects of life, familiar to us all, that tend to show that anatomy and biology do not necessarily have the force of law in the human species.

Femininity/Motherhood Dissociation

This dissociation can be observed on different levels: the psychological, the social, and even the physical. Physiological processes no longer control women's lives. Contraception, by putting an end to the diktat of nature, has revealed a truth which even a short time ago was unthinkable: feminine destiny is no longer linked to motherhood. Some women even deliberately choose to exclude it from their existence. It is certain, though, that those who have radically dissociated femininity and motherhood still represent only an infinitesimal minority of the population.[87] But is this any reason to treat them as if they were abnormal? Up till now, they have been studied more by psychologists than by historians or sociologists. Nevertheless, the examination of their unconscious should not rule out the need to inquire about their plans, their conception of married life as containing only two people, not three.

The only surveys on this theme come from the USA and Canada.[88] They cover couples who have been married for at least five years and who declare that they do not want children. From these in-depth studies, it emerges that these "child free" couples not only see themselves as being released from the worries inherent in child-raising, but also consider that the quality and intensity of their relation as a couple will be better protected if they remain childless. "Husband and wife, lover and mistress, are better friends, and as a couple can meet most, if not all, of each other's social and emotional needs." These dyadic couples are said to appear very happy and to consider that the birth of a child would upset their equilibrium. The women questioned regard themselves as "liberated' from their husbands, and on the same level of authority and competence.

Whatever the psychological origin of the common refusal of both members of a couple to have children, such couples prove that human happiness does not necessarily depend on the presence of a child in the home. And in particular, that women can find their equilibrium elsewhere than in motherhood, outside procreation. Even if the relations within the couple do not exclude mutual paternal-maternal feelings and even if the desire to have a child makes itself felt from time to time, after weighing up the advantages and disadvantages of parenthood, they finally decide against it.

We may contest this mode of life in the name of the interests of the species, but certainly not in the name of mental health. This would be to postulate that the desire for a child is a criterion of psychological normality, whereas it is well known that it is not unambiguous. Women who choose not to become mothers are not necessarily less well balanced than others.

The great majority of women do not have this negative attitude. Nevertheless, they have decidedly distanced themselves from motherhood. Western women are having fewer and fewer children, and they refuse to take the interests of the species into account. The birth rate is everywhere lower than two children per woman,[89] which tends to show that motherhood for them is now no more than one stage of their life among others. The time devoted to motherhood has become considerably shorter for two reasons. In the first place, women's expectation of life now borders on eighty years, and the education of two children represents no more than some fifteen years of active mothering, or less than a fifth of their life. So it is no longer reasonable to expect mothering to be the focal point of a woman's life. Formerly, a woman's interest was centred on her children; today, it is centred on herself: her emotional and professional life. She no longer builds her existence around her children, but obliges them to adapt to her plans for a personal life.

The time spent with their children has also decreased in women's day-to-day lives. As we have seen, the majority go on working after having had children, even though this means that they have to work miracles to reconcile opposing demands. In particular, much less time is spent alone with each child. Crèches, schools, and television have become substitutes for the old-fashioned mother. Today there remain the first and last meals of the day, bath time, homework and shopping time, and the weekends. All things considered, a mother is a mother barely a third of the time. Quality counts for more than quantity, and the father is expected to do his share.

In actual fact, motherhood does not fundamentally alter a woman's social life, any more than do the other stages of her biological life. On the contrary: the fact that women's first menstruation now takes place earlier, and their menopause later,[90] contributes to the unification of the stages of feminine life. An earlier[91] and longer sex life gives women a feeling of having a longer active life. The menopause does not change their status.[92] In the old days, it corresponded to a retirement from sexual activity; today it no longer marks any particular stage, whether professional, emotional or sexual. Mothers have difficulty in seeing themselves as grandmothers.

The control of nature or the detachment from physiological functions is made even more obvious by the new procreative techniques. In the nineteenth century, Pasteur's discoveries made bottle-feeding possible, and deprived women's breasts of their nourishing function. Today, a woman can become pregnant without making love,[93] borrow an egg from X, some sperm from Y, fertilize the whole *in vitro*, have the embryo reimplanted or get it carried by another woman. The time may perhaps not be so far off when an artificial mother could be substituted for a flesh and blood woman. After her breasts, it would be a woman's womb that becomes inessential: an option which every woman could freely choose!

All this implies a new conception of motherhood. The real mother would be less the one who passes on her genetic material, carries the child and gives birth to it, than the one who brings it up and gives it her love. The more "nature's imperatives" retreat, the closer the concept of motherhood comes to that of fatherhood.

After role-sharing, detachment from their physiological functions constitutes the most powerful factor in the resemblance between the sexes. Now, it is undeniable that all our efforts are converging, in the long term, to deprive our bodily organs of their imperialistic character. Being unable to do away with death, we prolong life, we make women fertile who only a few years ago could not have conceived. In short, we do everything to bend our bodies to our desires and to stop making a virtue of necessity. The importance we attribute to our body has not decreased, but has completely changed its meaning.

From a "technical" object, it has become an "aesthetic" object.[94] We no longer so much want to use it as to be astonished by it, to admire it, and cause it to be admired. In our civilization, no one is upset by a mother who does not breast-feed her baby, but we *are* shocked by a body that has been let go. Everything must be done to retard its old age, to hide its weaknesses, and to keep it seductive at all costs. Some people even say that this is a question of ethics!

Our dependence on our bodies is perhaps no less, but it no longer resembles our former dependence. We are gradually becoming better able to control our biological factors, and are finding arms against the unaesthetic. Sacrosanct nature is being manipulated, modified, and defied, according to our desires.

Even if our psyches sometimes have difficulty in keeping pace, we should be very naïve were we to think that there is an end to all this.

Individual Difference before Sexual Difference

The stereotypes of the manly man and the feminine woman have been shattered. There is no longer one obligatory model, but an infinity of possible models. Both men and women value their own particularity, their own balance between femininity and masculinity. "The differences necessary for them to exercise attraction over one another are developed by the couple in private, and less and less in public."[95]

The sharing of roles and feelings is making sexual discrimination more and more difficult. It has now lost its primary, fundamental character, and often seems secondary. The differentiation of individuals and groups evolves accoring to more subtle divisions than that of sex; divisions, for instance, such as age, culture, or sensitivity. And indeed, there is sensitivity in the way we perceive the masculine and feminine in ourselves.

In some societies, what distinguishes a man from a woman is not so much sex, as the power of fecundity. Sterile women have a particular status. Among the Samo of Upper Volta (Burkina Faso), they are classed as children. As Françoise Héritier says: "The event that gives a girl the status of a woman is not the loss of her virginity, or marriage, or even motherhood: it is conception. One pregnancy is sufficient, but it does not matter whether it is followed by a miscarriage or a birth. A sterile woman is not considered a real woman . . . she will die . . . an immature girl, and will be buried in the children's cemetery."[96]

Among the Nuer of the southern Sudan, on the other hand, sterile women are thought of as men, and have a right to all men's advantages. "If a girl marries and has no children, after several years she returns to her original family with the status of a man. She will be called 'uncle' by her nephews and nieces. She will be given a share of the cattle, will gradually acquire a herd, and will then pay the necessary dowry to get herself a wife. Her wives will call her 'my husband'. She engages a genitor who will also be her servant . . . Her wives will have children who will call her 'father'."[97]

It is not the same in our societies. Sterile women are neither identified with unmarried girls nor with men. Even though we may think that the distinction made by pregnancy is not so much that between the women's group and the men's group, as that between women who have conceived and all the others – both men and women – who have not had that experience, contraception and the category of voluntarily sterile women divest pregnancy of its characteristic of being a crucial experience, a necessary stage in the acquisition of femininity. A woman does not feel less of a woman because she does not want children. Women's femininity is not confined to their ovaries; they have maternal feelings for people other than their children. Moreover, the new procreative techniques are blurring our old criteria of fertility. When several women can participate in the maternal process, how is it possible to determine which one shall be called "fertile"? In the case of "shared motherhood", is the woman fertile who gives the egg, or is it the one whose womb receives the embryo? We cannot see this clearly, so we minimize the importance of the biological part and stress the desires. Between the genetic mother, the surrogate mother and the mother who brings up the child, it is finally the last who seems to us to deserve the name of mother – in which case, there is no longer any difference between motherhood and fatherhood.

Many societies make a distinction between the genitor, the man who gives his sperm, and the father, the man who gives his loving care. We now have to do the same with some women. We must now make a distinction between the genetrixes and the mothers, who give their love. The differences between father and mother are therefore no longer so much a matter of their physiology as of their gender identity. These differences are more individual than sexual. Even if the dominant model requires a masculine father and a feminine mother, we are more and more coming to realize that each is a unique mixture of two components, and that the images imposed upon them are disintegrating.

Bisexual humanity draws the sexes together into the greatest possible resemblance. In so doing, it permits the expression of all personal differences. It is no longer split into two heterogeneous groups, but is constituted of a multiplicity of individualities which at the same time resemble and are distinct from each other in all kinds of subtle ways.

II

THE COUPLE, OR
THE MUTATIONS OF THE HEART

The resemblance between the sexes is fraught with consequences for our desires. In the absence of a sense of alienation, of opposition, indeed for the lack of combatants, the dialectic of the One and the Other loses its original tension.

The traditional notion of the couple has been shaken. The permanence that used to be its characteristic has now simply become an ideal and is no longer an imperative, for we are refusing to accept the constraints that used to make it possible.

If reality does not turn out to be like the romantic fantasy of Philemon and Baucis, we split up. To hell with half measures and approximations! The ideal does not lend itself to compromise. The couple operate according to the principle of all or nothing: they prefer to have several tries, in the hope of achieving perfect unity, rather than to settle for the compromises inherent in longevity. Since the imperatives – social, economic, religious – formerly a strong incentive to permanency, have largely disappeared, it is now the heart alone that rules our life as a couple. Unlike the classical age, which was acutely aware of the haphazard quality of love and refused to create a union on so fragile a foundation, we now give absolute priority to the most irrational and inconstant part of ourselves. Here, as elsewhere, it is not so much our "passions" that now preside over our destiny as, in the final analysis, our "neuroses". We love, we evolve, we don't love any more. And then we start again.

The intermittences of our hearts are not a sign that our loves are fickle. They are contingent because of our need for perfection. It is because the unity we seek is far more demanding than it used to be that we have so much difficulty in achieving it and making it last. The quality and intensity of the bond take precedence over everything else, and so indifference, weakness or conflict shatter unity and put the survival of the couple at risk. What is the point of remaining two if in fact we are now only one? When hearts no longer communicate, when silence becomes established, then the couple breaks up, for it has no more *raison d'être*. It is unforgivable for estrangement to take the place of the desired intimacy.

The fact remains that the symbiotic unity we dream of is made even more difficult by our androgynous mutation. Our demands have increased, and are sometimes contradictory. Imperfect androgynes that we are, we are seeking at the same time self-sufficiency and the fused relationship which we see as the perfect interlocking of our two double natures.

We are thus confronted by a triple challenge: to reconcile self-love with the love of another; to deal with our conflicting desires for liberty and for symbiosis; and finally, to adapt our own duality to that of our partner, constantly trying to adjust our mutual evolutions.

This wager is made even more dangerous by the fact that the Ego has never been so strong, nor the need for love so exigent.

The Individual before the Couple

In the old days, the couple constituted the basic unit of society. It was formed of two moieties, both determined to play its "part", and was seen by each party as a transcendent entity. Socially, and even psychologically, it was understood that the One was incomplete without the Other. The bachelor, whether despised or pitied, was seen as an incomplete being. The use of a single patronymic for two people still reflects this all-embracing conception of the couple in which individualities are erased. This mental and social operation becomes more complicated to carry out when both members of the couple keep their own name and their independence.

Our present tendency is no longer towards the transcendental notion of the couple, it is rather towards the union of two people who consider themselves less as the two moieties of a beautiful unit and more as two autonomous wholes. It is hard to sacrifice the slightest part of oneself to a partnership. A hypertrophied ego and militant individualism are great impediments to the life of the couple as we would like it to be. It is true that our aims have changed, and that we are no longer prepared to pay any price for the presence of the Other by our side.

The Absolute Value of the Ego

The emergence of our androgynous nature multiplies our demands and desires. We want everything, because we experience ourselves as a totality. We have the more or less pronounced feeling of being a representative example of all humanity. A substitute for the divine totality. We want ourselves to be complete and self-sufficient, but our interiorized otherness makes our search for the Other less urgent and less piquant. These days, there is a limit to the price we are prepared to pay for the Other. He is desired if he enriches our being, but rejected if he demands sacrifices from it.

Our unprecedented aspiration towards totality makes it more painful than ever when we become conscious that something is missing. This is why most sterile couples will go to any lengths to put an end to the frustration that deprives them of something that is common to all humanity. Stoicism has gone; necessity is no longer a virtue. If nature plays us the dirty trick of amputating a part of ourselves, of forbidding us an experience that she permits other people to have, we jib, and take short-cuts.

When the Other is the cause of our frustration, we leave him. It is better to cultivate one's Ego than to suppress an aspect of one's personality. When we cannot manage to get someone to love us as we are, never mind, we are always prepared to love ourselves passionately.

The Ego has become our most precious possession, since it has at the same time an aesthetic, economic and moral value. In the old days it was "bad manners" to talk about it, and reprehensible to make it the foundation of one's existence. At all costs, one had to give the impression that the Other was more important than the Ego. But the new generations will have nothing to do with this moral standpoint – or this hypocrisy. They are less obsessed with making the most of the Other than with making the very most of themselves. Aims have changed radically: all we think of now is of making the best of our own lives and using all our capacities. To leave some of our potentialities undeveloped is an unforgivable crime against the new capitalism of the Ego. Parents, aware of their responsibilities, go frantic in the effort to make their children's lives as full as possible. They make them try everything, in the hope of discovering talents in them that will be "pluses" for their Ego. And so we see children rushing from a Judo session to a dancing class, from the pottery studio to a music lesson . . . even if they would rather stay at home and do nothing. But unproductive leisure causes the parents remorse and anguish; they sometimes "invest" more in their child's Ego than they do in their own.

The exploitation of the Ego demands a new methodology: narcissism. "Know thyself" and "love thyself" are the two prerequisites for any sort of cultivation of the Ego. False modesty is no longer the order of the day. Since incapacities and lack of appetite are ascribed to an unhappy Ego, one that has "got stuck", it is our duty to listen to it, look at it, dissect it, so as to be in a position to liberate it.

The Ego is the object of a cult and of a culture, because we stake our all on it. It is supposed to bring us pleasure, happiness, glory, and perhaps even eternity, more surely than *anything* or *anyone* else. Our supreme ambition, then, is to make it into a work of art, envied and admired by other people. Gilles Lipovetsky is right to emphasize that "these days the Superego presents itself under the guise of demands for fame and success which, if they are not achieved, unleash an implacable storm of criticism against the Ego."[1]

Today, there is no greater misfortune than the frustration and devaluation of the Ego. They lead to desperate reactions such as suicide or drugs. In the last resort, not to love oneself is lethal, and the *only* thing we ask of psychoanalysis is to teach us to put up with ourselves.

The Ego possesses moral value because self-love has become a code of ethics. The categorical imperative no longer sets out the conditions of the relationship between Ego and Other People, but those of my relationship with myself. It orders me to love myself, "to develop myself", "to enjoy myself". The aim of the moral code has shifted away from the Other and on to Oneself. "Authenticity is considered more important than reciprocity, knowledge of oneself more important than gratitude."[2]

When the Ego becomes our main preoccupation and the thing that matters more than anything else is "to develop oneself independently of the criteria of the Other", we are obliged to recognize that intersubjective relations are losing their value. "The space occupied by interhuman rivalry is gradually giving way to a neutral public relationship in which the Other has lost all consistency and is no longer hostile or competitive but indifferent, *desubstantialized*, like the characters of Peter Handke or Wim Wenders."[3]

The absolute value attributed to the Ego goes hand in hand with relative value allotted to the Other. "Grand passions" are no longer in vogue. Hate and jealousy are censured[4] and detachment praised – as a sign of self-control and an antidote to suffering. Couples who divorce make it a point of honour "to remain good friends", as if excessive attachment were an indication of the poverty and incompleteness of the Ego. However great the difficulties, it is good manners to give the impression of being sufficient unto oneself.

This egocentric moral code jeopardizes the Christian and Kantian ethic. The altruism on which this is based is hardly compatible with our militant individualism. By dint of proclaiming our duty towards our personal development (Me first! Ego!), the idea of sacrifice now only appears under its negative aspect of self-mutilation. We can only accept altruism if it serves Ego's aims: its aesthetic and its grandeur. A great gulf divides this standpoint from that of letting the Other come before Ego, a gulf we cross more and more rarely.

All this has a direct influence on our way of loving. "Oblative"[5] love – which for long has embodied the model of love – has serious limitations, as observed in the conjugal and even maternal relationship. In the old days, motherhood was defined in terms of devotion and sacrifices. You had children in order to obey God's commandment ("increase and multiply"), to give your husband some descendants, and to accomplish your destiny as a woman. The symbol of the good mother was the pelican, who opens her belly to feed her young. It was understood that the wellbeing of the child demanded the gift of the mother's person, and even of her life. Today, our society has a totally different conception of motherhood. In the first place, if you have a child it is primarily in order to satisfy a personal desire, and you are repelled by the idea of having a child you do not want, merely to please the Other. And you are even less willing to have one merely for the survival of the species, or for some other socio-economic necessity. More than anything else, you have a child for your own purposes, to satisfy and enrich your Ego. It is only honest to recognize that the desire for a child is profoundly egoistic and narcissistic, two feelings which, more than any others, guarantee the survival of the species. We have children because we want to re-produce ourselves, to see and admire ourselves in this Other who forms part of my Ego. If the birth rate in the Western world hovers at around two children per woman, it may also be because we want to reproduce ourselves in the masculine *and* in the feminine. The ideal is to have the experience of bringing up both a male and a female. After that, procreation becomes repetition. And if we have been lucky, most of us prefer to stop there, and kiss goodbye to our bisexual reproductive desire. With more than two children, the par-ents feel the burden is too heavy, the sacrifice of their Egos too great.

It must be admitted that the children we dream of having are con-ceived of not only as the Ego's masterpieces – the perfections that we are not but which we think we can achieve through them – but also as inexhaustible sources of love. In short, we procreate more from nar-cissism, to ensure our survival, to renew our pleasure, and less to give life to a human being whom we accept in advance with his failings and his inevitable hatreds. Mothers are prepared to sacrifice a great deal but there is a limit to their altruism, which is precisely that of their Egos. You can give everything providing you get some gratifi-cation from the giving. But when that is no longer the case, you withdraw what you have invested in the Other in order to protect yourself against anxiety, remorse, disappointment, and to preserve your own integrity. Even if most parents are prepared to make very generous gifts of love for the wellbeing of their child, without expect-ing any immediate return, their gifts are never totally gratuitous, nor are their narcissistic desires abandoned. They still hope that the real child will merge with the fantasy child. If this hope is crushed, if hatred is stronger than love, then the sacrifice of the Ego will be seen as useless, if not dangerous.

Whether we like it or not, it is no longer only children who "settle accounts". Parents do this too, even if in a less brutal and assertive way. Maternal love itself is not what it used to be, or, to be more precise, not what it was supposed to be. Mothers too do their "accounts", with a view to settling them. They have realized that they can make a total sacrifice without necessarily being given anything in return. They have sacrificed their Ego, but have no guarantee that their sacrifice has been of any use.

Up to the present, the image of the sacrificing mother had managed to remain the model. Women who rebelled against it did so among themselves, under their breath, in the closed circle of friendship, for fear of being misunderstood or rejected. Today we can tell our children publicly that they are going too far and making too many demands on our love. By calling her book *Moi, ta mère*[6] ("Moi" meaning both "Me" and "Ego"), Christiane Collange was giving us an opportune reminder – to the relief of some women and the outrage of others – that mothers too had an Ego that called for a minimum of consideration if it were not to disintegrate. The success of this courageous book is due to the fact that the author was saying aloud what people had been saying *sotto voce* for some time: We are willing to give you all our love,[7] on condition that you give us a sufficient amount back. If we see no tangible proof of your affection, we shall detach ourselves from the passion we feel for you, in order to suffer less from your apparent indifference.

Such unconditional, "oblative" love is even more limited in the marital relationship, especially as the Other is not part of oneself as the child is. Altruism is counterbalanced by the demand for reciprocity. Whether consciously or not, we make a strict evaluation of profit and loss: give, in order to receive – that is the condition for the survival of the couple.

Ideal Love, whose paramount virtue is to protect us from solitude, is generally perceived as a permanent dialogue that has its source in the respect and tenderness we feel for the Other, and is expressed through one's special feelings for him. Respect and dialogue imply the equality of the loving couple, and conjugal love must follow the absolute rule of reciprocity. *I love you as much as I love myself, on condition that you love me as much as you love yourself, and that you prove it to me.* Which means that when the sacrifice is reciprocal, we no longer feel it to be a sacrifice.

This rule implies that nothing is free, and that it is difficult for love to be unilateral. It is a rule that has always existed in marriage: even if people did not exchange an equal amount of love, both parties contributed something that was equivalent to what the Other was giving – a title, or social status, against a dowry. Or, more prosaically, board and lodging against household duties and the care of the children.

This rule is now more than ever being put to the test in the private life of the couple. More and more frequently, husband and wife both have a wage to contribute to the family finances, so the rule of reciprocity is no longer confined to proofs of love. These are manifested in what appear to be the most innocuous acts that constitute the essential framework of the life of the couple.[8] Has He done something for Her? – then she will soon have to pay him back by doing something similar for him, and vice versa. Even if they pretend not to be counting, they are. How shameful! some will say. No, for love can only be expressed in terms of proof, and its survival depends on reciprocity. If we don't want to see it wither, then we must constantly steer a middle course between its egotistic impulses and its desire to keep the union going.

A prolonged breach of the rule of reciprocity is always, in the last analysis, seen as an injustice, a proof of indifference or a lack of consideration. All of which invariably ends up by undermining the mutual understanding, and hence the *raison d'être*, of the couple. If the dispute becomes exacerbated, that is the end of the dialogue and the beginning of the worst of all constraints: the hostile confrontation.

Solitude, rather than Constraint!

The constant increase in the number of divorces is a phenomenon that has been common to all the industrialized countries, both in the East and in the West, for the last fifteen years or so. In Sweden, in the United States and in the Soviet Union, nearly one in every two marriages ends in divorce. France has been going the same way, because in 1984, there were 284,000 marriages and 130,000 divorces. The number of marriages is no longer greater than the number of couples that are dissolved by divorce or death. Divorce mainly affects young couples, after three or four years of marriage, and urban populations, which are less subject to the social, economic or religious pressures still exerted in certain regions.[9] But there is a fact of even greater interest: in all the countries where divorce exists, a vast number of women are the petitioners. Since divorce was instituted in France in 1884, the proportion of women petitioners has always been greater than that of men,[10] except in the periods immediately following the First and Second World Wars. The statistics tend to show that women feel the disadvantages of married life more bitterly than men do.

When we consider the life of couples at the present time, we can see that the rule of reciprocity is constantly flouted to the detriment of women. All the studies of couples' daily timetables show that it is work in the home that is the least equitably distributed between the sexes.

AVERAGE DAILY SCHEDULE OF
URBAN MARRIED COUPLES WITH TWO CHILDREN
(FRANCE 1974–1975)*

	Working Men	*Working Women*	*Non-working Women*
Child care	0 h 17	1 h 05	1 h 59
Other housework	1 h 13	3 h 53	5 h 53
Time spent out at work, including travelling time	6 h 48	4 h 52	—
Personal time†	11 h 06	10 h 50	11 h 19
Free time‡	3 h 52	2 h 39	3 h 52
Non-professional travelling	0 h 43	0 h 41	0 h 52
TOTAL	24 hours	24 hours	24 hours

* Marie-Thérèse Huet, Yannick Lemel, Caroline Roy, *Les Emplois du temps des citadins*, document "Rectangle", INSEE, December 1978.
† Sleep, meals at home and away from home, personal and medical care.
‡ Education, religion, clubs, entertainments, parties, sports, excursions, reading, television, music, DIY, handwork, and all other leisure pursuits.

While it is true that working women spend less time (in terms of statistics) at work than men do, we cannot but observe that they have eight and a half hours less leisure time per week.

This imbalance is roughly the same in the United States[11] and the

199

Soviet Union. In a large survey of 2,214 representative American couples, James Morgan observed that after they are married, men do half as many hours of housework a week as they did when they were bachelors (four hours a week instead of eight), while the reverse is true for women (forty hours a week against twenty for unmarried girls). True, this phenomenon is not new, for almost ninety years ago Durkheim wrote, in *Suicide*: "It must be admitted that married life, which is disastrous for women, is on the contrary, even when there are no children, beneficial for men." But women are resenting this inequality more and more. Its resulting fatigue generates latent discontent, which is becoming all the more apparent since women have gained their economic independence. All the surveys show that the higher their educational level and professional status, the less satisfied with their married life they declare themselves.

The fact of being on terms of equality with their male colleagues at work incites women to expect equality with their partners at home. Believing that they have no more maternal instinct than domestic instinct, that nothing in their nature predisposes them to wash nappies or to get up in the middle of the night, they have become more and more aware of the restricting aspect of these tasks when they are not shared. And when men balk at the idea of sharing, they consider that they are breaking the contract of solidarity and reciprocity, the basis of married life.

The fatigue felt by women who work outside the home causes them to feel resentful of their spouses. It does not take long before the era of dialogue is over and has given way to the kind of solitude against which women thought they had protected themselves by cohabitation or marriage, a solitude composed of hostility towards the Other who is seen as an exploiter.

In such conditions, why stay together?

When women enjoy relative economic independence, it is then very much in their interests to get a divorce. Separation is both a physical and psychological relief and a source of hope. They will still be responsible for their professional and family lives, but they will be rid of the burden of a partner who has become a stranger. Moreover, when a woman divorces her husband she is almost certain to gain custody of her children,[12] a priceless remedy against solitude.[13]

With or without children, separation also implies the hope of starting again more happily with someone else.[14] A temporary spell of (relative) solitude is preferable to sharing one's life with someone you no longer recognize as yours. The new conjugal morality is severely critical of marriages that are kept going by "force of circumstance". When your heart is no longer involved, staying together is thought hypocritical. A compulsory bond is seen as both moral cowardice and a serious emotional handicap.

By and large, the younger generations are more and more choosing the risks of solitude rather than those of a strained relationship, which they are finding it increasingly hard to bear. Three words explain this change of attitude: Liberty, completeness, and apathy, with its positive and negative connotations.

In the seventies, many feminists were in favour of solitude. Taking their inspiration from Virginia Woolf, they demanded the right to possess "a room of one's own", or even "a bed of one's own",[15] a place in which to live freely, for and by oneself. This claim went hand in hand with fierce criticism of the couple, which, as Évelyne Le Garrec put it, was seen as "an illusion that is bound to drive individuals to destroy themselves by merging into each other, which they would not do if it were not in the name of a religion or of an ideal. Évelyne Le Garrec denounces the myth of the Great Love, which she sees as really only a permanent battle in which each deceives the other, and in which the stronger takes over the weaker.

"When I wrote about the necessity of couples sharing duties, what was I doing?" she asks. "I thought that this would lead to the end of domination relationships ... I was wrong. When a couple fight each other they are wasting energy, which they will not be able to use elsewhere, on a daily battle which is never won but must always be recommenced ... It is playing the card of the reform of the couple, as workers play that of the reform of their company." But in vain.

At that period, many feminists made a positive choice to live on their own,[16] not only to ensure that their private lives were in keeping with their ideology, but also to regain possession of their own personalities, to become a free and autonomous "I". Évelyne Le Garrec insists that the couple annihilates the human person in an alienating confusion. "'I' disappears, absorbed into, swamped by 'We'. Never alone. For the couple doesn't cater for the amount of solitude that is indispensable to the existence of the individual. Even when absent, the Other is there, a reference point, his burdensome traces are all over the house, showing that he will always be back."

The couple, in fact, far from being a remedy against solitude, often secretes its most unpleasant aspects. It puts a barrier between oneself and other people, it weakens one's links with the community. By making us renounce our freedom and independence, it makes us even more fragile in the event of a break-up or of the death of the Other. "The man or woman who is left behind is then condemned to total solitude, to isolation and rejection, to be a complement without a direct object, the unusable left-over of a pair. Total solitude, because the individual does not exist in his own right, nor does the community exist in which he would still have had his place. When the 'We' has disappeared, what remains is a half of something, and it is sickly, crippled, non-viable, like a newborn baby with no one to feed and clothe it, tortured by fear."[17]

In order to fight against this solitude – the worst kind of alienation – the individual learns, not without pleasure, to live for himself (or herself), and to cultivate his Ego. There is no doubt that we are powerfully helped in this direction by our exaggerated narcissism and the ideal of completeness that we have acquired. It has become a categorical imperative for us to protect our Ego against the risk of the suffering inflicted by the Other. Some people, as for instance Jerry Rubin, the former American protest leader, have gone so far as to advocate the complete withdrawal from intersubjectivity. "To give up love so as to love myself enough not to need anyone else to make me happy."

Gilles Lipovetsky – who quotes Jerry Rubin – sees this narcissistic search for autonomy at all costs as a pathological, almost depressive state of apathy. To his mind, this excess of personalization is destabilizing. "It creates a purely here-and-now existence, a total subjectivity with neither aim nor meaning, intoxicated with self-love. The individual, confined within his ghetto of messages, henceforth confronts his mortal condition with no transcendent support, be it political, moral or religious."[18]

Nevertheless, we do not have to accept this pessimistic aspect of apathy. Originally, the Stoics and the Epicureans identified it with wisdom, which is to say quietude. The pursuit of autonomy does not necessarily imply an incapacity to establish a dual relationship, but rather the refusal to pay any kind of price for it. The tranquillity of the soul, so dear to Democritus, is on its guard against the passions, and against excesses of all kinds. More than anything it fears the loss of self-control, but it also seeks the serenity of the contented heart.

As imperfect androgynes, our completeness is never total. To have learnt how to cope with solitude is a strength, not an aim. It allows us to be extremely demanding in what we expect from the relationship of the couple; we now see it as the fusion of two entities who respect each other's liberty.

Less Passion, but more Tenderness

The Decline of the Passions

> *I turned to him, turned pale, turned red and turned aside,*
> *I felt confusion rising; my mind was stupefied.*
> *I could not speak or breathe; things swam before my eyes;*
> *All through my body ran at once both fire and ice.*[19]

Alas, we no longer react like Phaedra. Racine's heroine, who incarnates the chaos of absolute passion, finds only the faintest reflection in the women of today. At first sight, this makes us feel rather sad. Isn't there something wonderful about extremes of feeling? On second thought, we remember that Phaedra's passion is utterly devastating, and is couched in terms of appalling violence. "The violence of the insults which conclude her declaration to Hippolytus; the violence at the beginning of Act III where Phaedra is prepared to go to any lengths to satisfy her mad passion; the incredible violence of Act IV, when she discovers the agonies of jealousy."[20]

It may be objected that passion does not necessarily exclude tenderness. But tenderness is easily hidden under all kinds of contradictory sentiments. It does not play the star part. Its characteristic serenity is constantly giving way to a form of irrationality that can lead to murder or suicide. Like the Stoics, we consider passion to be a disease of the soul which is more likely than any other bond to curb our liberty. We want to "fall" in love, yet we want to avoid being so badly affected as to become alienated. Our ideal of self-control and fulfilment cannot accept such a painful feeling for long.

We find it difficult to imagine a twenty-first century Phaedra consumed by desire and prepared to kill herself, and we find it equally difficult to imagine the hero of *The Blue Angel*, the pathetic puppet of a *femme fatale*. When we are head over heels in love, we take care to limit any effects of this state that would be dangerous for our Ego. If it looks as if there is going to be more suffering than pleasure, we prefer to withdraw. Here too we do our arithmetic, which is hardly favourable to the excesses of passion that threaten the integrity of the Ego.

Passion is heading for extinction, and so is sensual ecstasy.[21] In our analgesic ethic, there is no room for the risks of suffering. Both men and women dream of other things than heartbreak. But even if we wanted to, we could not experience it any more. The conditions for passion no longer exist, either from the social or the psychological point of view.

We have never been so far away from the courtly eroticism so brilliantly described by Denis de Rougemont.[22] He has shown that desire feeds on its impossibility. Ordeals, obstacles, prohibitions, are the necessary conditions of passion. In loving her husband's son, Phaedra experiences a feeling that is doubly forbidden: by the law, and by nature. Adultery is culpable, incest is monstrous, two insuperable obstacles that excite an unavowable desire. Passion is indissociable from the transcendence of the moral and social law. Its real or imaginary transgression can only be paid for by death or its equivalent. Romeo and Juliet commit suicide to escape from the law of their fathers; Phaedra does so to punish herself for having had feelings that are in conflict with humanity. Madame de Lafayette's Princess of Clèves retires to a convent, because she knows that Monsieur de Clèves has been killed by his passion for her.[23] In any case, one must have a very elevated idea of morality to be a hero or victim of passion!

This is no longer the case today. At a time when incestuous couples confess their secrets to the television cameras, when marriage is no longer sacred, when fidelity attaches to successive objects, permissiveness has deprived passion of its most powerful driving force. By admitting that the heart is no longer outside the law, but above it, we have played a very dirty trick on desire. By giving it full rights, we have divested it of its force and substance. We barely give it a chance to come into existence. Everything goes too quickly to allow it to mature, to become exacerbated and invade the erotic scene. Our relationship with time has changed, for two reasons. In the first place, women are no longer "inaccessible", nor do they demand that their lovers undergo a long initiatory period before "giving themselves". And secondly, our relationship with temporality is now judged according to the personal gauge of the individual, and no longer according to that of society.

The preliminaries have been transformed: "Rather than following a single logical and chronological pattern, each couple now follows the anarchical disorder of its own desires. They can choose their own rhythm, work out the successive stages of their progress as a couple without reference to any social arbitration, for no one else will intervene to organize the moments of their *establishment*."[24]

From her in-depth study of several dozen young couples living in "concubinage",[25] Sabine Chalvon-Demersay notes that "events can follow one another extremely quickly: corners are cut, intermediary phases telescoped, without restraint, without obstacle, without delay. Desire merges into its immediate satisfaction."

Young people may decide to live together after an evening when they have experienced a *coup de foudre*, without giving themselves time to "fall in love". A young woman relates: "We were immediately on very *intimate* terms and felt there were very strong bonds between us. But we didn't have time to get to know one another. We short-circuited the whole *waiting* period, the time when you find out, when you *dream* about the other, when you wait for him to look at you. Within three days we were already an old married couple."[26]

Even if other couples put off the decision to live together, they rarely delay the moment of erotic satisfaction. Time no longer represents an obstacle to the appeasement of desire, but is seen as a sign of hesitation to commit oneself. The aim remains the same for everyone: setting up house, intimacy, complicity. If necessary, they will reject the passionate phase with its uncertainties, its disquiet, its strangeness, in order to be able to love each other more quickly.

When Sylvie says: "Within three days we were already an *old married couple*," she gives a very positive meaning to what the partisans of passion would see as distressing – not to speak of the eternal Don Juans . . .

Our mutant hearts no longer seek the torments of desire. We could almost say that they wouldn't know what to do with them. The resemblance model goes together with the eradication of desire. By integrating our own otherness better than we used to, we are limiting the strangeness and mystery peculiar to the other sex. As everyone is endowed with both masculinity and femininity, we like to get a given part of the One to harmonize with a given part of the Other. It is the multiplicity of given situations that makes the special character and mystery of couples. The most manly men may be loved for their femininity, the most feminine women for their manliness. Psychologically bisexual beings "adapt themselves" as best they can to their double desires in order to find peace of heart. Even if one may seek in the Other the qualities with which one is the least endowed, this complementarity does not exclude the complicity of resemblance, or even certain homosexual feelings.

We are far from the traditional approach to desire in terms of opposition, which was a characteristic of the complementary model. Not that lack and difference play no part at all in our affections, but they serve different ends from those of the warlike ideal[27] inherent in love-as-desire. Sexual conquest is no longer the apotheosis of our love life. The perception of a loving relationship is more important than sexuality. Even if they are indissociable at first, the heart takes precedence over the body. We have therefore reversed the causal factors: understanding between bodies is subordinated to the understanding of the hearts, which becomes the couple's great adventure.

This evolution of attitudes is reflected in literature and films, which no longer tell the same stories. Yesterday, their theme was the long process of conquest, strewn with pitfalls and resistance. The "happy ending" took effect when the hero and heroine were finally about to form a couple. On the pretext that happy people have no history, no one took any more interest in what was going to become of them. The only thing that counted was the meeting of their bodies, which implied the eternal fusion of their hearts. Today, sexual conquest fascinates us less than the life of a couple, with its difficulties and its breakdowns. We are interested in the problems of communication, in family life, in divorce, in the frustration of the heroes of everyday life. The happy ending has changed its nature: people triumph over the obstacles inherent in a life in common, or they separate to form a new couple. However that may be, if desire for the other is still the prime mover of affairs of the heart, it no longer constitutes its substance. However delightful it may be, the preliminary strangeness remains a phase that must be left behind. The aim of the union is of a completely different nature. These days we cannot wait to lay down our arms and try out our complicity. It is openness that governs our loving relationships. We open our heart more widely to the Other in the hope of finding our twin. It is when passion falls silent that true love can be born, and true love is no longer merely the desire for possession and submission.

The Desire for Tenderness

The Ancients made a radical distinction between love-as-friendship and love-as-passion. The first referred to a fraternal relationship, in which sex had no place. The second characterized the erotic relationship. It seemed to them that each of these kinds of love had such different origins that when passion died it was no longer appropriate to speak of love. Eros is either passionate or it is nothing. The sociologist Francesco Alberoni reproduces the classical distinction in these terms: "Love is a passion . . . Love is ecstasy, but also torment. On the other hand, friendship has a horror of suffering . . . Friends want to be together in order to be happy. If they are not, then they leave each other . . . Love is not necessarily a reciprocal feeling, and one of its characteristics is to try to become so. Friendship, on the contrary, always demands reciprocity . . . In love, we can hate the person we love . . . In friendship, there is no room for hate."[28]

There are several indications that seem to show that the loving relationships we are looking for are more inspired by the model of friendship than by that of passion. We no longer want torment, strangeness, mistrust; we prefer serenity, openness, confidence. When there is no reciprocity we lose interest, and we are no longer prepared to eat our hearts out over a love that is not returned. Like the friends described by Alberoni, lovers want to have similar images of themselves and of each other, or at least images that are not too discordant. We get together because we are alike, and because we want to see the same reality with the same eye. Lovers walk side by side in solidarity, and face life together.

The vocabulary used to describe them today is very revealing of what their relationship has become. We speak less of lovers or spouses than of companions. Whether married or not, the Other is seen as such. Originally, the word "compagnonnage" was used to designate the trade guilds "formed for the mutual aid and protection of workers sharing the same interests"; a "compagnon" was one with whom one shared one's bread ("pain"). By extension, it has become "one who shares the feelings or ideals of another person". The term implies the identity of condition of two human beings who have fraternal feelings towards each other.

There is an apparent paradox: the lovers are brothers. The sexual relationship becomes one of the components of this fraternal relationship which contains something like a slight whiff of incest. But family feelings take precedence over those suffered by the protagonists of Madame de Lafayette or Racine. We are less concerned to dominate and possess the Other than to be loved, protected, consoled, understood, and forgiven. As Theodor W. Adorno says, the only person who really loves us is someone to whom we can show our weakness without inciting him to force. More than ever, the model of love is that of the mother for her child: we imagine it as disinterested, "oblative", and as transcending all conflicts. The archaic desire for a return to the maternal symbiosis has never been so strong, both in men and in women. The desired fusion is of the same nature, with one major exception. We seek openness in our relationships, the milk of human kindness, the perfect complicity that united us to our mother, but at the same time we reject the constraints of dependence. Even if we have no intention of using it, we consider our liberty as the essential condition of our fused relationship. Without liberty, paradise becomes hell, and tenderness turns to hate. The Ego is only prepared to put up with the voluntary alienation that participates in its emotional development. Any compulsory bond is self-defeating.

For the couple to survive, each partner must not only be the loved child, but also the mothering mother. Since we want to receive all, we must also know how to give all. Now, as we have seen, our heightened individualism makes sacrifice and devotion more difficult. We passionately love to be loved, but are we capable of loving the Other for himself? Gratuitousness has its limits and so, with them, does the maternal tenderness we so passionately desire. The solution, which is always precarious, comes through subtle negotiations which are all directed towards the satisfaction of our Ego. And when it feels injured, misunderstood, or alienated, the couple loses its whole *raison d'être*.

Our awareness of the fragility of the couple is so acute[29] that we envisage a break-up as an integral part of any love story. And yet, if marriage and divorce have come to seem simple formalities,[30] that is not all they are. There is some justification for thinking that the reason young couples are marrying less and less is not only because they refuse to make a definite commitment[31] – which is the antithesis of liberty – but also because they dread the traumas of an official dissolution, such as is becoming more and more frequent. This adds to the distress of the divorce of their hearts. Marriage is frightening because it seems ever more linked to divorce, in other words, to failure.

Marriage – no longer being a divine bond, or an alliance between two families, or an economic union – is, for those who go in for it, the ultimate proof of tenderness. Often linked to the desire for a child, it is the fruit of a long process of maturation, and not the result of a sudden, passionate impulse. As cohabitation has become common, and as marriage is being postponed for longer and longer, it is easy to see that the time of the first passions is not that of the Institution. For such couples, the traditional honeymoon, which was supposed to prepare them for conjugal life, no longer makes sense. These days, a girl marries a lover whom she knows well, and who may be called a special friend.[32]

In one sense, present-day marriage bears more resemblance to that of the classical period – in that it rejects passion as its basis – than to marriage as we knew it before the 1960s. In those days, one married the person one loved in order to found a family. Today, marriage barely changes the life of a pre-existing couple. On the other hand, the nature of the marital bond has changed radically since a number of the *Mercure galant* declared in 1678: "There is nothing so common as marriage, and nothing so uncommon as to be happy within marriage. Love, which is supposed to be the first of its guests, is almost never found therein."

Today, love-as-tenderness *is* to be found within marriage; we stay married for as long as we find satisfaction in it. On the other hand, and soon, perhaps, there will be nothing "less common" than to get married. More and more couples are persisting in refusing marriage because they cannot see what it contributes to their condition. For many, "the Institution has lost all meaning and become pointless."[33]

However that may be, the loving couple remains "the first and last value on which a union, whether legitimate or not, is based."[34] Love would like to be intense but not passionate, a peaceful not warlike relationship. The union of hearts feeds on the openness of friendship. Contrary to what we have long been led to believe, friendship is not incompatible with eroticism. It is even friendship that gives eroticism a chance to last, among the pleasures of tenderness.

Between the Warm and the Comfortable

It is customary to contrast the warmth of the couple with the coldness of solitude. Not so long ago people had such a horror of solitude that they preferred to settle for partial harmony within marriage. Today, Louis Roussel observes, we expect the couple to be a total success in all spheres: emotional, sexual, intellectual, material . . . Nothing will be done to save a shaky couple. In the name of authenticity, they separate. It's either heaven or hell.

The spectre of solitude has given way to the hell of a failed life as a couple. Unlike our forebears, we can imagine nothing worse than conjugal disagreement. The end of symbiosis, marked by the absence of dialogue, plunges us into a kind of solitude that is far more unbearable than if we were really living alone, freed from the constraints imposed by the presence of the Other. It is no longer the harshness of the solitary life that we contrast with the pleasure of a harmonious, fused life, it is the distress caused by the failure of a loving relationship. This is what we now see as real coldness, by comparison with which solitude seems almost warm.

While it is true that our demands have never been so great – our grandparents may well regard us as spoilt children – this evolution nevertheless has many positive aspects. When we lament the growing number of separations and divorces, we should bear in mind the conjugal hells of former days, which were so many life sentences. How can we ever know how many lives were ruined by hatred, violence and suffering? Today, we no longer allow couples to be pushed to such extremes. When their disagreements become apparent, they face the fact, and leave each other as "good friends". And anyway, what is the good of trying to patch things up temporarily when their hearts are no longer on the same wavelength? An unstable couple has lost its reason for remaining a couple. To pretend to ignore this smacks of a hypocrisy which runs counter to our cult of authenticity.

The result is that the number of "one-person households" has vastly increased in the last thirty years. "Around 1950, in most industrialized countries, the fraction of the population living in such households was less than three per cent . . . Since then, their number has often tripled or quadrupled."[35] In France, nearly five million have been recorded, an increase of more than seventy per cent since 1962. One in four households consists of a single person, and this proportion rises to one in two in Paris, as in New York. People who, for want of a better term, are called "celibates", form an extremely heterogeneous population. They consist of those who do actually live on their own, those who live with one or several children, part-time couples, concubines, etc. But the phenomenon that we consider important is the growing number of people who accept the risks of solitude. Even if most of them hope it will be temporary – just a phase between two liaisons – solitude is becoming a commonplace experience that is likely to come everyone's way at one stage of life or another. Formerly, it was mainly the lot of elderly women; today it is spreading among the under-thirties and the divorced. Louis Roussel thinks that the propensity to live on one's own results partially from the earlier incidence of divorces mainly occurring among childless couples whose separation creates two one-person households. Moreover, the probability of an early remarriage has considerably decreased. Even though many divorcees subsequently start living with someone else, they often take the circuitous route of a period of true solitude.

This solitary transit time has now taken on a different meaning, for the image of the celibate individual has lost its negative connotation. In traditional society, living alone was thought abnormal and suspect. In the second half of the nineteenth century, "bourgeois statisticians tracked down the unmarried in prison, hospital, asylum and morgue registers, trying to show that they were harmful and unhappy."[36] According to some people, their mortality rate was higher than that of married men, who were better cared for by their wives. Others claimed that they were the most likely to commit suicide and turn to crime. The condition of "old maids" was said to be even worse, for they could not claim to be artists or perpetual students. Michelle Perrot sums up the way they were regarded thus: "The unmarried woman was at the same time in danger and a danger. In danger of starving to death and of losing her honour. A threat to the family and to society. She was idle, and unless she devoted her time to good works, she spent it in intrigue and gossip . . . With no family on whom to exercise her power, she lived as a parasite on other people's families . . . Not having a permanent home with them, unmarried women circulated. They were seen as busybodies, procuresses, abortionists, more or less witches."[37]

Today, the celibate has the same rights as the married, since it is estimated that more than thirty-six per cent of French men and women may never marry. Moreover, solitude is sometimes the result of choice. The higher the position in the social scale, the higher the rate of celibacy; from ten per cent among female factory workers it reaches twenty-four per cent among senior women executives.[38] This comes as no surprise when we read François de Singly's statistics, which show that matrimony is a handicap for such women. When unmarried, and therefore more available, women get better jobs than unmarried men. When married, they get worse jobs than married men.[39] Female ambition and high-status careers are powerful factors in favour of solitude or separate apartments. Even if some of these women occasionally complain, and lament the absence of a great love, in the last resort they prefer their liberty to a tie they consider mediocre.

There remain the true celibates, who are celibate by choice. Such people choose to exercise their right to absolute egotism. They value their freedom[40] more highly than anything else, and consider it jeopardized by a shared life. As champions of the non-shared bed, they consider that there is more warmth in their own nest than in that of only moderately happy couples. They like discoveries, adventure, and also silence, but more than anything else, they like not feeling obliged to do things to please the Other. True, in comparison with these triumphant solitaries, there are others[41] who feel frustrated and who have secret dreams of a great love. These people have not chosen their solitude, but carry it with them like a ball and chain. Even so, their situation is not as catastrophic as it was in earlier centuries, and it is not certain that conjugal life would suit them better.

Whether chosen or imposed, whether provisional or definitive, solitude has more and more come to be preferred to a forced tie. We are learning to plan it, to enjoy our egotism. Even if it is still seen as a hardship by some, it is no longer regarded as a social and economic calamity. Psychologically, it can even be a pleasure. Whether we like it or not, it is becoming part of our life, which "is being broken up into relatively brief alternating sequences of communal life and solitary life... Side by side with the people who still experience only one cycle of family life, there is an ever increasing number of people whose biography is made up of successive periods of shared and solitary living. Everything happens to them as if they disposed of several very short lives instead of one single history."[42]

It is still some people's privilege to live a single love story until they die. And, there is no reason to believe that they will be less numerous tomorrow than they were yesterday. But if married life turns out to be unbearable, or even merely disappointing, these days we prefer the lesser warmth of our "bed of one's own". If we can't have a perfect union with the Other, we find it preferable to try to be self-sufficient and to indulge our Ego. Turning in on ourselves like this reinforces our egotism and sometimes makes it difficult for us to establish new relationships. This is the price we have to pay for our mutation. Torn between our will to independence and completeness and our desire for ideal fusion, the logic presiding over our relations with the Other swings between two extremes: indifference and interaction. If I can't be warm with You, I choose to be comfortable with Myself. But we have certainly turned our backs on the old logic of opposition that generated hatred and war.

The only choice remaining is between the warm and the comfortable.

POSTSCRIPT:

Return to the Question of Power

Our general view of time and space has allowed us to glimpse a constant complementary relationship between the sexes. Powers have been apportioned in ways that swing between an almost perfect balance and the most flagrant inequality. One way requires mutual respect; the other, brutal oppression. Even when absolute patriarchy was established, here or there, with its determination to seize every power and with its logic of exclusion, man and woman – he marked with the positive sign and she with the negative – nevertheless continued to share the world between them. Even when they possessed all the privileges and considered themselves women's masters, men still had to come to terms with the sex on which they depended for their reproduction, for the management of their daily life, and for peace with other men.

In Western societies, which demand more in the way of democracy, women have taken advantage of the dominant ideology to put an end to the inegalitarian relationship that united them to men. Seeing their traditional functions depreciated, women were no longer content with the ancient distinction between the roles, even if they were equally shared, and revalued.[1] In fighting with all their strength against the complementary model that, as we have seen, distinguishes man from the primates, women have thus initiated a type of relationship between the sexes that has no precedent in the history of humanity. The world is less and less divided into complementary masculine and feminine spheres, and now offers a uniform aspect to which each sex has equal access. The question of equality is imperceptibly becoming that of the specific character of the One and the Other.

So far, since the resemblance model goes hand in hand with the withdrawal into oneself, it seems to have dissolved the question of power. As God is no longer to be reckoned with in the West, it is becoming impossible to say what powers one sex has over the other, since they both have access to the economic, political, social, cultural, etc., spheres. It looks as if there is only one type of power left that is exercised from individual to individual: the option of indifference that results from our liberty. We can refuse to form relationships just as easily as we can separate. But this liberty is not the power of one sex over the other, because it belongs to both.

There is still one essential difference, which, thanks to science, has turned into a fundamental inequality. The fact that women bear men's children is the "natural" constant that links them to their ancestors and distinguishes them from men. But an exclusive power of decision has been added to the eternal power of procreation, and it has no equivalent for the male sex. Even if women only rarely exploit their power, men are well aware that they possess it. But how long will men go on agreeing to share everything with women except what may be the essential thing: their reproduction, and in the first place the decision to procreate? Not only has the egalitarian ideal of resemblance caused men to lose all their traditional characteristics, but the discovery of contraception has, objectively, put them in a state of inferiority. If they want a child but their partner does not, they have to admit defeat.

From men's point of view, the equality of the sexes is a trap, so long as they feel that they have made all possible concessions and got nothing in return. Moreover, many men are not far from thinking that they have been cheated. It would be understandable if their private feelings about this new stage were similar to those of women when Absolute Patriarchy was the rule: that they have been dispossessed of their powers.

On the other hand, one might be surprised at men's silence since the beginning of this extraordinary mutation some twenty years ago. There have been no books, no films, no radical thoughts on their new condition.[2] Men have remained silent, as if struck dumb by an evolution which they do not control. Apart from those who put up a show of denying the change, and from a handful of individuals who militate for true parental equality, we have observed no collective masculine awareness of the new relations between the sexes. They either deny it, put up with it, or regress in silence.

The silence of half of humanity is never a good sign. We shall have to wait, then, until sooner or later men respond to the change that has been imposed on them. Their response will certainly depend on the way they adjust to their problems of identity. Will they become better able to cohabit with their inner femininity, or will they on the contrary become more anxious about their virility?

Depending on the answer to this question, we can imagine two kinds of evolution aimed at re-establishing the balance in their favour. This may be achieved either by reinforcing the complementary schema that has now been attenuated, or by developing further the egalitarian resemblance model. As it is most unlikely that men will be able to recreate a territory or an activity that is specifically theirs – symmetrical to motherhood for women – what remains is the hypothesis of a reaction pure and simple. Given an ideological about-turn, on the pretext of the necessity of a rise in the birth rate, men could impose a brutal retrograde step on women. They would only have to deprive them of the control of their fertility[3] (the abolition of contraception and of the right to abortion), in order to force them back to the home to look after the children whose numbers they would no longer control – a solution that is not impossible in times of crisis or war.

It is possible to formulate other hypotheses which, although they might involve limits to women's total control over their procreation, would still respect the liberties they have won. For instance, men might once again assume responsibility for procreation by the use of new and improved male contraceptives. However rare may be the cases where men are treated as simple genitors, there is still a demand for liberty. If there cannot be equality where reproduction is concerned, men could easily share the power of decision not to have a child, or more precisely the responsibility for such a decision. It is true that this is only a negative liberty. But it would be no less important from the symbolic and psychological point of view.

It is also possible that men would not be content with the power to say no, and would try to deprive women of the privilege of motherhood. Any evolution in this direction would imply an unprecedented outrage committed against Nature, of a kind that terrifies the average thinking man of the twentieth century. For all that, there are many arguments that can be put forward in favour of perfecting the procedure whereby an incubator can be used for nine months as an artificial mother for an embryo fertilized *in vitro*. The misfortune of women who cannot carry a pregnancy to term, the small number of surrogate mothers and of children offered for adoption, the so disputed "right" to parenthood, may encourage scientists to work in this direction. But there is no doubt that if we do get to the point of being able to do without women's bodies, it will be men who will get the greatest benefit in the long run. They will be able to have a child without a mother, rather as some women have children without a father.

So far, no one can envisage without horror the complete development of a foetus *in vitro*, in an aseptic environment, deprived of physiological and emotional exchanges with a mother. But if human desires prevail over the dread of the unknown – which would hardly be a novelty for the human species – it is conceivable that women will one day share their prerogative with a machine.

There is still another way of stealing women's maternal power from them, which would imply an incredible revolution in our mentalities, and in particular in those of men. This is the possibility of a pregnant man. Delirium? Science fiction? Perhaps not. The two scientists principally responsible for the first French test-tube baby, Amandine, have already expressed their doubts as to whether it is an impossibility.

In April, 1985, Michèle Manceaux asked the question in the women's magazine *Marie Claire*: "Are pregnant men really a possibility?" Professor René Frydman's simple answer was: "Two years ago, I did not think so. But now, frankly, I no longer know." A few months later, in February, 1986, Professor Frydman was distinctly more affirmative. Another magazine, *Actuel*, asked him the same question and he replied: "Technically, it is possible . . . Today, the myth of masculine pregnancy could become a reality."

The hypothesis of the biologist Jacques Testart is more explicit: "We can imagine a man asking to experience a pregnancy by receiving an embryo a few days old in his stomach. Before Amandine was born, a transsexual asked us to do this. But bear in mind that from the strictly medical point of view, masculine pregnancy (like a feminine pregnancy that takes place outside the genital system), presents fatal risks."[4]

Nevertheless, Testart adds: "Masculine pregnancy is not a mere fantasy. *Two physiological ideas show that it is possible*: in the first place, the human embryo is capable of developing to term outside the womb (in the abdominal cavity), and children have been born in this way by Caesarean section; next, the hormonal adjustments that occur during pregnancy can be provided without the presence of ovaries by means of the appropriate hormonal injections."[5]

For all that, while both these men – like other doctors, in America[6] and New Zealand – express a positive opinion on the future possibilities of the pregnant man, they add that such research is utterly inappropriate. René Frydman considers it "the world upside down", and thinks that "a doctor should not agree to transplant an embryo into the abdomen of a man." Jacques Testart places the hypothesis of masculine pregnancy among the "misuses" of *in vitro* fertilization.

It is hard to grasp the philosophical and moral principles behind the rejection of this hypothesis. To judge by most men's reaction to the idea, however, one begins to doubt whether any teams of scientists will be inclined to work on such a project. Nevertheless, what is found disgusting today may perhaps be found desirable tomorrow. The male unconscious[7] had for so long been haunted by fantasies of pregnancy that some men may indeed try to put an end to that longing and powerlessness that they now discuss more and more openly.

True, the fantasy and the reality are worlds apart, but no period was ever more favourable to the realization of desires and the overthrow of prohibitions. By opening the door of the nursery to men, and by allowing them to be so closely associated with childbirth, we have brought them nearer to the baby, bringing with it the risk of arousing hitherto unacknowledged desires for maternity. Who can say today that no one will not cross this ultimate frontier, thereby completely changing the immemorial hand dealt us by Nature?

When Western society recognized women's right to get rid of their foetuses, it admitted that an adult's desire took precedence over all other considerations, and that the life of a complete human being was more important than that of a potential human being. How can we tell whether humanity will not go one step farther along the path of absolute egotism,[8] and that we will not cause children to be born in conditions that are contrary to nature, at the risk of making them subject to dangers that are impossible to evaluate? But after all, who could have sworn, only a short time ago, that the first test-tube baby would become a beautiful child just like any other?

If tomorrow's humanity agrees to allow the birth of children mothered by a machine or by a man, it is probable that this will trigger a mutation of the species. Given that such children do not turn out to be monsters, the extreme similarity of the sexes and the radical individualism that must underlie it seem to us, on the face of it, a threat to our survival. How can we accept the end of the necessary link established by nature between a female mammal and her child? How can we think of the relationship between the sexes and the survival of societies if all the links of obligatory dependence between man and woman are broken?

If prudence dictates that we refuse such hypotheses, it is nevertheless true that the *status quo* we have now reached demands, here and now, a radical re-examination of our certainties. Yesterday, everyone still agreed that the complementarity of roles and functions was the surest sign of the distinction between man and primate.[9] Today, this sign is becoming obsolete. We have to observe – not without amusement – that from the simple viewpoint of complementarity, we are now closer to the primates than to the first man. It is as if the wheel had come full circle, at least from this angle.

And yet, even if we agree that we should call a halt, we would be extremely naïve if we thought that evolution will stop at our particular stage. Perhaps it is reassuring to remember that although some species became extinct because they were unable to adapt to ecological changes, other species appeared and the world did not come to an end. Tomorrow, the human species might well secure the means to bring about an even more radical mutation. The end of Man? No, a new Mankind.

NOTES

PREFACE

1. This no longer goes without saying, now that contraception allows a woman to remain childless if she so wishes.
2. Françoise Héritier, *L'Africaine, Sexes et signes*. Cahiers du GRIF, Brussels, no. 29, p. 10

PART ONE

CHAPTER I

1. "The great defect of Europeans is always to philosophize about the origins of things on the basis of what happens around themselves." *Essai sur l'origine des langues*, Chapter 8.
2. *Race et Histoire*, Gonthier, 1967, Chapter 4.
3. André Leroi-Gourhan, *Les Religions de la préhistoire*, PUF, 1964, p. 3.
4. *Male and Female*, Pelican Books, 1962, p. 31. (Our italics.)
5. *Le Fait féminin*, Fayard, 1978, p. 400.
6. *Ibid.*, p. 387.
7. *Ibid.*, p. 387.
8. *Male and Female*, p. 84. "Between husbands and wives sex is a hasty, covert, shameful matter . . . The sex act becomes a sort of shared excretion."
9. *Ibid.*, pp. 101–2.
10. Margaret Mead, *op. cit.*, pp. 82–3: "Love-making is conducted like the first round of a prize-fight, and biting and scratching are important parts of foreplay."
11. *Anthropo-logiques*, PUF, 1974, p. 14.
12. André Leroi-Gourhan, *Le Geste et la parole*, Albin Michel, 1970, Vol. I, p. 214.
13. Sarah Hrdy, *The Woman that Never Evolved*, Harvard U.P., 1981, pp. 8–9.
14. *My Friends the Wild Chimpanzees*, National Geographic Society, 1967.

15. It is true that we sometimes read that "in the Palaeolithic Age, men and women hunted and gathered equally." And yet, although palaeontologists consider that women hunted effectively, theirs was a very different kind of hunting from that of men. No doubt they hunted the small animals they came across on their gathering grounds, but it was only the men who went off on expeditions, sometimes very far away from their homes, to hunt big game.

16. Cf. André Leroi-Gourhan, Richard Leakey, Jane Goodall, Sydney Mellen, Serge Moscovici, etc.

17. At the time of going to press (1986), Alain Testart has just published an extremely abrasive essay on *The Basis of the Sexual Division of Labour among the Hunter-Gatherers.* He aims to show that the sexual division of labour is not a natural given, but a social given linked to a complex ideology that keeps women away from all the bloody operations of the hunters.

18. Helen Fisher, *The Sex Contract*, Granada, 1982.

19. For example, cf. Owen Lovejoy, a locomotion expert much quoted by Donald Johanson and Maitland Edey in their book *Lucy: The Beginnings of Humankind*, Simon & Schuster, 1981. Lovejoy thinks that locomotion is part of an overall survival strategy, closely linked with sex, and forms part of a complicated feedback loop.

20. For the whole of the following description, cf. Helen Fisher, *op. cit.*, pp. 50ff.

21. Table taken from Johanson and Edey, *op. cit.*, p. 342.

22. All these brilliant cultures, which took their names from French sites (Perigordian, Aurignacian, Solutrean and Magdalenian), evolved during a period that lasted about 25,000 years (from 35,000 BC to 10,000 BC).

23. Signs of it are already to be found in the preceding, Neanderthal, period.

24. There were two kinds of art: parietal art, executed on rock-shelter walls, and "mobiliary" art: decorated objects, statuettes . . .

25. André Leroi-Gourhan, *Le Fil du temps*, Fayard, 1983, p. 258.

26. It's always the same divine malediction that hangs over Eve!

27. Serge Moscovici, *Society against Nature*, Tr. Sacha Rabinovitch, Harvester Press, 1976, p. 90.

28. *Les Racines du monde*, Belfond, 1982, p. 206. André Leroi-Gourhan takes up the hypothesis of M. Gerasimov, who discovered, north of Lake Baikal, very long tents in which the objects were distributed differently in the sides respectively considered masculine and feminine.

29. In central Africa, many villages possess separate "refectories" for the two sexes.
30. André Leroi-Gourhan (duplicated lecture notes, 1956-7) says that among the African bushmen (hunter-gatherers with whom Palaeolithic societies have often been compared), when some big game is killed the hunter gives a specific part (the fat, the meat from the hindquarters, the entrails) to his wife, who shares it with the other women in the camp. The rest of the animal is shared between the chief, the adolescents (not yet incorporated into the hunters' group), and the hunters themselves, according to the strict rules peculiar to each category of people.
31. *Les Racines du monde*, p. 21.
32. Representing an erect phallus.
33. André Leroi-Gourhan, *The Art of Prehistoric Man in Western Europe*, Tr. Norbert Guterman, Thames and Hudson, 1968, p. 121.
34. Cf. the caves of Les Trois-Frères, Les Combarelles, Le Gabillou, Pech-Merle, Altamira, Rouffignac, etc.
35. *Le Fil du temps*, p. 288.
36. Edgar Morin, *Le Paradigme perdu*, Le Seuil, 1973, p. 71.
37. *Ibid.*, p. 72.
38. I object to the unpleasant habit of calling every woman of science who fights against sexist prejudices a "feminist", whereas every researcher who does the opposite is respectfully termed a "scientist".
39. Nancy Tanner and Adrienne Zilhman, *Women in Evolution: Innovation and Selection in Human Origins. Signs I* (3), 1970.
40. As Donald Johanson says, *op. cit.*, p. 329: "Increased parental care . . . requires a great IQ on the part of the human mother."
41. At Lascaux, the greater part of the compositions is taken up by the theme ox–horse. At Pech-Merle, by that of bison–mammoth.
42. *The Art of Prehistoric man . . .*, p. 118. (Our italics.)
43. Eleanor Leacock, "Women in Egalitarian Societies", in Bridenthal and Koonz, *Becoming Visible: Women in European History*, Boston, Houghton Mifflin, 1977.
44. André Leroi-Gourhan, *Les Racines du monde*, p. 211. He has calculated that the average ration of reindeer meat of the Magdalenians, in a temperate climate, was eight hundred grammes per individual per day.
45. Pathfinder Press Inc., N.Y. and Toronto, 1975.
46. George Allen and Unwin, 1927.
47. Françoise d'Eaubonne's subtler and better-documented book, *Les*

Femmes avant le patriarcat, Payot, 1976, was no more successful in achieving these aims.

48. Represented by Franz Boas, and his disciples Kroeber, Lowie, etc.
49. Françoise Picq, in her thesis: "Contesting the idea that evolution was the same everywhere, they refused to consider that matrilineal filiation generally preceded patrilineal filiation, reversed the chronological order, or denied any kind of regular order."
50. Robert Lowie, *Traité de sociologie primitive*, Payot, 1969, p. 102: "Even if paternity is not established, that does not prove the necessity of descendence on the mother's side, for biological paternity and sociological paternity are two different things."
51. Both are anthropologists at Rutgers University, New Jersey.
52. Edgar Morin, *op. cit.*, p. 78.
53. In some societies, the uncle may still today be considered as the father.
54. Edgar Morin, *op. cit.*, p. 173.
55. *Ibid.*, p. 174.
56. *The Second Sex*, Tr. H. M. Parshley, Penguin, 1972, pp. 102 and 109.
57. "A matriarchal society is one in which some if not all of the legal powers relating to the ordering and governing of the family – power over property, over inheritance, over marriage, over the house – are lodged in women rather than in men." (Margaret Mead, *op. cit.*, p. 275.)
58. "We may speak of matrilineal societies, in which a man inherits his name, his land, and his position, or any one of these from his mother's brother, through his mother. This may not mean a great deal of power for women, although it is a system in which women are sufficiently favoured so that polygamy, for instance, does not work well within it." (Margaret Mead, *op. cit.*, p. 275.)
59. Excavations of prehistoric tombs have shown that the dead were sometimes buried with certain objects of their everyday life: tools and jewels. So there could not have been much left to "bequeath" to their descendants – always supposing that they had any idea of doing so.
60. It was Morgan's observation of Iroquois society and its kinship system that inclined him to put forward the matriarchal thesis.
61. Françoise Héritier, *L'Africaine. Sexes et signes*, p. 10. (Our italics.)
62. "A form of social organization in which a male is the head of the family and descent, kinship and title are traced through the male line." (*Collins English Dictionary*.)
63. Evelyn Reed, *op. cit.*, p. 13: "To us, a mother is an individual woman

who bears a child ... But in primitive society motherhood was a *social* function of the female sex; thus all women were actually or potentially 'the mothers' of the community."

64. Cf. Michelle Zimbalist Rosaldo and Louise Lamphère, Editor's introduction in *Women, Culture and Society*, Stanford University Press, 1974.

65. Sarah Hrdy, *op. cit.*, pp. 16–25.

66. International Afar Research Expedition, directed by Yves Coppens, Donald Johanson and Maurice Taieb.

67. Yves Coppens, *Le Singe, l'Afrique et l'Homme*, Fayard, 1984, pp. 86–8. "Lucy was nearly one metre tall, walked upright, her brain was of hominoid organization and her hands were capable of precise prehension."

68. Vestiges of thirteen individuals were collected and nicknamed "the first family".

69. It is generally agreed that men are on average between 15% and 20% taller than women, and that this difference is now tending to decrease.

70. Cf. the very fine book by Henri Delporte, *L'Image de la femme dans l'art préhistorique*, Picard, 1979.

71. Some forty in France; thirty-five in the Siberian group.

72. Silhouettes in profile, ithyphallic figures, sometimes an isolated phallus or a face seen from in front or in profile.

73. Cf. the man lying wounded in front of a bison at Lascaux, the three Cougnac men, and the Pech-Merle one transpierced by assegais, etc.

74. *A History of Religious Ideas*, Tr. Willard R. Trask, Collins, 1979, Vol. I, p. 36. For her part, Françoise Héritier notes that the value attributed to tasks accomplished is everywhere unequal, and that this depends neither on the amount of work done nor on the skill involved. The women's contribution – gathering – sometimes represents three-quarters of the food resources of the group, but this does not alter the fact that only hunting enjoys any real prestige.

75. *L'Africaine. Sexes et signes*, p. 20.

76. The Venus of Willendorf, the Brassempouy head, etc.

77. It is hard to understand Leroi-Gourhan's remark: "To say that these statuettes are fertility symbols leads to what?" (*Les Racines du monde*, *op. cit.*, p. 89.)

78. *The Art of Prehistoric Man* ..., pp. 121–2.

79. André Leroi-Gourhan, *Les Racines* ..., p. 90: "These 'Venuses', whose bodies are so far removed from anatomical reality, are 'reconsidered' images of woman, surrealistic, symbolic works."

80. It is certain that this hypothesis can no longer be put forward for present-day primitive societies, who know the essential part played by the man in procreation, even if the precise biological facts are not understood by them all.

81. Mircea Eliade, *Patterns in Comparative Religion*, Tr. Rosemary Sheed, Sheed and Ward, 1979. Chapter 7 describes the history of beliefs about the origin of children.

82. Mircea Eliade, *A History of Religious Ideas*, Vol. I, Chapter 1.

83. The "Great Magician" of the Trois-Frères cave was made famous by the Abbé Breuil. This is a figure with the head of a stag, the ears of a wolf, and the beard of a chamois. Only its lower limbs, its penis, and its dancer's pose indicate that it is the figure of a human being.

84. *The Art of Prehistoric Man . . .*, p. 131.

85. *L'Image de la femme . . .*, p. 307. (Our italics.)

86. In the same way as the red ochre coating of the tombs was an evocation of blood and of the vital principle.

87. *Women of Value, Men of Renown*, Austin, Texas, 1976.

88. The Trobriand Islands are part of Papua New Guinea.

89. Annette Weiner, *op. cit.*, p. 20. (Our italics.)

90. *Op. cit.*, p. 228. Annette Weiner says that Trobriand women "function within that society not as objects, but as individuals with some measure of control."

91. *Op. cit.*, Book I, Part II, Chapter 2.

92. *Op. cit.*, p. 78.

CHAPTER II

1. This transitional period between the Palaeolithic and the Neolithic is also called the Epipalaeolithic. Unfortunately, while the two later stages have left us sufficient vestiges to enable us to venture hypotheses about the relations between men and women, this is not the case with the earliest one, which has all the characteristics of a transitional phase. This final stage of the hunters' civilization inaugurates a new kind of sedentary life which heralds the Neolithic culture. But so far as we can judge from the present state of our knowledge, they did not feel the same need as their Palaeolithic ancestors and their Neolithic descendants to express their beliefs.

2. In the literal sense, "neolithic" means the age of the new polished stone, as opposed to the chipped stone of the Palaeolithic. In actual fact, what is called "the Neolithic revolution" cannot be reduced to a transformation in lithic technique, or even to an economic transformation.

3. From the Greek *khalkos*, copper. The transitional period between the Neolithic and the Bronze Age.
4. The Bronze Age and the Iron Age (2000–500 BC).
5. Gabriel Camps, *La Préhistoire. A la recherche d'un paradis perdu*, Perrin, 1982, p. 263.
6. *Ibid.*, p. 411.
7. André Leroi-Gourhan: "It is highly probable that agriculture was a feminine invention." See also Vere Gordon Childe, *Man Makes Himself*, C. A. Watts, London, 1956; Elise Boulding, *The Underside of History*, Boulder, Westview Press, 1977.
8. Lewis Mumford, *The Myth of the Machine*, Harcourt Brace, 1966–7, p. 132.
9. Lewis Mumford has very charmingly tried to recreate the Neolithic garden. Drawing on the work of Edgar Anderson, he believes that the earliest gardens must have started out simply as plots of uncultivated land that were protected because they produced edible leaves or fruits; and that they contained a mixture of different botanical species in which, either as weeds or cultivated plantlets, foods, condiments, spices, medicines, useful fibres and flowering plants grew side by side.
10. Jean Guilaine, *Premiers Bergers et Paysans de l'Occident méditerranéen*, Hachette, 1976, p. 16.
11. Ceramics appeared at the same time as the first agriculture. Jacques Cauvin discovered in Syria the oldest ceramics so far known, which he has been able to date between 8000 and 7000 BC. But cultures possessing ceramics only began to spread around 6000 BC.
12. For Vere Gordon Childe and George Thomson, there is no doubt that pottery was a feminine occupation, fire being the prerogative of women. This hypothesis is not absurd, since we know that in the ancient Indian civilization it was always women who were in charge of fire.
13. Lewis Mumford suggests a religious origin to stockbreeding. Taking up Edward Hahn's hypothesis, he thinks that the aurochs was first domesticated for religious, not economic reasons. This animal's horns were supposed to correspond to the horns of the moon. (*Op. cit.*). It is true that we find traces of a cult of the bull (in Anatolia, from the sixth millennium) as far afield as south-west Asia, and that it was still very much alive in Minoan Crete (cf. Jacques Cauvin, *Religions néolithiques de Syro-Palestine*, Maisonneuve, 1972, pp. 103–4, and Charles Picard, *Les Religions pré-helléniques*, PUF, 1948). But in the Neolithic era the cult of the bull gave way to that of the goddess.

According to P. Ducos, *L'origine des animaux domestiques en Palestine*, Delmas, Bordeaux, 1968, the sheep was the earliest domestic animal (between 9000 and 8900 BC in the north of Iraq), followed by the goat (before 7000 BC in Palestine).It is known that there were also pigs on the Lebanese coast at the beginning of the seventh millennium, and towards 6500 BC at Jarmo, in Mesopotamia. The ox appears only later, towards 5000 BC, in Palestine.

14. It was not until the beginning of the eighth millennium, in the Euphrates region (at Mireybet), that feminine representations in the form of stone statuettes and terracotta figurines appeared for the first time. Cf. Jacques Cauvin, *Les premiers Villages de Syrie–Palestine du IXe au VIIe millénaire avant J.-C.*, Lyon, 1978.

15. Gabriel Camps, *op. cit.*, p. 414.

16. *Ibid.*, p. 415: "Among the north African populations that were composed more of shepherds than of agriculturists . . . no feminine statuette belongs to the era of the beginning of the Neolithic."

17. In the Jericho region, a limestone statuette from this era has been found; it has strongly marked features, and a prominent posterior that prefigures the style that became prevalent in the fifth millennium. This is the very beginning of the explicitly feminine figurations of the Near-East, from Palestine to Anatolia, which are all very much alike.

18. It would have had between 5,000 and 7,000 inhabitants.

19. Gabriel Camps, *op. cit.*, p. 411: "The sanctuaries have revealed great numbers of figurines, in stone or terracotta. Those made of unfired clay usually represent men or animals. The fact that they are found in remote corners or outside the sanctuary, and their slight artistic interest, incline us to think that they are merely humble ex-votos. The stone statuettes, on the contrary, seem to have occupied the place of honour . . . And these almost always represent a feminine figure. They are true deities."

20. She is called the *Potnia Theron*, which means "Mistress of the wild beasts".

21. Jacques Cauvin, *Religions néolithiques . . .*, p. 88.

22. The ethnologist Camille Lacoste-Dujardin notes that in the patriarchal societies of the Maghreb, in which mothers exercise enormous power over their sons, the masculine myths and imagination are haunted by the mortiferous ogress who displays aggressive femininity.

23. With excessive development of fat on the buttocks.

24. Jacques Cauvin, *op. cit.*, p. 102.
25. Dr Wolfgang Lederer, *The Fear of Women*, Grune and Stratton, N.Y., 1968. It is probable that before she became a cow the goddess was a sow, because of that animal's fertility. This would explain why the sow, and especially its sex organs, was a sacred animal until the great religions declared it impure.
26. The Great Goddess sometimes has her abode in a tree, like Artemis later. She is portrayed as a bare tree trunk or dressed in foliage. The presence of the goddess beside a symbol of the vegetable kingdom confirms the meaning attributed to the tree in archaic mythology; that of an inexhaustible source of cosmic fertility.
27. Charles Picard, *Les Religions pré-helléniques*, pp. 74–8. In Cnossos, a Potnia with lions has been found, and another surrounded by doves. Cf. Jean Przyluski, *La Grande Déesse*, Payot, 1950, p. 96: "In a general way, the goddess is represented with wild beasts or domesticated animals. We may suppose that there are connections between these two series which may be explained by the development of techniques. The capture of live game preceded domestication. But between hunting and stockbreeding, there was a place for the activity of the tamer, and these three phases of technical evolution are reflected in the attitudes of the goddess, who was in turn huntress, tamer, and mistress of domestic animals."
28. Charles Picard, *op. cit.*, p. 109. See also the polyandric triad of Indian and Assyrian mythology.
29. Jean Przyluski, *op. cit.*, p. 27.
30. Mircea Eliade, *Patterns in Comparative Religion*, p. 262.
31. *Ibid.*, p. 243: "What we are concerned with is the idea that children were not conceived by their father, but at some more or less advanced stage of development, they were placed in their mother's womb as a result of a contact between her and some object or animal in the country round about."
32. Armenian and Peruvian legends. According to Malinowski, in the Trobriand Islands it is a spirit that penetrates the woman's body to fertilize her, even if the natives readily acknowledge that the spirit has easier access to women who have had relations with men.
33. Mircea Eliade, *op. cit.*, p. 247. The ritual of paternal adoption – which was practised in Greece and Rome – consisted in the father raising the child above the earth (which signifies its recognition) and then putting it down again, as if to show that the earth is its real mother. In this telluric view, human motherhood is seen as the continuation of divine creation, whereas paternity is only a social function. Mircea

Eliade points out that until recently this practice was still customary among the Abruzzi, the Japanese and the Scandinavians.

34. It is quite clear that these "broody" fathers, and all the members of their society who surround them and celebrate them as if they were the real mothers, do know the biological truth. What matters, though, is to elevate the father to the rank of procreator.

35. Mircea Eliade, *op. cit.*, p. 62.

36. *Ibid.*, pp. 331–2: "It is not so long since the custom still prevailed in Eastern Prussia for a naked woman to go to the fields to sow peas. Among the Finns, women used to bring the first seed to the fields in a cloth worn during menstruation . . . Again, with the Germans, it is women, and particularly married and pregnant women, who sow the grain."

37. In pre-Homeric mythology, all the gods belong to the earth and have a part in life as they do in death. The chthonian religion does not separate a dead man from the community of the living because he has his dwelling in the womb of the maternal earth. Hence the generalized pre-Homeric custom of carefully burying the dead. But this practice was later abandoned in the culture of the Homeric epic (the dead would be cremated), in which the interdependence of the dead and the living had completely ceased. In Homer, the Olympian gods belong entirely to life. They have nothing to do with the dead. It is true that while the religion of the pre-Homeric Earth gave pride of place to the maternal and the feminine – the masculine is always subordinate – the new Greek religion reversed the situation. The gods seized the goddesses' powers, as men seized those of women.

38. Charles Picard, *Les Religions pré-helléniques, op. cit.*, p. 87.

39. Pierre Vidal-Naquet, *Le Chasseur noir*, 1981; republished LD/ Fondations, 1983, p. 272: Matriarchy existed only in myths and legends. The Greek cities were opposed to them.

40. *The Iliad* mentions Amazons against whom King Priam fought.

41. When a society becomes profoundly laicized, like ours, the power of one sex over the other loses its most valuable legitimacy. By abolishing the divine foundation of power, all idea of the "natural" superiority of the One to the Other is undermined.

42. Françoise d'Eaubonne, *op. cit.*, p. 82, points out that the sexual specificity of tasks – stockbreeding by men, agriculture by women – obtained until a very much later period in some regions of Europe. The first British peasants, in megalithic times, left traces of the cultivation of wheat by women, and sheepbreeding by men.

43. Daniel Faucher, *Histoire générale des techniques*, Vol. I, PUF, 1962.

44. *Ibid.* The representations of the most primitive ploughshares, those of the cave art of the Maritime Alps and southern Sweden, date from the beginning of the Bronze Age.
45. Daniel Faucher points out that it is in ancient Mesopotamia and in Egypt that the earliest use of the swing-plough is found, and that the plough did not supersede it until the historic period.
46. Daniel Faucher: "It is probably no exaggeration to say that the swing-plough created the field."
47. As was still recently the case in Borneo. Cf. Mircea Eliade, *Patterns . . .*, p. 258.
48. Cf. Malinowski's studies of the Trobriand Islanders, or those by Spencer and Gillen of the Arunta at a time when these populations had not yet come into contact with Europeans.
49. The Trobrianders said that a woman becomes pregnant when a matrilineal ancestral spirit sends a "child-spirit" into her body.
50. Jean Przyluski, *op. cit.*, p. 161.
51. *Ibid.*, pp. 161–2. For a long time – contrary to the evidence – people refused to extend the consequences of the common experience to their heroes and kings. "Even after the beginning of the Christian era, the Andhra kings of India were still the sons of the horse, begotten by a horse that had been offered up as a sacrifice. Readily accepted for animals, the principle of procreation by the father can only have been extended to men slowly, with repugnance, and with the exclusion of exceptional individuals."
52. *Le Chasseur noir,* pp. 285–6. Pierre Vidal-Naquet points out that it was S. Pembroke who reconstructed this myth in *Women* (1967).
53. *Ibid.*, p. 286.
54. Legend has it that Cecrops was the first mythical king of Attica and the founder of Athens, then called Cecropia.
55. Max Escalon de Fonton, *La fin du monde des chasseurs et la naissance de la guerre, Courrier du CNRS*, July 1977.
56. Gabriel Camps, *op. cit.*, p. 311: "Sometimes there were veritable massacres, the best example of which is to be found in the subterranean burial ground in the Roaix caves, in the Vaucluse. There, the upper layer contains several dozen piled-up skeletons that had been buried at the same time, as well as many very elongated arrowheads, scattered among the bones."
57. Françoise d'Eaubonne, *op. cit.*, p. 59, finds them "in a hundred different countries, as far as China and the mysterious isles so frequently referred to by the Arab travellers of the eleventh and twelfth centuries."

58. *Ibid.*, p. 60: "We may cite, as a matter of interest, the Dahoman battalions, the Ethiopian gynaecocracy reported in 1600 by two explorers, the female warriors of Monomatopa, as well as the pre-1917 women's battalions in Russia, etc."

59. Jean Markale, *Women of the Celts*, Tr. A. Mygind, C. Hauch, P. Henry, Gordon Cremonesi, London, 1975, p. 32, quotes the historical example of Boadicea, queen of the Iceni, who, having seen her daughters raped by Roman legionaries, led the great revolt of AD 61 against Roman rule in Britain. "This revolt united all the people of the island after the slaughter of the Druids . . . by the army of Suetonius Paulinius."

60. André Pelletier, *La Femme dans la société gallo-romaine*, Picard, 1984, p. 13.

61. *Plutarch's Lives* (Caius Marius), The Dryden translation revised by Arthur Hugh Clough, Dent, Everyman's Library, Vol. II, p. 90, 1962 reprint.

62. Françoise Héritier points out that in certain Amerindian societies, the women used to hunt and also go to war with the men.

63. Françoise Héritier, *Le Fait féminin*, p. 399, admits that "There were indeed, here and there, warrior women," and that in certain societies (Amerindian and Gallic) women did accompany men when they went hunting or to war. But: "They did not lead them. They accompanied them." And it was only unmarried girls or young concubines who were allowed to do so, "so long as they had not acquired the normal status of married women."

64. A. Moret, *Mélanges offerts à Jean Capart*, Brussels, 1935, p. 312.

65. *Ibid.*, p. 325: "Cave bas-reliefs of this period describe the processions and ceremonies of the mystical marriage that unites the Great God and the Great Goddess."

66. Françoise d'Eaubonne rightly points out that in the megalithic period in western Europe and the African coast (from the end of the third millennium until the beginning of the first), divine dualism also existed. It was represented by two different types of mineral formations: *menhirs*, phallic columns with an ovoid top (verticality), and *dolmens* (horizontality). She expresses surprise that so little interest has been taken in the feminine symbolism of the dolmen, whereas anyone can see the phallic aspect of the menhir. And she reminds us that for the Khassi, of Assam, dolmens are the representations of the Great Mother of the clan, and menhirs those of the Great Father. (*Op. cit.*, pp. 88 and 98.)

67. Jean Przyluski, *op. cit.*, p. 153.

68. *Ibid*, p. 162. The unisexual dyad is also found in Greek, Latin, Etruscan, and even Japanese mythology.
69. Jean Przyluski, *op cit.*, p. 163: "The couple formed by the goddess and a young god serves as a transition between the two conceptions. The young god is both son and lover, because he was at first a substitute for a goddess who was the daughter of the Great Mother."
70. Cf. Pauline Schmitt-Pantel, *Une histoire des femmes est-elle possible?* Rivages, 1984; Jean-Pierre Vernant, *Myth and Thought among the Greeks*, Routledge, 1983; Pierre Vidal-Naquet, *Le Chasseur noir*; Nicole Loraux, *Le lit et la guerre*, 1981.
71. *Myth and Thought . . .* , Chapter 5.
72. *Ibid.*, p. 133: Vernant cites the case of marriage, in which "this orientation of the man towards the exterior and the woman towards the interior is reversed. In marriage, in contrast to all other social activities, it is the woman who is the mobile social element, whose movement creates the link among different family groups, whereas the man remains tied to his own hearth and home. The ambiguity of the female status lies thus in the fact that the daughter of the house . . . can nevertheless not fulfil herself as a woman in marriage without renouncing the hearth of which she is in charge."
73. *Ibid.*, p. 141: As goddess of the hearth and home, Hestia presides over the meals that are at the same time closed and open on to the outside. On the one hand, when the ancients sacrificed to Hestia, they took their meals together and would not allow any stranger at their table. At the same time, however, it is also the function of the hearth, the meal and the food, to open "the domestic circle to those who are not members of the family", to enrol them in the family community.
74. *Ibid.*, p. 142. (Our italics.)
75. *Le Chasseur noir*, p. 191.
76. *Ibid.*, p. 205.
77. *Le lit et la guerre*, pp. 37–67.
78. *Ibid.*, p. 39: "True, the censorship forbade the actual birth to be depicted; time, on the steles, is immobilized into a before or an after: her waistband ungirded, her hair undone, the suffering woman abandons herself to the arms of her waiting-maids . . . or else the dead woman casts a vague eye on the newborn baby . . . This is what really matters: just like the soldier, whose image is for ever that of a combatant, the new mother has won honour in death."
79. Nicole Loraux cites P. Chautraine, *Dictionnaire étymologique de la*

langue grecque, Paris, 1968: "All the derivations of *lokhos* relate either to childbirth or to military usage."

80. *The Medea of Euripides*, Tr. Rex Warner, John Lane, The Bodley Head, 1944, p. 18.
81. Nicole Loraux, *op. cit.*, p. 45.
82. *Ibid.*, p. 66.
83. Jean-Pierre Vernant, *Myth and Society in Ancient Greece*, Tr. Janet Lloyd, Methuen, 1982, p. 54: "The status of women, like that of their sons, whether legitimate or bastards, thus depended to a large extent upon the *time* or honour in which they were held by the head of the family."
84. *Ibid.*
85. Jean Przyluski, *op. cit.*, p. 170.
86. Indira Mahindra, *The Rebellious Home-Makers*, S.N.D.T. Women's University, Bombay, 1980, pp. 36–40.
87. History mentions the names of Shashiyasi, Vadhrimati and Vishpata.
88. Jean Markale, *Women of the Celts*, p. 31. He points out that in this moderate patriarchal system, the basis of the family was the couple. The woman had a theoretical right to choose her own husband, but in any case she could not be married without her consent. In contrast to Roman law, an Irish woman "did not become a member of her husband's family." She still owned her own property and could get a divorce easily. And even though the man was termed "the head of the family", there existed two cases in Irish law in which he was no longer the head of the couple. The first was when the wife was as well off and of just as good a family as he; here the spouses were completely equal. The second was when she was better off than her husband, in which case she was the uncontested head of the family. This situation is inconceivable in later patriarchal societies which set their seal, in the name of God, on the idea of the natural inferiority of women.

PART TWO
CHAPTER I

1. There are very many forms of patriarchy. The most moderate – those which grant women a certain number of prerogatives – may allow relatively balanced relations between the sexes. There are others, on the other hand, in which man sets himself up as absolute master and appropriates all powers. These systems result in extreme dissymmetry between the sexes, and may be called absolute patriarchies.

2. Germaine Tillion, *Le Harem et les Cousins*, Le Seuil, 1966, p. 6.
3. Jean Guilaine, *La France d'avant la France, du néolithique à l'âge du fer*, Hachette/Littérature, p. 39: As early as "the fifth millennium, in Europe, the exchange of women between communities may have contributed to the spread of new ideas and techniques."
4. We shall be concentrating on absolute patriarchy, because the caricatural ideology that underlies it makes it easier to perceive the basic principles of the system.
5. A myth abounding in meaning, analysed by Phyllis Chesler in *Women and Madness*, Allen Lane, 1974. The ethno-psychoanalyst Georges Devereux has also written at length about this myth in his *Baubo, la vulve mythique*, J.-C. Godefroy, 1983.
6. Phyllis Chesler, *op. cit.*, p. xiv.
7. J. Guilaine, *op. cit.*, sees proof of this in the wealth of the Armorian tombs, which lends credence to the suggestion of a hierarchized society in which the warrior chief is the object of particular respect (p. 160).
8. Jean Markale, *op. cit.* "The blonde Iseult is the sun personified."
9. In *Homer's Odysseys*, Tr. George Chapman, *To Earth, the Mother of All*, George Newnes, 1904, p. 564.
10. The following account is taken from Fatna Aït Sabbah, *La Femme dans l'inconscient musulman*, Le Sycomore, 1982, pp. 179–81.
11. Jean Markale, *op. cit.*, Chapter 6.
12. Abraham's "dates are a matter of controversy – fifteenth or twenty-first centuries BC, with modern scholarship veering to the fifteenth century BC." Peter Calvocoressi, *Who's Who in the Bible*, Penguin, 1988.
13. Mircea Eliade, *A History . . .* , p. 172. "He . . . manifests himself as 'the god of my/thy/his father' (*Gen.* 31, 5) . . ." "The god of thy father Abraham" . . . "The god of Isaac . . ."
14. André Chouraqui, *Des hommes de la Bible*, Hachette, 1985.
15. Jean Markale, *op. cit.*, p. 118.
16. A fourteenth-century work, *Le Songe du verger*, Book I, Chapter CXLVI.
17. Émile Benveniste, *Indo-European Language and Society*, Tr. Elizabeth Palmer, Faber, 1973. Benveniste points out that in Indo-European the name of the father (*Pater*) is solidly established. Its use in mythology is significant: it is the permanent qualification of the supreme God. But in its original representation it excludes the relation of physical paternity. The word *atta* designates the foster-father who brings up the child.

18. *Genesis* 2, 18–23. After God had made the woman out of his rib, Adam exclaimed: "This is now bone of my bones, and flesh of my flesh: she shall be called Woman because she was taken out of Man."

19. Myth related by Serge Dunis, *Sans tabou ni totem*, Fayard, 1984, p. 50. (Our italics.)

20. Aryan narratives also deny women's participation in the creation of the universe and of human beings. Creation, according to Manu, was a specifically masculine undertaking: "Learn . . . that the being whom the divine male, called Viraj, produced by himself, is I, Manu, the creator of the entire universe." (*The Laws of Manu*, Book 9, verses 34–6.)

21. Jean-Pierre Vernant, *Myth and Thought* . . . , p. 143; defines the institution of the *epikleros* by reference to the laws of Manu: "He who is without a son may instruct his daughter to provide him with one . . . The day the girl . . . gives birth to a son, the maternal grandfather becomes the father of the child."

22. Penguin Classics, 1956, Tr. Philip Vellacott, pp. 169–70. (Our italics.)

23. For Aristotle, form, "essence", is "the act", or rather the perfection, that bears the stamp of the divine. Matter, on the other hand, is merely being *in posse*, indeterminacy, which is characterized by passivity.

24. *De Generatione Animalum*, Book I.

25. *De Anima*, II.

26. *Metaphysica, De Generatione* . . .

27. *De Generatione* . . .

28. *Ibid.*

29. *Metaphysica.* "Para Phusin" generation. For example, when a horse begets a mule.

30. *De Generatione* . . . "The first genetic deviation is the birth of a female instead of a male."

31. *Ibid.* In this respect, it is difficult not to recall the theories about the feminine sex put forward by Freud, who was perhaps the last great theoretician of patriarchy.

32. *Ibid.* Females are by nature weaker, and indeed colder, and their nature must be considered as a natural defect. There will also be a monstrosity when a male child resembles his mother.

33. Indira Mahindra, *The Rebellious Home-Makers*, pp. 45–6. In the absence of any definite historical reference, the laws of Manu have been approximately dated to 1200–1500 BC.

34. *The Laws of Manu*, Book 9, lines 33–7, 44.

35. The *Koran*, Tr. N. J. Dawood, Penguin Books, 1987.

36. *Ibid.*

NOTES to pp. 72-75

37. *Op. cit.*, p. 78.
38. Geneviève Delaisi de Parseval sums up very charmingly the three principal theories of conception. There is the one in which *the woman simply serves as a hotel:* her uterus harbours the foetus, but it is fed entirely by the father or fathers. There is the one in which *the woman serves as a hotel-restaurant and provides half-board:* the father and mother are both said to contribute to the growth of the foetus. There is the one in which *the woman serves as a hotel-restaurant and provides full board:* the mother provides everything the foetus needs. Here, the father is considered unnecessary, if not dangerous. (*La Part du père*, Le Seuil, 1981, pp. 42–3.)
39. Quoted by Margaret Mead, *op. cit.*, p. 52.
40. Cf. Lévi-Strauss, *Introduction to a Science of Mythology*, I, 2, 3.
41. "A custom . . . whereby a man imitates the behaviour, etc., of his pregnant wife and at the time of birth is put to bed as though he were bearing the child." (*Collins English Dictionary.*)
42. Quoted and italicized by Bernard This, *Le Père: acte de naissance*, Le Seuil, 1980, p. 184.
43. Quoted and italicized by Bernard This, *op. cit.*, p. 185. He adds: "In the fourteenth century, Marco Polo describes similar events in a province in China. Others have studied couvade in southern India, Malaysia, and America. In all these places, when the baby is born, the father lies down and looks after it."
44. *La Part du père*, p. 68. "The European rite seems to be concerned only with the pseudo-maternal, peri- and post-natal couvade (the initiatory couvade where the man takes on the work of the woman who gives birth), and this differs from other practices, notably those of South America, in which a phase of pre-natal taboos may be observed." But this is of no great importance, because in every case the father mimes one or several stages of motherhood.
45. *The Politics of Reproductive Ritual*, University of California Press, 1981.
46. Geneviève Delaisi de Parseval, *op. cit.*, pp. 75–6.
47. *The Savage Mind*, Weidenfeld & Nicolson, 1966.
48. Geneviève Delaisi de Parseval, *op cit.*, p. 95.
49. Margaret Mead, *op. cit.*, p. 110.
50. *Ibid.*, p. 111: "Sometimes more overtly, sometimes less, these initiations go on, as the initiates are swallowed by the crocodile that represents the men's group and come out new-born at the other end; as they are housed in wombs or fed on blood, fattened, hand-fed, and tended by male 'mothers'. Behind the cult lies the myth that in some way all of this was stolen from the women; sometimes women

were killed to get it. Men owe their manhood to a theft and theatrical mime, which would fall to the ground in a moment as mere dust and ashes if its true constituents were known."

51. J. G. Frazer, *The Golden Bough*, Macmillan, 1963, pp. 911–12, quoted and commented on by Bruno Bettelheim in *Symbolic Wounds*, Thames and Hudson, 1955.

52. *La Production des grands hommes*, Fayard, 1982.

53. Note the close analogies with Aristotle's theory.

54. The Baruya think that the women's milk comes from the men's sperm.

55. *La Production . . .* , pp. 91–2. This custom, which disappeared after the arrival of the Europeans in 1960, still subsists, according to Godelier, in the Anga tribes who live in the mountains and forests, where they are less accessible to the influence of the Europeans.

56. *Ibid.*, p. 12: "In their eyes, every aspect of masculine domination, whether economic, political or symbolic, is explained by the different place occupied by each sex in the process of the reproduction of life."

57. Margaret Mead, *op. cit.*, p. 275. We may add that this notion, common to patriarchal societies, sometimes contains a few variants. In matrilineal-type social structures, the girl child is dependent on her maternal uncle, and her mother is dependent on her brother. But whatever the modality, ethnologists observe that basically there is everywhere domination by men over women.

58. Georges Duby, *The Knight, the Lady and the Priest*, Tr. Barbara Bray, Penguin Books, 1985, p. 18.

59. Claude Lévi-Strauss, *The Elementary Structures of Kinship*, Tr. James Harle Bell, John Richard von Sturmer and Rodney Needham, Beacon Press, Boston, 1969, pp. 60–1.

60. *Ibid.*, p. 37: "Only limitations born of the environment and culture are responsible for their suppression. Consequently, to our eyes, monogamy is not a positive institution, but merely constitutes the limit of polygamy in societies where . . . economic and sexual competition reaches an acute form."

61. *Ibid.*, p. 38.

62. Helen Fisher, *The Sex Contract*, pp. 10–11: "Nature has provided the human female with a clitoris, a bundle of nerves designed solely for sex." While men's orgasms follow the same principle as those of women, women's sex organs generate more intense pleasure than those of men. "At orgasm a man normally feels three or four major contractions followed by a few irregular minor ones, all localized in the genital area. Then sex is over. The blood totally diffuses, the

penis goes limp, and the male must start from the beginning to achieve orgasm again. The female pattern is very different. She normally feels five to eight major contractions and then nine to fifteen minor ones, and they diffuse throughout the entire pelvic area. But for her, sex may have just begun. Unlike her mate, her genitals have not expelled all the blood, and if she knows how, she can climax again soon, and again and again if she wants to."

63. *Ibid.*, p. 11: "As recently as 1966, not one man or woman among the inhabitants of a rural Irish island had ever heard of female orgasm. But sexual behaviour in that region was severely repressed."

64. Lévi-Strauss, *The Elementary Structures . . .* , p. 39.

65. *Ibid.*, p. 39: "The Pygmies . . . say that 'the more women available, the more food'."

66. *Ibid.*, p. 68.

67. *Ibid.*, pp. 115-16. (Our italics.)

68. *The Knight, the Lady and the Priest*, pp. 104-5.

69. Georges Duby, *William Marshal, The Flower of Chivalry*, Tr. Richard Howard, Faber, 1985, pp. 135-6.

70. Georges Duby, *The Knight . . .* , pp. 41-2.

71. *Ibid.*, pp. 100-6: Indeed, the rights of wives had been so effectively suppressed by those of the husband that in the eleventh century some fathers saw this as an intolerable threat to the property of their own line. Such a father's answer to his son-in-law's threats was to reduce the right of a married daughter to the inheritance to the minimum, "limiting her claim to property that had once formed her mother's dowry and now formed her own."

72. *Ibid.*, p. 94.

73. Georges Duby, *William Marshal . . .* , pp. 119-20.

74. *Ibid.*, p. 47.

75. *Ibid.*, p. 53.

76. Lord Raglan, *Jocasta's Crime*, Methuen, 1933.

77. Lippert, *Evolution of Culture*, New York, Macmillan, 1931, shows that in the laws of Manu it is said that "a child belongs to its father in the same way as the owner of the cow becomes the owner of the calf." Quoted by Evelyn Reed, *op. cit.*, p. 422.

78. Georges Duby, *The Knight . . .* , p. 46.

79. See Nancy Marval, *The Case for Feminist Celibacy*, quoted by Sarah Hrdy, *op. cit.* In 1986 it was reckoned that there were 80 million excised women in the patriarchal world and several tens of millions veiled, to conceal them from the gaze of men who are not their husbands.

80. The lover was only charged with being an accomplice to the act of adultery, and more often men were only punished if they had committed adultery in the conjugal domicile.
81. Lévi-Strauss's italics, *op. cit.*, p. 115, note 1.
82. *Ibid.*, p. 116: Describing the case of the Menangkabau of Sumatra, where a husband is called *orang samando*, "borrowed man", Lévi-Strauss stresses the fact that in such systems "it is the brother or eldest son of the mother's family who holds and wields authority." In all other known cases, matrilineal descent is accompanied by patrilocal residence. "The husband is a stranger . . . sometimes an enemy, and yet the woman goes away to live with him in his village to bear children who will never be his." In such cases, "matrilineal descent is the authority of the woman's father or brother extended to the brother-in-law's village."
83. G. Murdock, quoted by Lévi-Strauss, *ibid.*, pp. 116–17.
84. *Ibid.*, pp. 116–17. (Our italics.)
85. *Ibid.*, p. 117. (Our italics.)
86. *Ibid.*, p. 115.
87. Serge Moscovici, *Society against Nature*, pp. 113–14.

CHAPTER II
1. The Greek philosophical and medical thought of Aristotle or Hippocrates conceives of the equilibrium of the world and the health of the human body as a harmonious mixture of opposites. Wisdom and medicine have no other aims than to re-establish the "natural" equilibrium, threatened by one excess or another. The principal categories are those of hot and cold, dry and wet, each related to the masculine or the feminine, and assigned a positive or negative value. Aristotle, and his contemporaries also, thought that the hot and the dry are positive, the cold and the wet are negative. No one will be surprised that the male should be on the right side and the female on the wrong. But even though the proportions vary, complementarity still persists in the logic of opposites.
2. Having defined Émile at some length as an active, impetuous, strong, courageous and intelligent creature, Rousseau paints the portrait of a passive, timid, weak and submissive wife. "Specially created to please the opposite sex", Sophie is to be brought up to be a coquette, not very intelligent, and to be content to play second fiddle . . . It is her "nature" not to have been created for herself, but "to be subdued by her man . . . to be agreeable to him . . . to give in to him and even to bear with him when he is unjust".

3. Quoted by Indira Mahindra, *op. cit.*, p. 51.
4. Georges Duby, *The Knight* . . . , p. 212.
5. *Ibid.*, p. 46.
6. George Duby, *op. cit.*, p. 216.
7. The pseudonym of the author of *La Femme dans l'inconscient musulman*, Le Sycomore, 1982.
8. *The Perfumed Garden*, by Sheikh Mohammed.
9. *Comment le vieillard retrouvera sa jeunesse par la puissance sexuelle*, by Ibn Suleyman, better known under the name of Kamal Pact.
10. Fatna Aït Sabbah notes that these two books are available in the streets and bookshops of the medinas at an absurdly low price.
11. The author tells us that these manuals are to be found everywhere in bookshop windows and at the entrance to mosques.
12. *The Koran*, Tr. N. J. Dawood, Penguin Books, 1987 reprint, Sura 4, p. 366. Polygamy gives man the right to share his favours among four legitimate wives, as well as innumerable concubines.
13. Georges Duby, *op. cit.*, pp. 213–15. This sort of Christian para-liturgy, first set down between 1050 and 1170, was addressed to an aristocratic audience and performed in a church. It has four characters: Adam, the husband; Eve, the wife; God, or good; Satan, or evil.
14. Quoted by Georges Duby, *op. cit.*, p. 61.
15. *Ibid.*, p. 65.
16. *Ibid.*, p. 65.
17. *Ibid.*, p. 66.
18. *Ibid.*, p. 72.
19. *Les Rôles masculins et féminins*, PUF, 1964.
20. *Anthropo-logiques*, p. 34. Fatna Aït Sabbah also talks of "a reification of women as a condition of patriarchal strategy", *op. cit.*, p. 78.
21. Helene Deutsch, *The Psychology of Women*, Vol. I, Grune & Stratton, N.Y., 1944, Chapter 8.
22. Georges Balandier, *op. cit.*, p. 34.
23. Fatna Aït Sabbah, *op. cit.*, p. 58. This destructive intelligence characteristic of the feminine sex is called *Kayd* in the *Koran* and is one of the key concepts in the Muslim order.
24. Georges Duby, *The Knight* . . . , p. 106.
25. Camille Lacoste-Dujardin, *op. cit.*, p. 79, makes the same observation about societies in the Maghreb. Marriage, she says, is not a consequence of the "couple" (a Eurocentric notion), but a step taken to increase the patrilineal family. And Wédad Zénié-Ziegler reports this dialogue with a group of Egyptian peasant women: "With us

fellaheen, a girl isn't allowed to say no to her parents." "Are you forbidden to love?" "Yes, we are forbidden to love. There are no discussions. A girl has to accept the man she is given, even if he is deformed, deaf, blind or an imbecile." (*La Face voilée des femmes d'Égypte*, Mercure de France, 1985, p. 36.)

26. Denis de Rougemont, *Love in the Western World*, Tr. Montgomery Belgion, Princeton U.P., Revised edition, 1983.

27. *Ibid.*, p. 19. Denis de Rougemont envisages *Tristan* not as a piece of literature, but as typical of the relations between man and woman, in a particular historical group – "the dominant social caste, the courtly society, saturated with chivalry, of the twelfth and thirteenth centuries."

28. *Ibid.*, p. 39.

29. *Ibid.*, p. 40.

30. *Ibid.*, p. 53. See also the Marquis de Sade and Georges Bataille on the link between desire and death.

31. *The Perfumed Garden*, quoted by Fatna Aït Sabbah, *op. cit.*

32. *Op. cit.*, p. 25.

33. Godelier, *La Production des grands hommes*, p. 109. The menstrual blood which is opposed to sperm is an indispensable condition for the manifestation of the creative power of the woman's womb. In this substance, then, she possesses a power that is different from that of men, and necessary for the reproduction of life.

34. *Ibid.*, p. 227. The flute is the symbol of the power to make children be born, and grow.

35. *Ibid.*, p. 119.

36. *Ibid.*, pp. 234–6.

37. Cf. the work of Melanie Klein.

38. Fatna Aït Sabbah, *op. cit.*, p. 107.

39. See the innumerable legends of the *Vagina dentata*. In India, many tales tell of women whose vagina is full of teeth that cut off the man's penis (cf. Wolfgang Lederer, *The Fear of Women*, p. 45).

40. In the fabulous kingdom of Prester John, throughout the Middle Ages it was serpents which were to be found in the vagina. Elsewhere, it was wild beasts which guarded its entrance.

41. One should not think, however, that fear of the feminine sex is confined to primitive societies. Ours have nothing to envy them in this respect, as many an obscene ditty sung in doctors' common rooms bears witness.

42. Serge Dunis, *op. cit.*, pp. 197–8. *Po* means "shadows".

43. Everything that follows is taken from Serge Dunis, *op. cit.*, pp. 199–200, and p. 415.

44. *Ibid.*, p. 211. Taranga is a name designating both penis and vulva. She possesses the distinctive chignon of the chiefs (*tikitiki*). Which suggests her bisexual nature, all the more so as there is no mention of Maui's father.

45. *The Second Sex*, pp. 177–8.

46. We will not deny that in other societies, the feminine, and even maternal, figuration of death has a soothing, consoling function.

47. Cf. the work of Robert Stoller, of which more later.

48. Margaret Mead, *op. cit.*, p. 156.

49. "Let us now consider why the femininity complex of men seems to much more obscure than the castration complex in women, with which it is equally important." Melanie Klein, *Contributions to Psychoanalysis 1921–1945*, Hogarth Press, 1947, p. 207.

50. Marcel Griaule, *Conversations with Ogotemmêli*, Tr. Ralph Butler, Audrey Richards, Beatrice Hook, OUP, 1965.

51. George Groddeck, *Le double sexe de l'être humain* in *Nouvelle Revue de psychanalyse*, no. 7, spring 1973, pp. 193–8.

52. Roger Lewinter, *Groddeck: (anti) judaïsme et bisexualité*, in *Nouvelle Revue de psychanalyse*, no. 7, spring 1973, p. 200.

53. *The Ritual, Couvade and the Fear of Retaliation*, Hogarth Press, 1931.

54. *Psychanalyse et Anthropologie*, Gallimard.

55. Maurice Godelier, *op. cit.*, p. 84.

56. Rita Thalman, *Être femme sous le IIIe Reich*, Laffont, 1982, p. 66.

57. *Ibid.*, p. 84. On Hitler's accession to the Chancellorship, the decree of 7 April 1933 began the purge of women in the form of suspensions and dismissals.

58. *Ibid.*, p. 92. Law of 25 April 1933, supplemented by an order of 28 December.

59. Free seats for entertainments (!), priority in holiday centres (!), transformation of Mother's Day into a national holiday in 1935, award of medals, etc.

60. Who said that however high the rank enjoyed by a woman among the members of her own sex, she would still be far from equalling the most mediocre of men.

61. Maurice Godelier, *op. cit.*, p. 122. "It is in the forest that man receives from the big trees the sap that is going to become his sperm, it is in the forest that he hunts, kills, tests his strength, his resistance, and his mastery over the means of destruction."

62. In her study of the patriarchal societies in the Maghreb, Camille Lacoste-Dujardin stresses the profound dichotomy that exists between the masculine and feminine universes, the absence of

communication that makes the choice of a partner impossible, the severe disapproval of conjugal intimacy, the lack of expectation of affection from this relationship, and finally, the total ignorance of any such thing as the ideology of the couple. (*Op. cit.*, pp. 79, 92, 223.)

63. *L'Africaine, op. cit.*, p. 9.

CHAPTER III

1. Bossuet, *Politique tirée des propres paroles de l'Écriture Sainte (1709)*, Books II and III.
2. There is no power that does not come from God.
3. Jean Lacroix, *Paternité et démocratie*, in Revue *Esprit*, May 1947. And Albert Camus, in *The Rebel*, writes of the execution of Louis XVI: "God totters, and the law, in order to assert its equality, has to strike the final blow against him by making a direct attack on his representative on earth."
4. Robespierre had asserted the necessity of this fundamental act in advance, and proclaimed in the Convention that the Republic could only be found innocent if the king was guilty. For the nation to live, he said, the king must die. (Speech of 3 December 1792.)
5. Article quoted. Lacroix reminds us that the Constitution of 3 September 1791 calls for the establishment of national holidays "to foster fraternity between citizens".
6. Jean Lacroix, article quoted. "The most characteristic feature of modern consciousness is no doubt that faith in man implies the end of faith in God."
7. Jean Dupuy *La laïcité dans les déclarations internationales des droits de l'homme*, in *La Laïcité*, PUF, 1960.
8. André Latreille, *L'Église catholique et la laïcité*, in *La Laïcité, op. cit.*
9. Jean Dupuy, *op. cit.* These were the American and Brazilian delegations, supported by most Latin American countries.
10. *De l'égalité des deux sexes*, Reissued 1984, Fayard.
11. Thomas, *Sur le caractère, les moeurs et l'esprit des femmes*, 1772.
12. *Sur les femmes*, 1 April 1772.
13. Jean-Marie Dolle, *Diderot, politique et éducation*, Vrin, 1973.
14. *Correspondence with the Abbé Galiani*, Letter 107, 14 March 1772.
15. Women had few defenders among the revolutionaries. Among them we may cite the Abbé Grégoire, Pierre Guyomar, Saint-Just, Chabot, Cambacérès, Charlier.
16. *Lettres d'un bourgeois de New Haven à un citoyen de Virginie*, in *Recherches sur les États-Unis*, Book I, 1788.

17. *Ibid.* (Our italics.)
18. *Mémoire sur l'éducation des femmes*, which accompanied the plan for the general organization of Public Education presented to the Assemblée nationale on 20–21 April 1792. (Our italics.)
19. Article 1: Woman is born free and remains the equal of man. Article 2: The aim of all association is the preservation of the natural rights of woman; these rights are liberty, property, security, and above all, resistance to oppression.
20. The plan was adjourned by the Convention in August 1793.
21. Cf. Article 212 of the Civil Code.
22. There are still today a few Swiss cantons where women do not have the right to vote.
23. In 1914, American women had the right to vote in every State except New Mexico.
24. German women were given the vote in 1919 by the Weimar Constitution.
25. The English electoral law of 1918 granted the vote to all men over 21 and to women over 30. The age limit was abolished in 1928.
26. Mill was elected the member for Westminster in 1865, where he advocated the right of women to vote, but where, though highly respected, he made no great mark. He published *The Subjection of Women* in 1869.
27. In 1879, Bebel published a very important book: *Women in the Past, Present and Future*, Tr. H. B. A. Walther, London 1885.
28. On 20 April 1945, women voted in the municipal elections, and later that year, 21 October, in those for the Constituent Assembly.
29. Irène Joliot-Curie for Scientific research, Suzanne Lacor for Public Health, and Cécile Brunschvicg for National Education.
30. Madame Peyroles in the Constituent Assembly, 19 March 1946. France was one of the last democratic countries in Europe to grant women this right.
31. Title of a novel by Colette Yver (1913). The word refers pejoratively to women intellectuals.
32. The suffragette party made itself known to the world in 1905. The militant women organized tumultuous marches in London.
33. Léon Abensour, *Histoire générale du féminisme*, Ressources, 1921. Norway, liberated from Sweden, gave women the vote in 1907.
34. Tocqueville, *De la démocratie en Amérique*, Flammarion, 1981. "In almost all Protestant nations, girls are infinitely more the mistresses of their own actions than they are among the Catholic peoples . . ." Women's independence "is even greater in the Protestant countries

which, like England, have kept or acquired the right to govern themselves. Liberty then penetrates into families through political habits and religious beliefs."

35. "Instead of making her distrust herself, they continually try to increase her confidence in her own forces . . . to give her an early knowledge of everything."

36. 30 October 1867: Victor Duruy circular on secondary education for girls.

37. 21 December 1880: Camille Sée law establishing secondary education for girls, and at the same time laws concerning the obligatory establishment of training colleges for girls, laws making primary schools free, compulsory, and secular.

38. In 1889, the Neo-Malthusian Paul Robin opened an information centre in Paris where contraceptives were sold. Nelly Roussel, Madeleine Pelletier, Marie Huot and Jeanne Dubois also joined in the battle.

39. It was in the country of Malthus that the brothers Drysdale founded the first Neo-Malthusian organization in 1877.

40. The first clinic where midwives taught the use of contraceptives was opened in 1878. In 1895 the Neo-Malthusian League was recognized by royal decree as being in the public interest.

41. The first German Neo-Malthusian league was founded in 1892.

42. A couple called Humbert were sentenced to five and two years of prison respectively, for propaganda against the advocates of an increased birthrate.

43. At the 1930 Lambeth Conference, the Anglican Church agreed that birth control served a useful purpose, in spite of the opposition of a minority (193 in favour, 67 against).

44. Maria-Antonietta Macciocchi, *Les Femmes et leurs maîtres*, Christian Bourgois, 1978. It should be noted that the Pétain regime did not weigh so heavily on women as did the three Fascist countries mentioned.

45. Liberalization of marriage and divorce; contraception and abortion on demand.

46. On 19 December 1917 and 17 October 1918, Lenin promulgated two decrees that granted women the right to economic, social and sexual self-determination.

47. At the 1932 Congress of Kiev, abortion was decried. There was talk of the preservation of the race. In 1944, legal abortion was abolished, and anyone helping a woman to have an abortion became liable to two years' imprisonment. In March 1934, the former Tsarist

legislation penalizing homosexuality was readopted and sentences of between three and eight years' imprisonment could be given. In 1936, a new law made divorce subject to fines, and was reinforced in 1944 by a severer law. Illegitimacy was once again penalized and both mother and child were stigmatized. The father was no longer held responsible. The laws of 1936 and 1946 gave benefits to mothers of six children, etc.

48. Women of the privileged classes were called "mistress of the house".

49. In 1877, the Swiss biologist Herman Fol had once and for all put an end to the millenarian polemic by observing for the first time the penetration of the sperm in the starfish. He showed that the paternal and maternal reproductive cells (the gametes), although so dissimilar (ovum and sperm), have precisely equivalent nuclei and contribute equally to the constitution of the nucleus of the egg. It must be said, however, that this discovery, which demonstrates the strictly equal participation of father and mother in the formation of the progeniture, was received with something less than passionate interest.

50. *Le Paradigme perdu, op. cit.*, p. 78. (Our italics.)

51. In 1966, she founded the first great feminist movement: NOW (National Organization of Women).

52. In May 1968, Anne Tristan and some women friends founded the "Féminin-Masculin-Avenir". After 1970, the press wrote of the MLF (Mouvement de libération de la femme), but the MLF was a nebula of small, short-lived groups.

53. Anne Tristan and Annie de Pisan, *Histoires du MLF*, Calmann-Lévy, 1977.

54. Until now, successive generations have been immersed in a flood of images, films and books that endlesly relate the horrors of the Second World War.

55. Cf. the slogan of the neutralist "Greens": "Better red than dead."

56. 43.65 % of them worked in agriculture.

57. Table of working women published by *L'Express*, 3–9 March 1975:

	France	Germany	Italy	GB	USSR	USA	Sweden
% of women in the working population	38	36.9	27.8	37.2	51	37	40.7
% of working women in proportion to the female population	52.3	45.5	18	48.4	90	24.5	61
% of married women among the female working population	62	59.6	51.4	64		23.4	59

58. In 1983, 60% of mothers of children under eighteen months were gainfully employed, compared with 40% in 1970. (Figures from the US Bureau of Labor Statistics.) In 1983, 70% of mothers of nursery school children were in full time employment.
59. In 1975, Germany had only 20,438 places in crèches for 9.5 million working women, and England 29,902 places for 9.3 million working mothers. On the other hand, Sweden had 36,000 places in crèches for 1.6 million working mothers, and France 51,064 for 7.9 million.
60. Nicole Marc and Olivier Marchand note that between 1975 and 1982 there was an increase of 10% in the number of women with one child who were working, and an increase of 15% in women with two children. (*Economie et Statistiques*, no. 171–172, November–December 1984.)
61. *Population et Sociétés*, no. 186, December 1984. In 1982, 52% of babies had working mothers.
62. Of the 20,840 managers of the 4,300 largest businesses in France, only 810, or 3.9% are women. (*Nouvel Économiste*, March 1985.)
63. Figures published in 1984. In 1983, 43.3% of women in management were under thirty-five, 33% under twenty-five.
64. *Femmes made in USA*, Autrement, 1984. "According to the Department of Commerce, the receipts from these businesses founded and run by women amount to more than forty billion dollars."
65. Evelyne Sullerot, *Histoire et Sociologie du travail féminin*, 1971 edition, p. 102. In Paris, at the end of the nineteenth century, the average wage for men was almost double the average wage for women. In Germany, women's wages were often only a quarter of that of men doing the same jobs.
66. *Ibid.*, pp. 97–8. In the nineteenth century, women were given the dirtiest, most repugnant jobs. They were sewer cleaners, oil purifiers, rag pickers, street sweepers . . .
67. At the beginning of the nineteen eighties, the wife's wage represented about 40% of the total family budget.
68. When the expenses they incur through working are deducted from their pay (loss of social and tax advantages, cost of child-minders, transport, canteens, etc.), it is seen that they are left with a more or less derisory sum.
69. *Op. cit.*, pp. 87–8. Edgar Morin rightly points out that the same does not apply to men, because they have access to feminine culture through their early links with their mother.
70. Ivan Illich, *Gender*, Marion Boyars, 1983. N.Y. Pantheon, 1983.

71. After the Neo-Malthusian militants of the beginning of the century, we would like to pay homage here to the anarchists, to some Freemasons, to all the doctors in the Family Planning movement, and to Dr Étienne Baulieu, who perfected the French Pill.

72. According to Professor Baulieu, who was working in the USA in 1961, Dr Pincus was particularly impressed by Margaret Sanger's arguments about the dangers of world over-population. (Article in *Science et Avenir*, no. 48.)

73. Mrs MacCormick was the first to finance this research, and the Searle company gave generous aid to Pincus. When they felt that this was a business that would pay dividends, other pharmaceutical companies also became interested.

74. At a Cabinet meeting on 9 June 1967, General de Gaulle is said to have declared: "The Pill is for amusement."

75. Abortion was legalized in Japan in 1968.

76. Loi Veil, 17 January 1975, voted for by all the Left and a minority of the Right.

77. Denmark (1978), Italy (1978), Luxembourg (1978), The Netherlands (1981).

78. The Portuguese law of 27 January 1984 authorized abortion for therapeutic reasons but refused it for economic reasons.

79. In Ireland, abortion became a crime punishable by life imprisonment in March 1983.

80. Mary Jane Sherfey, quoted by Sarah Hrdy, *The Woman that Never Evolved*, p. 178.

81. Evelyne Sullerot, *Pour le meilleur et sans le pire*, Fayard, 1984, p. 66.

82. *Ibid.*, p. 70: "It is hard to believe that in America only twenty years ago people were publishing little manuals on how to catch a husband."

83. The proportion of working women aged between twenty-five and thirty went up from 45.3% in 1962 to 71.1% in 1982.

84. With the exception of a few Mediterranean countries in which the divorce laws have only recently been modified.

85. There was a spectacular increase in the number of divorces in the year following the 1965 change in the Soviet law which made the procedure much easier. 1965: 360,000 divorces; 1966: 646,000 divorces; 1979: 950,000 divorces.

86. Premarital conceptions continued to increase between 1965 and 1972, at which date contraception was better controlled. From 65,000, the number rose to 108,000, which means that about 30% of all babies were born less than seven months after the marriage of

their parents. (Cf. Evelyne Sullerot, *op. cit.*, p. 50.)

87. Seven out of ten children born outside wedlock are recognized by both their parents.

88. During this period, a third of all Swedish children were born outside marriage.

89. Jean-Louis Flandrin, *Le Sexe et l'Occident*, Le Seuil, 1981, and Elisabeth Badinter, *The Myth of Motherhood*, Tr. Francine du Plessix Gray, Souvenir Press, 1981.

90. Sabine Chalvon-Demersay, *Concubin–Concubine*, Le Seuil, 1983.

91. Evelyne Sullerot, *op. cit.*, p. 94.

92. *The Elementary Structures*, p. 115.

93. *Ibid.*, p. 117.

94. Dossier, *Le Monde de l'éducation*, (March 1985): In 1984 there were a million single parents, of whom 821,000 were women.

95. Lévi-Strauss, *op. cit.*, Introduction, Chapter 2.

96. A television programme on FR3 on 14 September 1984: A brother and sister living together had just had a little girl, and asked the President of the Republic to give them permission to marry. Cf. also *le Monde-Dimanche* of 20 September 1981, the article by Alain Woodrow: "Incest, the last taboo?" which reported the views of people living in an incestuous situation.

97. Both quotations are taken from *le Monde-Dimanche*.

98. In *The Origin of the Family*, Engels qualified the appearance of the patriarchal family as a "great historical defeat of the feminine sex".

PART THREE

CHAPTER I

1. Alain Finkielkraut, *La nostalgie de l'épreuve*, in *Le Genre humain*, no. 10, June 1984, Éditions Complexe: "What is the masculine? This is a question that Western societies no longer know how to answer."

2. Georges Balandier, *Anthropo-logiques*, p. 61.

3. Étienne Baulieu and France Haour in *Le Fait féminin*, pp. 134–6: Testosterone is the androgenic hormonal secretion in men. Oestradiol and progesterone are the feminizing hormones. "The sex hormonal differences lead to a whole network of biochemical and functional consequences that are very different in men and women." (p. 138.)

4. *Ibid.*, pp. 135–6. "Oestradiol and progesterone are produced in the male sex, but in very much smaller quantities than those observed in women. Equally, we find a low level of testosterone in the female sex … Typically feminine hormones, such as prolactin, which stimulates

mammary development and lactation, and oxytocin, which induces the uterine contractions at parturition, are present in not inconsiderable quantities in the male sex."

5. Odette Thibault in *Le Fait féminin*, p. 218. Overall, women's muscular strength is about 57% of that of men. Aggressivity is partly associated with the male hormones.
6. Étienne Baulieu and France Haour, *ibid.*, p. 146.
7. Odette Thibault, *ibid.*, p. 215.
8. Evelyne Sullerot in *Le Fait féminin*, p. 483.
9. *Op. cit.*, p. 31. (Our italics.)
10. *Ibid.*, p. 182. "In very simple societies, a few men may shy away from the responsibility, become tramps or ne'er-do-wells or misanthropists who live in the woods by themselves. In complex societies, a large number of men may escape the burden of feeding females and young by entering monasteries – and feeding each other."
11. In some rare cases, the father is given custody of the children and the mother is "obliged" to pay him alimony.
12. *L'Africaine . . .*, *op. cit.*, p. 20.
13. When we observe, for example, the attitude of Israeli women to their husbands and sons, we can see just how far the man who risks his life for his family is seen as a king.
14. Margarete Mitscherlich, *La Fin des modèles*, Édition des Femmes, 1983.
15. *Ibid.*, p. 65.
16. The following analysis is taken from an article by James Levine, *La nouvelle paternité aux États-Unis*, in *Les Pères aujourd'hui*. International colloquium, Paris, 17–19 February, 1981. Institut national d'études démographiques, 1982.
17. The evolution of the American law began in 1973. Eleven of the fifty states allowed mothers and fathers joint custody of their children. California even made it the expected form of custody.
18. Violette Gorny, *Le Divorce en face*, Hachette, 1985. While a decree of the supreme court of appeal of 2 May 1984 forbade alternate custody, which was judged upsetting for children, on the other hand it recognized the benefits of joint custody, which makes both parents responsible for important decisions and envisages the possibility of the child living with each parent alternately.
19. "I have an idea," writes James Levine, "that there will be more doctoral theses on fatherhood written in our country this year than in all the previous twenty years put together." In June 1984 he organized a discussion on fatherhood in the six largest cities in the

United States. And on that occasion, he published the first national guide on the subject: *Fatherhood USA*, Bank Street College of Education.

20. Tr. Elliot Philipp, Allen & Unwin, 1975. The French original (*J'attends un enfant*) is revised annually, as also is *J'élève mon enfant*, Paris, Horay, 1965.

21. Geneviève Delaisi de Parseval and S. Lallemand, *L'Art d'accommoder les bébés*, Le Seuil, 1980, pp. 53–4, point out that most manuals suggest that fathers can, if need be, feed, amuse, and take the baby for walks, but that they are "constitutionally" incapable of changing its nappies.

22. Geneviève Delaisi de Parseval, *La Part du père, op. cit.*

23. *Ibid.*, p. 284: Delaisi de Parseval notes that this point must be treated with caution. Everything depends on the individual's libidinal evolution.

24. *Parenthood as a developmental phase*, in *Journal of the American Psychoanalytical Association*, 1959.

25. Dr Michael Yogman, *Présence du père*, in revue *Autrement*, no. 72, September 1985, p. 142.

26. The new methods of touch developed by Frans Veldman, which he called *haptomania* (the study of touch), were shown on French television in September 1984.

27. The following year, Publicis returned to the theme: "It takes two to bring up a child."

28. In 1974, *La Ligue du droit de la femme* created the notion of sexism, and announced its determination to "target" every sign of sexual discrimination.

29. The word "sexisme" appeared for the first time in the *Robert* dictionary in 1977, with the following definition: "Attitude of discrimination towards the feminine sex. See *Phallocentrisme*." The term "discrimination" became, in everyday language, a synonym of "segregation: the act of separating one social group from the others and treating it worse."

30. See particularly Luce Irigaray, Hélène Cixous, Annie Leclerc in France.

31. Some examples: In 1976, women were permitted to become police inspectors; in 1980, Micheline Colin became a fire chief; in 1984, men were allowed to train as midwives.

32. In spite of the decree of 30 July 1946 cancelling the reductions in women's wages, in spite of the law of 1972, women still earn less than men. In 1980 the gap varied between 20% and 30% according to professional category.

33. The governing class is predominantly male in all Western countries.
34. *Générations nouvelles et mariage traditionnel*, in *Institut national d'études démographiques*, Cahier no. 86, PUF, 1978.
35. It will be observed that the question was formulated in the most neutral and impersonal way possible.
36. A 1983 survey, published in 1984, which covered all social categories, confirmed the foregoing results. In their answers to the question: "Do you think that all jobs should be shared indiscriminately between men and women?" 64% were in favour, of whom 73% were working women and 70% were women under forty.
37. *Demain les femmes*, Laffont-Gonthier, 1965, p. 106. She has often repeated this proposition, notably in *Le Fait féminin*, p. 483.
38. According to the *Robert* dictionary, a woman is an androgyne when her morphology resembles that of a man, and a man is an androgyne when he presents superficial feminine characteristics.
39. Serge Dunis, *Sans tabou ni totem*, p. 263: "To be born to oneself is to accept one's sexuality . . . to go beyond the man/woman division and accept the bisexual structuring of the personality by the integration of the father and the mother."
40. Tr. Walter Hamilton, Penguin Classics, reprinted 1987, pp. 59–62.
41. The other two species were composed either of two male parts or of two female parts. Cut in two, they seek their other half of the same sex. These are the homosexuals.
42. Divisions and enumerations do not go very far towards the knowledge of men and women. And how do we proceed from the simple to the complex, when the simple no longer exists, and everything has become complex, "compound"?
43. Suzanne Lilar, *Le Malentendu du deuxième sexe*, PUF, 1962, dismisses equally the traditionalists who identify every individual with his or her natural difference, and the feminists who refuse to see any sense in the biophysiological.
44. Étienne Wolff, *Les Changements de sexe*, Gallimard, 1946, p. 59. He observes that the presence of nipples and glandular tissue in men is manifest proof of the morphological bipotentiality of the somata.
45. Letter to Fliess, 4 January 1898: "I embraced your stress on bisexuality and consider this idea of yours to be the most significant one for my subject since that of 'defense'. If I had a disinclination on personal grounds, because I am in part neurotic myself, this disinclination would certainly have been directed toward bisexuality . . . " *The Complete Letters of Sigmund Freud to Wilhelm Fliess, 1887–1904*, Translated and Edited by Jeffrey Moussaieff Masson, The

Belknap Press of Harvard U.P., 1985.

46. In his correspondence with Fliess, Freud thinks that repression presupposes bisexuality (4 January 1898).

47. In particular, *Three Essays on the Theory of Sexuality*, Tr. James Strachey, Imago, 1949, and *Un enfant est battu* (1919), in *Névrose, Psychose et Perversion*, PUF, 1973.

48. This proposition is illustrated in *The Psychogenesis of a Case of Female Homosexuality*, in which Freud says that the aim of the psychoanalytic treatment of homosexuality is "the re-establishment of full bisexual functioning . . . Seeing that throughout life, human sexuality normally oscillates between the masculine object and the feminine object."

49. Extract from Christian David's admirable report on psychological bisexuality, *Revue française de psychanalyse*, 5–6, 1975, p. 720.

50. *Revue française de psychanalyse*, 3, 1975.

51. The "normal" man is a manly man. A "normal" woman is a "feminine" woman (Helene Deutsch).

52. "Normality", here, is understood in its double sense of both a person's "nature", and his "mental health".

53. *Rapport sur la bisexualité psychique, op. cit.*, p. 728. (Our italics.)

54. *Ibid.*, p. 702. Christian David reminds us that as from 1928, Melanie Klein gave equal importance to the femininity complex of men and the castration complex in women.

55. *Ibid.*, p. 703. (Our italics.) Christian David adds: "Unless, that is, we want to approve the Nietzschean approach to love: 'Love – its means is war; its principle is mortal hatred between the sexes.'"

56. *Anthropo-logiques*, p. 21.

57. Cf. Part Two, Chapter 2.

58. Cf. *Male and Female*. The seven peoples are the Polynesian Samoans, the Manus of the Admiralty Islands, the Arapesh of New Guinea, the Mundugumor of the Yuat River in New Guinea, the Iatmul of New Guinea, the Tchambuli of New Guinea, and the Balinese.

59. *Ibid.*, p. 148.

60. *Ibid.*, pp. 148–9. Margaret Mead points out that "if breast-feeding were completely superseded as a form of feeding infants . . . and fathers and brothers were to take over an equal responsibility for the child, this biological regularity would disappear. Instead of girls learning that they simply were, and boys that they must become, emphasis would shift to such matters as relative size and strength; the preoccupations of the developing child would alter, and so might the whole psychology of the sexes."

61. *Ibid.*, pp. 157-8.
62. Cf. two articles: *Création d'une illusion: l'extrême féminité chez les garçons*, in *Nouvelle Revue de psychanalyse*, no. 4, 1974, and *Examen du concept freudien de bisexualité*, in *Nouvelle Revue de psychanalyse*, no. 7, 1973.
63. J. Money, J. G. Hampson, J. L. Hampson, *Imprinting and the Establishment of Gender Role* in *Arch. Neurol. Psycha.*, 77, 1957, pp. 333-6.
64. Robert Stoller, *Faits et hypothèses: un examen du concept freudien de bisexualité*, in *Nouvelle Revue de psychanalyse*.
65. *Ibid.* Conversely, when the original symbiosis is conspicuously lacking, with a frigid mother, the daughter will devote her energies to an endless search for a good mother in homosexual adventures.
66. It is not absurd to think that the men who declare themselves (or who are accused of being) "macho", or "phallocrats", are precisely those who have the greatest fear for their sexual specificity, a sign of the fragility of their sense of male identity.
67. From this point of view, their position is precisely symmetrical to that of the male chauvinists who consider that this model constitutes the suppression of masculine values and nature.
68. *Anthropo-logiques*, pp. 35-6.
69. *La cohésion sociale dans les sociétés polysegmentaires* (1931), in *Oeuvres*, Éditions de Minuit, 1968, Vol. III, p. 15.
70. Edgar Morin, *Le Paradigme perdu . . .* , p. 87, note 1.
71. Serge Dunis, *Sans tabou ni totem*, p. 263.
72. With the fundamental changes brought about in sexuality which we have seen in Part I, Chapter 1, and in particular with regard to the disappearance of oestrus in women.
73. Even if we have different ways of satisfying them according to the culture we belong to.
74. The first publications date from 1955.
75. *Intersexuality* is defined by a discrepancy in the occurrences normally present to characterize the somatic sex. Sometimes the external genital organs show an ambiguity that may be noticed immediately or later. Sometimes the external genital organs seem normal, but the development of the secondary sexual characteristics at puberty does not harmonize with the appearance. Intersexuality must be distinguished from transsexualism, which is the feeling of belonging to the opposite sex, in spite of a normal sexual morphology, and which is most often associated with the desire to change one's sex.

76. Reported by Robert Stoller in his preface to *Recherches sur l'identité sexuelle*, Gallimard, 1978, p. 13.
77. Money speaks of "gender role", and Stoller of "gender identity". Stoller uses the word "identity" to mean the organization of the psychological components necessary to preserve one's consciousness that one exists.
78. Robert Stoller, *Recherches sur l'identité sexuelle*, p. 12.
79. Robert Stoller, *Création d'une illusion: l'extrême feminité chez les garçons, Nouvelle Revue de psychanalyse*, no. 4, 1971.
80. Robert Stoller notes the rarity of cases of transsexual girls.
81. The little boy is a phallic substitute for the mother, who treats him as a transitional object.
82. Robert Stoller, *Création d'une illusion . . .*, p. 70.
83. The category of ambiguous individuals who do not suffer if the sex in which they were brought up is modified.
84. *Recherches sur l'identité sexuelle*, pp. 72–9. Four different kinds of clinical situations are cited in support of this conviction: girls suffering from vaginal aplasia but normal from every other point of view; subjects who are biologically neuter but whose external feminine genital appearance raised no doubts in their parents' minds; biologically normal girls whose external genital organs are masculinized and who have been brought up without question as boys; girls who are biologically normal but who have no clitoris.
85. Sydney Mellen, *The Evolution of Love*, W. H. Freeman, 1981, pp. 165–6.
86. *Ibid.*, p. 166.
87. The statistics are rare, and difficult to establish, for a sufficient lapse of time is necessary to be sure that a woman will not become a mother. What we do have are the surveys on the number of children women want. The most recent one, published in *le Nouvel Observateur* (14 January, 1983), shows that 4% of those polled did not want to have children.
88. Cf. the work of Jean E. Veevers, e.g., *Childless by Choice*, Butterworth, 1980.
89. *Population et Sociétés*, October, 1985, published the latest figures known in 1983–4: West Germany 1.27; Denmark 1.4; France 1.81; Italy 1.53; The Netherlands 1.47; Great Britain 1.77; Canada 1.68; USA 1.75; Australia 1.93, etc.
90. G. Doucet and Dr D. Élia, *Femme pour toujours, la ménopause oubliée*, Hachette, 1985.
91. Two recent surveys demonstrate this. One published in *Parents*, in

May 1982, covering a thousand young people between the ages of fifteen and eighteen, reports that a majority of both girls and boys have their first sexual experience during this period. This was confirmed more recently (1983) by a survey covering 5,110 lycée students, carried out by the magazine *l'Étudiant.*

92. *Le Fait féminin*, pp. 468–9. Massimo Livi Bacci says that the age at first menstruation has gone down by two or three years in the last century, while the age at menopause has gone up from 46 to 49.

93. A man can become a father without having any sexual contact with his wife. In the last ten years, 10,000 children have been born by artificial insemination, and the reason why people have recourse to surrogate mothers is "the taboo on the genetic father having sexual relations with the mother of his child". Paul Yonnet speaks of a process of "degenitalization". Cf. "Mères porteuses, père écarté", *Le Débat*, Gallimard, no. 36, September 1985.

94. Kant, *Critique of Judgement*, 39 and 17: "Beauty is purposiveness without purpose."

95. Evelyne Sullerot, *Demain les femmes*, Laffont, 1965, p. 106.

96. Françoise Héritier, *Le Fait féminin*, p. 392. She shows that the fate of the sterile woman is tragic. As the Samo fear that a body that has never known the pain of childbirth will experience this suffering after death, in some parts of Samo territory it is the custom, before a sterile woman is buried, to subject her to an operation that aims at "breaking her loins".

97. *Ibid.*, p. 401. (See also: Lucy Mair, *An Introduction to Social Anthropology*, O.U.P., second edition, 1985.) (Tr.)

CHAPTER II

1. *L'Ère du vide*, Gallimard, 1983, p. 81.

2. *Ibid.*, p. 67: "But while the figure of the Other is disappearing from the social sphere, another *division* is simultaneously reappearing: That between the conscious and the unconscious . . ."

3. *Ibid.*, p. 78.

4. Fewer and fewer *crimes passionnels* are being committed in our societies.

5. *Robert* dictionary: "*Oblatif:* that which is offered to satisfy other people's needs to the detriment of one's own."

6. Fayard, 1984.

7. Giving the child all one's love does not mean that we give him all the love that is *necessary* for him to live happily, but that we give him all that we *can* or know how to give. Maternal love is very different from

one woman to another. Some women dispense it almost without counting, but there are others who can only give what they themselves have received, which is sometimes very little.

8. Sabine Chalvon-Demersay, *op. cit.*, p. 57: "We no longer set a paid job against a household task, but a job one does now against its equivalent in the future. 'I'll do the dishes today; you'll do them tomorrow. I'll clean the house today; next week it'll be your turn. If I look after the baby today, then you'll have to tomorrow.' When anyone does a job, he thereby puts someone else in his *debt*, and this debt will only be cancelled by the later performance of a similar task."

9. Vendée, for instance, a region with a strong religious tradition, has the lowest divorce rate in France.

10. This phenomenon was already observed in the period when the revolutionary law of 1792 was in force. In 1979, 64% of petitioners for divorce were women.

11. James Morgan, Ismaïl Sirageldin, Nancy Baerwaldt, *Productive Americans*, University of Michigan, 1966.

12. Mothers are given custody of their children in 85% of cases.

13. On the other hand, unless they are divorcing in order to set up house with another woman, most men have everything to lose from separation. Apart from losing their home comforts, they are faced with real solitude. Since fewer than 10% of divorced fathers are given custody of their children, we are not over-dramatizing when we say that some fathers feel bereft of their children. So, if they do not find married life unbearable, why should they give it up?

14. Wives aged between twenty-five and thirty-five are the most frequent petitioners in divorce cases, and do in fact bring two thirds of such cases.

15. Évelyne Le Garrec, *Un lit à soi*, Le Seuil, 1981.

16. In 1978, Gisèle Halimi suggested that the abolition of the patriarchal family might well necessitate the abolition of the cohabitation of couples for a generation.

17. Évelyne Le Garrec, *op. cit.*

18. *Ibid.*, p. 69.

19. Racine, *Phèdre* (1677), Act I, Scene 3. (*Phedra*, Tr. Robert David Macdonald, Amber Lane Press, Oxford, 1985, p. 21.)

20. Notes by Jean Balou, *Nouveaux Classiques illustrés*.

21. For Anne Martin-Fugier, *Les Indépendantes*, Grasset, 1985, p. 149, "Passion is already dead."

22. *Love in the Western World*, cf. Part II, Chapter 2.

23. Because she also knows that passions feed on obstacles. "Am I to hope," she confides to Monsieur de Nemours, "for a miracle, and shall I ever be able to prepare myself for a certain end to this passion? – this would bring me great joy. Monsieur de Clèves was perhaps the only being in the world capable of preserving love in marriage . . . Perhaps, too, his passion only lasted because he found none in me. But I would not have the same means to preserve your passion: I believe, even, that the obstacles were the cause of your constancy." *The Princess of Clèves.*
24. Sabine Chalvon-Demersay, *Concubin–Concubine*, p. 100. (Our italics.)
25. Her study covers seventy people aged between twenty and thirty-five who had been living together for several years.
26. *Op. cit.*, p. 102. (Our italics.)
27. *Vocabulaire de la psychanalyse*, by Laplanche and Pontalis, article *Desire*: "Desire seeks to impose itself without taking any account of the language and the unconscious of the other."
28. *L'Amitié*, Ramsay, pp. 14 and 43.
29. Only 15% of couples living together, and not even one in three married couples, consider that "two people can remain really united" for ever. Evelyne Sullerot, *Pour le meilleur et sans le pire, op. cit.*, p. 91.
30. In 1977, a survey conducted by Louis Roussel showed that 80% of young people under thirty saw marriage as only a simple formality.
31. *Concubin–Concubine*, p. 91.
32. Michel Lévy notes that "More and more frequently, marriage now takes place during the communal life of couples, instead of marking its beginning." *Population et Sociétés*, October, 1985, no. 195.
33. *Concubin–Concubine*, p. 131.
34. Evelyne Sullerot, *Pour le meilleur et sans le pire*, p. 93.
35. Louis Roussel, "Les ménages d'une personne: évolution récente", *Population*, no. 6, 1983, p. 996. On p. 998, he publishes the table on the following page.
36. Dossier in *le Nouvel Observateur*, on celibate adventurers, no. 2228, 8–14 November, 1985.
37. *Autrement*, dossier no. 32, June 1981: *Célibataires*, p. 223.
38. François de Singly, *Mariage, dot scolaire et position sociale*, in *Économie et Statistiques*, no. 142, March 1982.
39. *Ibid*, p. 10. Almost 28% of unmarried women are senior or middle executives as against 8% of unmarried men; 14% of married women are in the executive class as against 21% of married men.

PERCENTAGE INCREASES IN THE NUMBER OF
ONE-PERSON HOUSEHOLDS

	1st period (a)	2nd period (b)	Total
Austria	37.4	11.3	52.9
Canada	91.0	107.3	295.4
Germany	48.3	39.4	106.7
The Netherlands	81.3	22.2	121.2
Norway	33.7	55.5	107.9
Sweden	47.7	48.9	119.9
Switzerland	79.3	76.1	217.0
USA	61.1	64.2	164.5

(a) 1960 or 1961 to 1970 or 1971
(b) 1970 or 1971 to 1980 or 1981, except for The Netherlands: 1971–1978.

40. The unmarried buy three times as many books as the married, go to restaurants twice as often, go to the cinema nine times more often. They spend ten times more than married couples at weekends and on holiday.
41. See particularly the problems of the celibate in rural districts, where there are three times as many celibates as in the towns.
42. Louis Roussel, article quoted, p. 1012.

POSTSCRIPT

1. See the extreme value attached to the mother in the nineteenth century.
2. It is a woman, Coline Serreau, who has expressed her thoughts on the new relations between men and babies in her film *Trois Hommes et un couffin* (*Three Men and a Baby.*)
3. In the USA and Europe there have already been trends of moralistic opinion in favour of an increased birth rate and the abolition of the right to abortion.
4. Jacques Testart, *De l'éprouvette au bébé spectacle*, Éditions Complexe, 1984, p. 103.
5. *Ibid.*, p. 103, note 17. (Our italics.)
6. Dr Cecil Jacobsen, Director of the Reproductive Genetics Center in Vienna, Washington: Dr Landrum Shettles, Director of the Gynecology/Obstetrics department at the Women's Hospital in Las Vegas. These two American doctors gave an interview to the magazine *Actuel*, in which they seem far less hesitant than their French colleagues about the possibility of pregnant men.
7. Roberto Zapperi, *L'Uomo incinto*, Cosenza, 1979.

8. Psychoanalysts speak of perversity.
9. As we have seen, among the primates the quest for food is individual and there is no trace of sexual specialization, whereas techno-economic complementarity is specific to the relations between man and woman. (Part I, Chapter 1.)

BIBLIOGRAPHY

Abensour, Léon, *Histoire générale du féminisme*, Ressources, 1921.

Aït Sabbah, Fatna, *Le Femme dans l'inconscient musulman*, Le Sycomore, 1982.

Alberoni, Francesco, *L'Amitié*, Ramsay, 1985.

Badinter, Elisabeth, *The Myth of Motherhood*, Tr. Francine du Plessix Gray, Souvenir Press, 1981.

Balandier, Georges, *Anthropo-logiques*, PUF, 1974.

Beauvoir, Simone de, *The Second Sex*, Tr. H. M. Parshley, Penguin, 1972.

Bebel, August, *Women in the Past, Present and Future*, Tr. H. B. A. Walther, London, 1885.

Benveniste, Émile, *Indo-European Language and Society*, Tr. Elizabeth Palmer, Faber, 1973.

Bettelheim, Bruno, *Symbolic Wounds*, Thames and Hudson, 1955.

Bord, Janet and Colin, *Earth Rites*, Granada, 1982.

Boulding, Elise, *The Underside of History*, Boulder, Westview Press, 1977.

Bridenthal and Koonz, *Becoming Visible: Women in European History*, Boston, Houghton Mifflin, 1977.

Briffault, Robert, *The Mothers*, Allen and Unwin, 1927.

Calvocoressi, Peter, *Who's Who in the Bible*, Penguin, 1988.

Camps, Gabriel, *La Préhistoire. A la recherche d'un paradis perdu*, Perrin, 1982.

Cauvin, Jacques, *Religions néolithiques de Syro-Palestine*, Maisonneuve, 1972.

Chalvon-Demersay, Sabine, *Concubin–Concubine*, Le Seuil, 1983.

Chesler, Phyllis, *Women and Madness*, Allen Lane, 1974.

Childe, Vere Gordon, *Man Makes Himself*, C. A. Watts, London, 1956.
Dawn of European Civilization, Routledge, 1957.
What Happened in History, Penguin, reprinted 1982.

Chouraqui, André, *Des hommes de la Bible*, Hachette, reissued 1985.

Condorcet, *Lettres d'un bourgeois de New Haven à un citoyen de Virginie*, in *Recherches sur les États-Unis*, Book I, 1788.

Coppens, Yves, *Le Singe, l'Afrique et l'Homme*, Fayard, 1984.

Crosland, Jessie, *William the Marshal, The Last Great Feudal Baron*, Peter Owen, 1962.

Delaisi de Parseval, Geneviève, *La Part du père*, Le Seuil, 1981.

Delaisi de Parseval, Geneviève and Lallemand, S., *L'Art d'accommoder les bébés*, Le Seuil, 1980.

Delporte, Henri, *L'Image de la femme dans l'art préhistorique*, Picard, 1979.

Deutsch, Helene, *The Psychology of Women*, Vol. I, Grune and Stratton, N.Y. 1944.

Devereux, Georges, *Baubo, la vulve mythique*, J.-C. Godefroy, 1983.

Dolle, Jean-Marie, *Diderot, politique et éducation*, Vrin, 1973.

Doucet, G., and Élia, Dr D., *Femme pour toujours, la ménopause oubliée*, Hachette, 1985.

Duby, Georges, *The Knight, the Lady and the Priest*, Tr. Barbara Bray, Penguin Books, 1985.

William Marshal, The Flower of Chivalry, Tr. Richard Howard, Faber,

Dunis, Serge, *Sans tabou ni totem*, Fayard, 1984.

Dupuy, Jean, *La laïcité dans les déclarations internationales des droits de l'homme*, in *La Laïcité*, PUF, 1960.

Eaubonne, Françoise d', *Les Femmes avant le patriarcat*, Payot, 1976.

Eliade, Mircea, *A History of Religious Ideas*, Tr. W. R. Trask, Collins, 1979.

Patterns in Comparative Religion, Tr. Rosemary Sheed, Sheed and Ward, 1979.

Le Fait féminin, Edited by Evelyne Sullerot, Fayard, 1978.

Faucher, Daniel, *Histoire générale des techniques*, Vol. I, PUF, 1962.

Fisher, Helen, *The Sex Contract*, Granada, 1982.

Flandrin, Jean-Louis, *Le Sexe et l'Occident*, Le Seuil, 1981.

Frazer, Sir James, *The Golden Bough*, Macmillan, 1963.

Freud, *The Complete Letters of Sigmund Freud to Wilhelm Fliess, 1887–1904*, Translated and Edited by Jeffrey Moussaieff Masson, The Belknap Press of Harvard U.P., 1985.

Three Essays on the Theory of Sexuality, Tr. James Strachey, Imago, 1949.

Godelier, Maurice, *La Production des grands hommes*, Fayard, 1982.

Goodall, Jane, *My Friends the Wild Chimpanzees*, National Geographic Society, 1967.

Gorny, Violette, *Le Divorce en face*, Hachette, 1985.

Griaule, Marcel, *Conversations with Ogotemmêli*, Tr. Ralph Butler, Audrey Richards and Beatrice Hook, OUP, 1965.

Guilaine, Jean, *La France d'avant la France, du néolithique à l'âge du fer*, Hachette, 1983.

Premiers Bergers et Paysans de l'Occident méditerranéen, Hachette, 1976.

Hisham Ibn Muhammad al-Kalbi, *The Book of Idols*, Tr. Nabih Amin Faris, Princeton, 1952.

Héritier, Françoise, *L'Africaine. Sexes et signes*, in *Cahiers du GRIF*, no. 29. Autumn 1984.

Homer, *Homer's Odysseys*, Tr. George Chapman, George Newnes, 1904.

Hrdy, Sarah, *The Woman that Never Evolved*, Harvard U.P., 1981.

Illich, Ivan, *Gender*, Marion Boyars, 1983.

James, E.O., *The Cult of the Mother Goddess*, Thames and Hudson, 1959.

Johanson, Donald, and Edey, Maitland, *Lucy: The Beginnings of Humankind*, Simon and Schuster, 1981.

Kelly, Amy, *Eleanor of Aquitaine*, Harvard U.P., 1981.

Klein, Melanie, *Contributions to Psychoanalysis, 1921–1945*, Hogarth Press, 1947.

Lacoste-Dujardin, Camille, *Des mères contre les femmes; maternité et patriarcat au Maghreb*, La Découverte, 1985.

Lacroix, Jean, *Paternité et démocratie*, in *Esprit*, May 1947.

Latreille, André, *L'Église catholique et la laïcité*, in *La Laïcité*, PUF, 1961.

The Laws of Manu, Tr. G. Bühler, Oxford, Clarendon Press, 1886.

Lederer, Wolfgang, *The Fear of Women*, Grune and Stratton, N.Y., 1968.

Le Garrec, Évelyne, *Un lit à soi*, Le Seuil, 1981.

Leroi-Gourhan, André, *The Art of Prehistoric Man in Western Europe*, Tr. Norbert Guterman, Thames and Hudson, 1968.

Le Fil du temps, Fayard, 1983.

Le Geste et la parole, Albin Michel, 1970.

Les Racines du monde, Belfond, 1982.

Lévi-Strauss, Claude, *The Elementary Structures of Kinship*, Tr. James Harle Bell, John Richard von Sturmer and Rodney Needham, Beacon Press, Boston, 1969.

Introduction to a Science of Mythology, Vols. I, II and III: Tr. John and Doreen Weightman: *The raw and the cooked*, Cape, 1970, *From honey to ashes*, Cape, 1973, *The origin of table manners*, Cape, 1978. *Race et Histoire*, Gonthier, 1967.

The Savage Mind, Weidenfeld and Nicolson, 1966.

Lilar, Suzanne, *Le Malentendu du deuxième sexe*, PUF, 1962.

Lipovetsky, Gilles, *L'Ère du vide*, Gallimard, 1983.

Loraux, Nicole, *Le Lit et la guerre*, in *L'Homme*, Jan.–Mar. 1981.

Lowie, Robert, *Traité de sociologie primitive*, Payot, 1969.

Macciocchi, Maria-Antonietta, *Les Femmes et leurs maîtres*, Christian Bourgois, 1978.

Mahindra, Indira, *The Rebellious Home-Makers*, S.N.D.T. Women's University, Bombay, 1980.

Markale, Jean, *Women of the Celts*, Tr. A. Mygind, C. Hauch, P. Henry, Gordon Cremonesi, London, 1975.

Martin-Fugier, Anne, *Les Indépendantes*, Grasset, 1985.

Mead, Margaret, *Male and Female*, Pelican Books, 1962.

Mellen, Sydney, *The Evolution of Love*, Oxford, W. H. Freeman, 1981.

Mill, John Stuart, *The Subjection of Women*, Dent, Everyman's Library, 1929.

Mitscherlich, Margarete, *La Fin des modèles*, Édition des Femmes, 1983.

Money, J., Hampson, J. G., Hampson, J. L., *Imprinting and the Establishment of Gender Role*, in *Arch. Neurol. Psych.*, 77, 1957.

Moret, Alexandre, *Mélanges offerts à Jean Capart*, Brussels, 1935.

Morin, Edgar, *Le Paradigme perdu: La nature humaine*, Le Seuil, 1973.

Moscovici, Serge, *Society against Nature*, Tr. Sacha Rabinovitch, Harvester Press, 1976.

Mumford, Lewis, *The Myth of the Machine*, Harcourt Brace, 1966–7.

Ouvry-Vial, Brigitte, *Femmes made in USA*, Autrement, 1984.

Paige, Karen, and Paige, Jeffrey, *The Politics of Reproductive Ritual*, University of California Press, 1981.

Pelletier, André, *La Femme dans la société gallo-romaine*, Picard, 1984.

Picard, Charles, *Les Religions pré-helléniques*, PUF, 1948.

Poulain de la Barre, *De l'égalité des deux sexes*, 1673. Reissued, Fayard, 1984.

Przyluski, Jean, *La Grande Déesse*, Payot, 1950.

Reed, Evelyn, *Woman's Evolution*, Pathfinder Press, N.Y. and Toronto, 1975.

Reik, Theodor, *The Ritual, Couvade and the Fear of Retaliation*, Hogarth Press, 1931.

Rocheblave-Spenlé, Anne-Marie, *Les Rôles masculins et féminins*, PUF, 1964.

Ross, Anne, *The Pagan Celts*, Batsford, 1986.

Rougemont, Denis de, *Love in the Western World*, Tr. Montgomery Belgion, Princeton U.P., Revised edition, 1983.

Schmitt-Pantel, Pauline, *La différence des sexes. Histoire. Anthropologie et Cité grecque*, in *Une histoire des femmes est-elle possible?*, Rivages, 1984.

Stoller, Robert, *Sex and Gender*, London, Maresfield, 1984.

Sullerot, Evelyne, *Demain les femmes*, Robert Laffont, 1965.
Histoire et Sociologie du travail féminin, Stock, 1971.
Pour le meilleur et sans le pire, Fayard, 1984.
and see *Le Fait féminin*

Tanner, Nancy, and Zilhman, Adrienne, *Women in Evolution: Innovation and Selection in Human Origins*, in *Signs, I (3)*, 1970.

Testart, Alain, *Essai sur les fondements de la division sexuelle du travail chez les chasseurs-cueilleurs*, Éditions de l'École des hautes études en sciences sociales, 1986.

Testart, Jacques, *De l'éprouvette au bébé spectacle*, Éditions Complexe, 1984.

Thalman, Rita, *Être femme sous le IIIe Reich*, Robert Laffont, 1982.

This, Bernard, *Le Père: acte de naissance*, Le Seuil, 1980.

Tillion, Germaine, *Le Harem et les Cousins*, Le Seuil, 1966.

Tocqueville, Alexis de, *De la démocratie en Amérique*, GF/Flammarion, 1981.

Tristan, Anne, and Pisan, Annie de, *Histoires du MLF*, Calmann-Lévy, 1977.

Veevers, Jean E., *Childless by Choice*, Butterworth, 1980.

Vernant, Jean-Pierre, *Myth and Society in Ancient Greece*, Tr. Janet Lloyd, Methuen, 1982.

Myth and Thought among the Greeks, Routledge, 1983.

Vidal-Naquet, Pierre, *Le Chasseur noir*, reissued LD/Fondations, 1983.

Weiner, Annette, *Woman of Value, Men of Renown*, Austin, Texas, 1976.

Wolff, Étienne, *Les Changements de sexe*, Gallimard, 1946.

Zapperi, Roberto, *L'Uomo incinto*, Cosenza, 1979.

Zimbalist Rosaldo, Michelle, and Lamphère, Louise, *Women, Culture and Society*, Stanford U.P., 1974.

INDEX

ABOUT THE AUTHOR

Elisabeth Badinter holds a doctorate in philosophy and teaches at the École Polytechnique. She has written extensively on women and the family, including *The Myth of Motherhood* (1982). She is married with three children and lives in Paris.